ANGLO-SCOTTISH RELATIONS
FROM 1900 TO DEVOLUTION AND BEYOND

PROCEEDINGS OF THE BRITISH ACADEMY · 128

ANGLO-SCOTTISH RELATIONS FROM 1900 TO DEVOLUTION AND BEYOND

Edited by
WILLIAM L. MILLER

Published for THE BRITISH ACADEMY
by OXFORD UNIVERSITY PRESS

Oxford University Press, Great Clarendon Street, Oxford OX2 6DP

Oxford New York
Auckland Bangkok Bogotá Buenos Aires Cape Town Chennai
Dar es Salaam Delhi Hong Kong Istanbul Karachi Kolkata
Kuala Lumpur Madrid Melbourne Mexico City Mumbai Nairobi
São Paulo Shanghai Singapore Taipei Tokyo Toronto

Oxford is a registered trade mark of Oxford University Press
in the UK and certain other countries

Published in the United States
by Oxford University Press Inc., New York

British Library Cataloguing in Publication Data
Data available

ISBN 0–19–726331–3   978–0–19–726331–0

Typeset in Times
by J&L Composition, Filey, North Yorkshire
Printed in Great Britain
on acid-free paper by
Creative Print and Design (Wales)
Ebbw Vale

Contents

List of Figures

Notes on Contributors

John Curtice, FRSE is Professor of Politics and Director of the Social Statistics Laboratory at the University of Strathclyde, and Deputy Director of the Centre for Research into Elections and Social Trends. He is a co-editor of the British Social Attitudes series and a co-director of the Scottish Social Attitudes survey.

Richard J. Finlay is Professor of Scottish History at the University of Strathclyde and author of *Modern Scotland, 1914–2000* (London, 2004).

Robert Hazell is Director of the Constitution Unit and Professor of Government and the Constitution in the School of Public Policy at University College London. He is the director of a five-year research programme into the Dynamics of Devolution funded by the Leverhulme Trust.

David Heald is Professor of Financial Management at Sheffield University Management School. From 1990 to 2003 he was Professor of Accountancy at the University of Aberdeen. He has published extensively on public expenditure, public sector accounting and the financing of devolved government. He directed a project on financing devolution in the United Kingdom, forming part of the Economic and Social Research Council (ESRC) Devolution and Constitutional Change Programme.

Anthony Heath, FBA is Professor of Sociology at the University of Oxford and a Professorial Fellow at Nuffield College. He was the co-director of the British Election Studies and is now working on national identity in England as part of the ESRC Devolution and Constitutional Change Programme. His recent books include *The Rise of New Labour* (Oxford, 2001), (editor) *Ireland North and South* (Oxford, 1999) and (editor) *Understanding Social Change* (Oxford, 2005).

Asifa Hussain is Lecturer in Management at the University of Glasgow. Formerly she was Ministry of Defence Post-Doctoral Fellow and later directed an ESRC project under the Devolution and Constitutional Change Programme in the Department of Politics. She has published widely on ethnic minority issues in journals such as *Management in Medicine, Policy Studies, Defence and*

Security Analysis, *Armed Forces and Society*, *Journal of Political and Military Sociology*, and *Scottish Affairs*. Her doctorate was published as *British Immigration Policy Under the Conservative Government* (Aldershot, 2001).

Charlie Jeffery is Professor of Politics at the University of Edinburgh and directs the ESRC research programme on Devolution and Constitutional Change. He writes on Germany and on comparative territorial politics, and has recently edited special issues of *Regional Studies*, *Representation*, and *Regional and Federal Studies* on themes in UK territorial politics.

James G. Kellas is Honorary Fellow, and former Professor of Politics, of the University of Glasgow. His *Scottish Political System* (Cambridge, 4 editions 1974–89) remains the standard work on pre-devolution Scotland. His more recent publications include *The Politics of Nationalism and Ethnicity* (Basingstoke, 1998) and *Nationalist Politics in Europe: The Constitutional and Electoral Dimensions* (Basingstoke, 2004).

Angela McCarthy curently holds the J. D. Stout Research Fellowship in New Zealand Studies at the Stout Research Centre, Victoria University of Wellington. She is the author of *Irish Migrants in New Zealand, 1840–1937: The Desired Haven* (Woodbridge, 2005), and has published numerous articles on Scottish and Irish migration. In 2006 Manchester University Press will publish her collaborative book with Enda Delaney on twentieth-century migration from Scotland and Ireland.

Neil MacCormick, FBA, FRSE is Leverhulme Personal Research Professor and Regius Professor of Public Law in the University of Edinburgh. From 1999 to 2004 he was (SNP) Member of the European Parliament for Scotland.

David McCrone, FRSE is Professor of Sociology at the University of Edinburgh and director of the University's Institute of Governance. He is co-ordinator of the Leverhulme Trust research programme on Constitutional Change and National Identity (1999–2004). He was a member of the Expert Panel that devised procedures and standing orders for the Scottish Parliament, and advisor to its Procedures Committee. His recent books include *Living in Scotland: Social and Economic Change Since 1980* (Edinburgh, 2004), *Understanding Scotland: The Sociology of a Nation* (Edinburgh, 2001), *New Scotland, New Society?* (Edinburgh, 2001), *New Scotland: New Politics?* (Edinburgh, 2001), and *The Sociology of Nationalism: Tomorrow's Ancestors* (London, 1998).

Iain McLean is Professor of Politics at Oxford University and a Fellow of Nuffield College. His recent work under the Leverhulme Trust's Nations and Regions Programme has concerned the union and the forces tending to strengthen or weaken it, from 1707 until the present. He is a specialist adviser on regional finance to the Treasury Committee of the House of Commons.

Alasdair McLeod was from 2001–4 a Research Assistant at the Centre for Regional Public Finance, University of Aberdeen, working with David Heald on an ESRC project on financing devolution in the United Kingdom, part of the ESRC Devolution and Constitutional Change Programme. Previously he was a finance civil servant in the Scottish Office, where he was closely involved in the management of the Scottish block and in formula negotiations, and latterly in the Scottish Executive.

William L. Miller, FBA, FRSE is Professor of Politics at the University of Glasgow. His (co-authored) books include *Political Culture in Britain* (Oxford, 1996), *Values and Political Change in Postcommunist Europe* (Basingstoke, 1998), *Models of Local Governance* (Basingstoke, 2000), and *A Culture of Corruption? Coping with Government in Postcommunist Europe* (New York, 2001). He is currently working on studies of public attitudes in east Europe and east Asia, and on the attitudes of ethnic minorities in Scotland.

James Mitchell is Professor of Politics at the University of Strathclyde and has recently completed an ESRC-funded project on Devolution and the Centre. His chapter draws on work under that project. His most recent book is *Governing Scotland: The Invention of Administrative Devolution* (Basingstoke, 2003).

Philip Schlesinger, FRSE, FRSA, AcSS is Professor of Film and Media Studies at the University of Stirling and Director of Stirling Media Research Institute. He has served for two terms on the board of Scottish Screen (1997–2005) and is presently a trustee of the Research Centre for Television and Interactivity and a member of the Scottish Advisory Committee of Ofcom. His most recent research monographs are the co-authored *Open Scotland? Journalists, Spin Doctors and Lobbyists* (Edinburgh, 2001) and *Mediated Access: Broadcasting and Democratic Participation in the Age of Mediated Politics* (Luton, 2003). He is currently working on three studies: the European public sphere; cultural creativity and policy; and the representation of exile.

Shawna Smith is currently a D.Phil. student and research officer in the Department of Sociology at the University of Oxford.

John Tomaney is Co-Director of the Centre for Urban and Regional Development Studies at the University of Newcastle upon Tyne. Professor Tomaney is co-author of *Local and Regional Development* (London, 2006).

Barry K. Winetrobe is Reader in Law at Napier University. He writes widely on parliamentary and constitutional issues, most recently contributing a chapter on Scottish devolution to the 5th edition of J. Jowell and D. Oliver's *The Changing Constitution* (Oxford, 2004), and a chapter comparing Westminster and Holyrood legislative process in a forthcoming Hansard Society book edited by A. G. Brazier, *Parliament, Politics and Law-making: Issues and Developments in the Legislative Process.*

1

Introduction: From Last Empress to First Minister

WILLIAM L. MILLER

THIS IS THE SECOND OF TWO VOLUMES reviewing the relationship between Scotland and England since the Union of the Crowns in 1603. Both volumes arise from a two-part conference organised by the British Academy and the Royal Society of Edinburgh to mark the 400th anniversary of that union. The first session was held in London on 17–18 September 2003 and focused primarily on the first three centuries; the second was held in Edinburgh on 6–7 November 2003 and focused primarily on the fourth. The chapters in this volume are revised versions of papers originally given at that second session.

Individual chapters range in focus from the late nineteenth century to the foreseeable future. They cover topics from the monarchy, constitution, parliamentary procedure, public policy, and finance to the attitudes, experiences, and identities of the ordinary Scots and English—both as majorities and as minorities in each other's country.

Several themes cut across the particular concerns of individual chapters. Though seldom the prime concern of any particular chapter, they form a persistent and inescapable background that defines and limits the possibilities of change in the relationship between Scotland and England. They include: (1) the natural inequality of the union in consequence of population sizes; (2) trends in culture and identity; (3) the changing role of the state; (4) cross-border sympathy; and (5) the pressure of adversarial politics.

The Gini Coefficient

Most obviously, there is the extreme disparity in population size—which mattered more in the democratic fourth century of the union than it did in earlier times. The union of Scotland and England no longer joins two crowns

Proceedings of the British Academy, **128**, 1–13. © The British Academy 2005.

or two parliaments in what nineteenth-century Scots (if not English) liked to portray as an 'equal partnership'. Instead it joins 37 million electors in England to 4 million in Scotland—along with 2 million in Wales and just one million in Northern Ireland. It is not just the ratio of size between the largest and the smallest that is significant—the ratio of Germans to Maltese in the European Union is greater than that of the English to the Northern Irish—but the lack of any medium-sized members. The UK is a union equivalent to an EU with a Germany and a Malta but no intermediate-sized state larger than the Netherlands.

However generous the largest partner may try to be, the brutal population facts mean that it can only be a union dominated by England. Economists and sociologists use Corrado Gini's 'Coefficient of Inequality' to measure the concentration of income or wealth within countries. It ranges from zero, representing complete equality, through to 100 per cent, when one individual holds all the wealth or income. In 1979 the Gini Coefficient for income inequality in Britain stood at around 25 per cent, rose sharply in the 1980s, and has stabilised at a new high under Blair of close to 35 per cent.[1] The same measure can be applied to calculate the concentration of democratic political power (based on population) within a union such as the UK or the EU, or the concentration of military power (based on military expenditure) within an alliance such as NATO.

The Gini Coefficient for the inequality of population size (and thus political power) across the 25 countries of the EU in 2004 is 65 per cent. It is inevitably an unequal union. But across the four countries within the UK the Gini Coefficient is 83 per cent—consequently a far more unequal union. To get a comparable figure we have to turn to the distribution of military expenditures within NATO. On 2002 expenditures, that produces a Gini Coefficient of 82 per cent. So, England within the UK is as much a natural hegemon—however benign—as is the USA within NATO.

That extreme disparity in population size has wide-ranging consequences for the relationship between Scotland and England.

Even if Scotland were independent, England would still be there. David McCrone quotes the remark by a Canadian Prime Minister about 'a mouse in bed with an elephant' adding that 'sharing the British island will always raise matters of *realpolitik* regardless of constitutional status'. But before devolution the size disparity had a less subtle and more immediate impact. While Scottish MPs could tip the balance in parliament when two parties were approximately equal in England, English MPs could easily outweigh even a decisive majority of Scottish MPs. That became painfully visible after

[1] A. Shephard, 'Inequality under the Labour Government', IFS Briefing Note 33 (London, Institute of Fiscal Studies, March 2003).

1979. McCrone himself attributes the rising pressure for devolution not to the election of a handful of nationalist MPs but to the Conservative government's failure to win seats in Scotland. This failure meant that it could not avoid overruling a decisive Scottish majority of MPs on issues such as the Poll Tax.

When devolution came, the extreme disparity in population size not only permitted an asymmetric model, it required one. A balanced symmetry of government between Scotland and England would have been an offence against common sense. John Tomaney points out that the 'founding text of English regionalism', *Provinces of England*, first published in 1919, begins by 'rejecting the idea of an English parliament', proposed by the Speaker's conference on devolution that same year, on the grounds that an English parliament would 'dominate the federation in the manner that Prussia had dominated the German Empire before 1914'. In fact the 1997–9 devolution settlement introduced great changes into the government of Scotland without (at that time) any significant change to the government of England. Elected regional assemblies are a separate issue and there are no proposals for any exact equivalent of the Scottish Parliament. Devolution remains, and must remain, asymmetric.

But long before devolution, size differences had a critical impact upon union administration. David Heald and Alasdair McLeod argue that the persistent use of very simple 'rule of thumb' formulae for allocating government expenditures between Scotland and England was caused in part at least by size. Scotland was so small that more complex negotiations would be a misuse of high-level UK or English political/managerial personnel when the expenditures involved were so small. It would require the Treasury to 'devote disproportionate resources, at a time when it can least afford them, to protracted and difficult negotiations over a relatively small part of total public expenditure'. The Scots could afford to give priority to such negotiations. The English could not. A 'rule-of-thumb' calculation was an efficient use of English top-level administrative capacity.

A switch to a needs-based allocation would not eliminate the pervasive impact of size. Heald and McLeod argue that England's size would probably mean that 'needs' would be determined by what was regarded as 'need' within England. Even a generous, UK solidarity approach would be on the basis of formulae determined in England. England would set the criteria for needs-based calculations.

Moreover, the extreme disparity in size meant that per capita over-expenditure in Scotland would produce hardly any detectable per capita under-expenditure in England—even if the English had cared to look for it, which for most of the twentieth century they did not. So only Scotland, not England, would be sensitive to territorial variations in expenditure. Even when a formula was in place, Iain McLean notes that Baldwin 'allowed public spending in Scotland to rise above [the formula]—on the grounds that "political unrest was not in the interests of the Union" '.

Inevitably, the growth of English regionalism charted by John Tomaney has had an impact on Scotland's relationship with England by changing the sizes in these comparisons. Reducing Scottish expenditure per capita could produce no detectable impact on English expenditure per capita, but it could be used to finance a significant growth in per capita expenditure within the North-East region.

Again, size produces asymmetric migration—or rather asymmetries in the visibility of migration. More Scots migrated to England than the reverse. But Scots migrants were relatively isolated and invisible within the much larger population of England. On 2001 Census figures only one and a half per cent of the English population were born in Scotland, but over 8 per cent of the Scottish population were born in England. And over 12 per cent of the population of Scotland's capital city were English immigrants.

Size also produces asymmetric identities. England is ever present in Scottish consciousness. For Scots, England is the 'significant other' that helps to define their Scottish identity. But for the English, Scotland is usually irrelevant. Anthony Heath and Shawna Smith point out that the English (like many outside the UK) have generally found it difficult to distinguish Britain from England. That may be changing under the stress of devolution, but they still find much greater 'pride in Britain' within England than within Scotland. Scotland has no significant role in defining English identity. If the English ever used a 'significant other' in constructing their identity it lay outside the British Isles—across the Channel or across the Atlantic.

Moreover, as the chapter by Heath and Smith shows, there is an inevitable asymmetry in the very nature and character of Scottish and English nationalism. Scottish nationalism is the nationalism of the underdog; English nationalism is the nationalism of the top dog. In their words, Scottish nationalism has a 'more benign, inclusive character', while English nationalism has 'worrying features . . . parallels with the far right' or 'the French Front National'. Happily, such English nationalists form a much smaller part of the population of England than Scottish nationalists within Scotland—though size disparity again means that they are not so few in absolute numbers.

The English seldom have cause to think about Scotland at all. The British Broadcasting Corporation's motto is 'Nation shall speak peace unto nation', but the English hear very little from Scotland. Size means England is sufficiently important that the Scottish press, radio, and television carry English as well as Scottish news. Moreover, culture was treated as a 'devolved' matter under the 1998 Scotland Act, but broadcasting was explicitly 'reserved' to Westminster. Philip Schlesinger describes how the BBC's Director-General

prevented BBC Scotland from broadcasting its own Six O'Clock News programme in Scotland. Conversely, however, the English press, radio, and television carry very little about their very small northern neighbour.
Post-devolution, David McCrone complains that 'the media . . . carry less
explicit Scottish news than ever before'.

In consequence of these asymmetries of immigration and identity, size
has created asymmetries of conflict and harassment. Asifa Hussain and
William Miller's focus groups and interviews with English migrants in
Scotland show that they had experienced a considerable degree of harass-
ment—albeit mainly low-level harassment, irritating rather than threatening.
By contrast, one of the Scottish migrants, whose long-term reflections on life
in England are recounted by Angela McCarthy, was very explicit: 'hating the
English' they said, was 'a one-way thing'.

Divergent Identities, Convergent Societies

Culture and identity are not merely conceptually and empirically distinct,
they seem to be trending in opposite directions: cultures are merging, identities diverging. Territorial identities remain strong. Indeed, John Curtice
shows that by some (not all) measures they are increasingly strong. The numbers who feel exclusively 'Scottish, not British' (in Scotland) or exclusively
'English, not British' (in England) have grown since measurements began in
1992, though they now appear to have stabilised at a post-devolution high.
But, paradoxically, the content and meaning of these identities have faded.

The people of Scotland and England have sharply different feelings about
such pure symbols as the Union Jack, the Saltire or the St George's Cross.
But this is identity, not culture. John Curtice shows that the political values
of the Scots and English, even their 'social and moral outlooks' have converged to the point where they are indistinguishable. They are now remarkably similar, both on the left–right egalitarian dimension of political values
and on a liberal–authoritarian dimension.[2]

The territorial nature of society—in Scotland and England, as elsewhere—has been attenuated. Scottish society, culture, and values at the start
of the twenty-first century are remarkably similar to contemporary English
society, culture, and values—and remarkably different from Scottish society,
culture, and values at the start of the twentieth century. Richard Finlay suggests that 'much of nineteenth- and early twentieth-century Scottish identity

---

[2] For similar conclusions based on an earlier survey, see W. L. Miller, A. M. Timpson, and
M. Lessnoff, *Political Culture in Contemporary Britain: People and Politicians, Principles and
Practice* (Oxford, 1996), pp. 366–73.

focused on the nation's presbyterian inheritance'. Scotland, he writes, at that time celebrated 1707 and indeed 1688 but not even 1603—tainted as 1603 was by the 'despotism' and later Catholicism of the Stuarts. Threatened by an influx of Irish Catholics, presbyterian Scotland still saw itself as by right an equal partner (with England) in a Protestant British alliance against continental Catholicism. And it was suspicious even of episcopalian insensitivity towards Scottish traditions. Indeed, a strongly British identity in nineteenth-century Scotland co-existed with the lack of—even the conscious rejection of—a pan-British culture.

But by the end of the century both Scotland and England had become secular multicultural societies. There was far too much internal diversity for anyone seriously to claim that either society had a 'national character'. We are so familiar with the concept of internally diverse, multicultural societies that it is easy to overlook the fact that individual-level diversity has been accompanied by territorial convergence. Both Scotland and England now have diverse multicultural societies but the difference between them is slight. The big differences now lie within, not between, Scottish and English cultures. James Kellas finds it 'difficult to distinguish between the two nations'.

That too has important consequences for the relationship between Scotland and England. Tracing attitudes to devolution from the late nineteenth century onwards, James Mitchell argues that Dicey viewed Scottish nationalism as 'benign' because, unlike Irish nationalism, it was not 'secessionist'. Yet Dicey accepted the 'democratic sentiment' of the age and placed popular sovereignty above parliamentary sovereignty. He accepted that ultimately the people should decide all political issues. But there remained the question which so bedevilled nationalist and unionist discourse at that time: 'which people?' should decide. Secession would make a difference because different people had different cultures that would be reflected in secessionist states. Secession was therefore as much about culture and values as about territory.

Now that Scottish and English culture and values have converged to the point where they are indistinguishable, the old nineteenth-century question is less relevant. It matters much less, if at all, 'which people' decide. Thus a unionist Prime Minister (John Major) could, in 1993, issue a statement supporting Scottish secession provided only that the Scottish people (not as Dicey would have argued, the British people) wished it.

The Changing Role of the State

In 1900 the people of Scotland and England owed a common allegiance to the Empress of India. It was true that it was a recently acquired title. But

Richard Finlay shows that Queen Victoria had a talent for interpreting and manipulating history, adopting national identities and evoking a significant response. If she had had access to jet aircraft instead of railway trains she might have spent more time in India and less in Scotland. Britain itself was only a fragment of Her Majesty's, mainly Asian, empire, while Europe was home to Britain's traditional enemies, even if some significant European powers were occasionally temporary allies.

It was also true that she reigned but did not rule. But neither did the people. Less than a tenth of the UK population voted in the parliamentary election of that year. Most adults of voting age were not entitled to vote. And the role of the state remained, as it had been for several centuries, to make and enforce laws, to define morality and religion (including religious belief as taught in schools), to make war, and to expand its empire.[3]

David McCrone goes further and argues that Britain in 1900 was neither a state nor a nation. The union was 'an imperial rather than a state arrangement', that 'being British was much more of an imperial than a national reality'. Vestiges of that remained until the 1980s. By the close of the century, however, the concept of allegiance had been hollowed out. To the dismay of the new Labour Prime Minister, citizens were far more interested in rights than duties. Scotland and England were no longer part of a global empire but part of a modest European state that was permanently locked in a co-operative relationship with the whole of Europe. Their world was no more global than it had been at the start of the century—indeed, arguably less global. But it was a world modelled on the concept of clubs that nations clamoured to join rather than empires they sought to leave.

And the essential role of the state in the post-imperial world had changed not once but twice since the start of the century. It no longer claimed the monopoly of making and enforcing laws (many of which were now made by supra-state clubs). It could no longer define morality and religion, which had been largely privatised. It could no longer control a military empire—even if that had remained an ambition, which it had not.

Instead the focus turned first towards extending the provision of welfare services, good government and civil rights for its citizens. The state was re-defined as the 'welfare state'. Later the focus again turned outwards, towards ensuring that its citizens gained maximum advantage from co-operative globalisation. The post-welfare state became the 'mentor state'. It assumed the roles of business advisor and advocate—to encourage (largely private) economic development, to help its citizens cope with economic change (though

---

[3] This traditional view of the role of the state is set out in K. Minogue, 'State' in J. Kuper (ed.), *Political Science and Political Theory* (London, 1987), pp. 235–40.

more by education, training, and opportunities than by welfare), and to ensure that its citizens' case was advocated persuasively (rather than by force) within global and regional clubs that it could influence but not threaten.

The role of the state interacts with the nature of society in its impact upon the implications of secession and consequently upon tolerating a right of secession. When territorial societies differ sharply, when the state claims a monopoly on making and enforcing laws, and when its role includes defining and enforcing morality, religion, and culture, secession means a great deal more than territorial separation. When none of these conditions apply, secession is reduced to an administrative technicality.

Dicey feared that secession would make Ireland less British. At that time Scottish secession might even have made both Scotland and England less British. That was not just because these societies were culturally different but also because the state embodied the national culture. But by the end of the century the changing role of the state combined with the territorial convergence of society and culture to almost eliminate the potential impact of Scottish secession on the functional Britishness of either Scotland or England. James Kellas cites even leading SNP politicians now talking of 'a "British society" in conjunction with a Scottish state'. Former, and once again, leader of the SNP, Alex Salmond frequently claims to be an 'Anglophile'. SNP Vice-President Neil MacCormick in this volume advocates a reversion from the 1707 Union of Parliaments to the 1603 Union of Crowns (though not of governments)—which Richard Finlay tells us was despised and rejected in nineteenth-century Scotland as being incompatible with Scottish culture! No doubt a sympathetic, frequently resident but non-governing Victoria was preferable to a powerful 'absentee' ruler like James. But it is yet another indicator of the lack of contemporary antagonism between Scotland and England—not least amongst nationalist politicians.

Secession has therefore changed its meaning since Dicey's day. It has gone from being a malign threat, through being 'benign', to being almost irrelevant. Arguably a British government has implemented devolution not so much because it fears Scottish nationalism and secessionism as because it no longer fears them. Apart from identity-shock, separation between Scotland and England would be more velvet than even the 'velvet divorce' between the Czech and Slovak Republics—though perhaps even less necessary and even more regretted.

Scotland and England began and ended the century bound together, within something called Britain. By the end of the century Scotland and England had changed. But what Britain was, and what Britain was for, had also changed. That permitted, if it did not actually encourage, some remarkable changes in the relationship between Scotland and England. The century opened with a Britain that was a 'multinational' state, a single 'union-state'[4] (though not, as it was often called, a 'unitary-state') with significantly different societies and cultures in Scotland and England. The century ended with Britain coming close to being a 'multi-state' but 'union-society'—with different governments north and south of the border but societies and cultures indistinguishable in everything except symbolic identity.

In this situation government itself lacks any intrinsically national or territorial culture. Robert Hazell and Barry Winetrobe argue that there was a determination that the 1997 devolution plan, unlike the earlier 1979 plan, would be 'not like Westminster' but would result from a 'home-grown process'. But it was to differ from Westminster not on a national or territorial dimension so much as on a modernisation or civil-rights dimension. Indeed devolution was only 'part of a wider package of reform'. Ideally it would serve as a model and a testing ground for reform at Westminster itself. The 1997 devolution plan was 'home-grown' and 'tailor-made' in origin but nonetheless had ambitions to be universalist in application.

There is nothing intrinsically Scottish about the Scottish Parliament and its procedures. Hazell and Winetrobe catalogue the Holyrood parliament's successes and its failures, but its successes (such as they may be) are there to be transferred and to be copied. It was never designed to be a 'Scottish Parliament for a Scottish people', as the post-1922 Irish parliaments were claimed by their leaders to be respectively 'a Catholic (or Protestant) Parliament for a Catholic (or Protestant) people'. Instead it was to be a 'modern parliament for a modern (and incidentally multicultural) Scotland'.

Cross-border Sympathy

As in any union, some friction is to be expected. But in a period of constitutional change and partial separation, the degree of cross-national or cross-border sympathy is more remarkable than the degree of friction.

Angela McCarthy's analysis of interviews with Scottish immigrants in England reveal 'predominantly favourable accounts of life in England' and indicate that 'Scots did not receive a hostile reception'. The English immigrants in Scotland studied by Asifa Hussain and William Miller do report considerable experience of harassment in Scotland. But they rate the conflict between themselves and Scots as far less serious than the sectarian conflict between Protestant and Catholic Scots. And so do the Scots themselves. Almost unanimously these English immigrants claim to feel 'at ease living in

[4] S. Rokkan and D. Urwin (eds), *The Politics of Territorial Identity* (London, 1982), p. 11.

Scotland'. On balance they feel Scotland has got 'more welcoming' to non-Scots since devolution, that it has got easier to criticise Scotland and things Scottish since devolution, and they themselves even feel marginally more at ease since devolution if that were possible. Very few look forward to returning to England. They do not feel—as they might well have done—at all like Russians in post-Soviet Central Asia or the Baltic states after control from Moscow was withdrawn.

The extreme disparity in size makes England a natural hegemon within the UK. But it is a very sympathetic hegemon—when it thinks of Scotland at all. John Curtice shows that the public in England are as favourable to Scottish devolution as Scots themselves.[5] In this respect sympathy is fully reciprocated: Scots are even more favourable to English devolution than the English themselves. Moreover Curtice shows that the 'West Lothian Question' ('why should Scottish MPs be able to vote on purely English affairs when, after devolution, English MPs cannot vote on devolved matters?') is not an issue between the Scottish and English public. Scotland's very small number of MPs at Westminster (now reduced still further as a consequence of devolution) reduces its practical importance and keeps it away from the forefront of either public's mind. But both the Scottish and the English public regard it as an anomaly. And both would accept a restriction on the rights of Scottish MPs at Westminster to remove that anomaly. It is government, opposition, and party that take sides on this issue, not countries or nations.

David McCrone claims that 'the scale of grievances in Scotland ... is simply not sufficient' to endanger the union and 'if anything' devolution has reduced them. James Kellas finds it 'difficult to imagine an independent Scotland pursuing an anti-English policy'. The SNP's Neil MacCormick feels that the personal and family cross-border connections merit 'some political recognition and even celebration'; he looks forward to a continuing 'union' with England even after independence, albeit the formerly despised Union of Crowns rather than a union of governments.

Size and scale have long encouraged Scots to match English sympathy with Scottish deference. The Scottish Parliament and Executive have sought to avoid unnecessary friction by focusing on strictly devolved matters and the business of governance rather than seeking to push back the boundaries of devolution by acting as a 'forum of the nation'. There have been exceptions such as the Scottish Parliament's 2003 debate on Iraq, but that ended with a vote affirming Westminster's responsibility for the issue. More surprisingly, Philip Schlesinger shows how 'most of the Holyrood political class have been

---

[5] For similar conclusions based on an earlier survey, see W. L. Miller et al., *How Voters Change: The 1987 British Election Campaign in Perspective* (Oxford, 1990), p. 285.

reluctant to explore the boundaries between the devolved and the reserved', even on less life-and-death issues such as broadcasting—though that may owe as much to the 'spectre of independence' that 'has haunted the calculations of devolutionist politicians' as to ingrained habits of deference to London. Conversely, he also recounts at least one post-devolution success for classic informal pre-devolution-style 'Scottish lobbying' in Westminster.

As long as the union persists, however, squabbles over finance provide at least some potential for internal tension. In the words of David Heald and Alasdair McLeod 'a UK government that wished to make the union unworkable could do so', though thus far they have not so wished. Iain McLean is less optimistic: any simple rule-of-thumb formulae that allocate higher per capita government expenditure to Scotland than England have 'no defenders outside Scotland' and are perceived 'in the rest of the UK to be defending the indefensible'. Moreover, he writes, in an attempt to stave off proposals for devolution successive Secretaries of State publicised (within Scotland) the supposed Scottish bias. Outside Scotland this was greeted with less scepticism and more interest, especially in the North-East region. To avoid the build-up of cross-border resentment McLean argues that government should either move to some form of equal revenue apportionment or to a credible needs-based formula that would legitimate unequal expenditure.

The Barnett formula was devised in the 1970s to progressively reduce the anti-English bias in per capita expenditures. But David Heald and Alasdair McLeod argue it may soon go too far and stir up legitimate resentment in Scotland and Wales—precisely because it will get too close to equal per capita expenditures. Equal per capita expenditures will be perceived as unfair in parts of the UK where relative poverty or the relative cost of public services mean that equal per capita expenditures do not provide equal access to services for those who need them. Unfortunately there is no universally agreed basis for calculating need.

The problem is not in fact one of expenditure but mainly one of justification or legitimacy. Because Scotland is so small, the Scottish bias in per capita expenditures has little or no detectable impact on per capita expenditure in England. But since the debate over devolution has made the bias visible, it could be a source of English resentment, even if its elimination would provide no detectable per capita benefit to the English. It has to be quietly forgotten, or eliminated, or justified.

But is justification possible? Charlie Jeffery poses the 'blunt' question: 'why should taxpayers in the southern half of England pay for everyone else's needs?' Tony Blair has justified political devolution on grounds of subsidiarity: 'finding different levels of politics appropriate to different types of issue'. But, Jeffery maintains, the issue of 'solidarity' or 'common standards' has not been addressed.

The combination of subsidiarity and solidarity is particularly difficult to justify. It means conceding local control in the interests of subsidiarity, yet asking richer areas to subsidise poorer areas in the interests of solidarity. It sounds rather too much like taxation without representation. Indeed it is taxation without hands-on control. So it requires a transcendent sense of community.

That seems unlikely. And yet Jeffery presents hard survey evidence from Canada, Australia, and post-unification Germany as well as Britain to show that subsidies from richer to poorer areas do have broad consensus support even in federal systems, and certainly in Britain. He attributes that to the co-existence of British identities with English/Scottish identities and a sense of 'common UK statehood'. English/Scottish identities justify subsidiarity but they do not exclude simultaneous British identities that justify solidarity. Moreover, public acceptance of policy diversity is bolstered by the fact that some peculiarly Scottish policies have majority approval throughout England as well as Scotland—and vice versa. It is not the case that the public in one country disapprove of policies that have only been adopted by government in the other country.

The best example of reactive and antagonistic English responses to Scottish devolution remains the coalition of North-East MPs and local authority leaders whom John Tomaney describes as 'the chief opponents of the Scotland Bill in 1977' which they 'effectively killed' by a rebellion on a parliamentary guillotine bill that had become necessary to end obstruction in the House. Yet Tomaney presents a wealth of evidence to suggest that the North-East's 'regionalism of discontent' was not rooted in antipathy towards Scotland but in 'a long and distinctive debate about the merits of regional government' that 'can be traced throughout the [twentieth] century'. Although Tomaney himself might not approve the phrase, his account suggests that North-East regionalism was as much anti-English as anti-Scottish—and more pro-North-East than anti-anything. After 1977 North-East politicians quickly switched from opposing Scottish devolution to copying the techniques and strategies of the Scottish devolutionists—including the creation of a 'Campaign for a Northern Assembly', succeeded by a 'North East Constitutional Convention' to parallel the 'Campaign for a Scottish Assembly' and the later 'Scottish Constitutional Convention'.

The Pressure of Adversarial Politics

Finally, a significant feature of the relationship between Scotland and England is inconsistency. Parties and politicians have frequently changed their political positions on Scottish administration, devolution or secession.

Sometimes that has been for reasons of principle. David Heald and Alasdair McLeod, as well as Iain McLean, point out that Lord Barnett himself later became a severe critic of his own formula for allocating expenditure between Scotland and England. But then he had only intended it to be a short-term stop-gap until a better but more complex formula could be implemented.

Sometimes, parties and politicians—notably the Liberals and the SNP—have compromised tactically, backing what they regarded as a second-best option rather than risk losing everything. That was notably true of the SNP in the 1997 referendum when they backed a vote in favour of Labour's devolution plan, a plan whose aims included the elimination of Scottish separatism.

But James Kellas argues that for Labour and the Conservatives especially, the opposition imperative or calculations of party advantage—that is, the mechanics of adversarial politics rather than principle or ideology—explain their changing positions on devolution. Scotland was not their main concern. Scottish government was not a core issue for them and their Scottish policy was determined by the opportunity to harry their opponents at Westminster and/or maximise their chances of winning a majority in future elections to the Westminster parliament.

In government, unionist politicians were also frequently ambivalent between a policy of concession and a policy of confrontation—sometimes with bizarre results. Richard Finlay describes the English reaction when the 'Stone of Destiny' was (briefly) taken from Westminster Abbey in 1950 by nationalist students from Glasgow University. The Archbishop of Canterbury reportedly said: 'there could be no simpler, more elementary illustration of the spiritual causes of the world's evil than the stealing from Westminster Abbey of the Coronation Stone.' As time went by the event was largely forgotten by most and regarded as a student prank by those few who were aware of it. Then in 1996 the stone was suddenly but permanently relocated to Scotland. An oddly nationalist act, as James Kellas points out, by a Conservative Secretary of State who was strongly opposed even to devolution, let alone nationalism.

AN EVOLVING UNION

2

Scotland and the Monarchy in the Twentieth Century

RICHARD J. FINLAY

AT AROUND 7 P.M. ON 22 JANUARY 1901, news began to filter into Glasgow, the Second City of the Empire, that Queen Victoria had died.[1] The news was not unexpected, but it did cause a bit of a commotion because nobody quite knew what to do. There were few people who could remember a time when Victoria was not the monarch and the development of public royal protocol over her long reign did not extend to what ought to be done in the event of her death. How were people supposed to act? It was especially problematic for Glasgow's entertainment managers. By the time that news got round the various theatres, most shows had already started and the ticket money was collected in. Should the news be broken to the audience and ought the shows to be cancelled as a mark of respect? A more immediate worry for some hard-pressed theatre managers was the question of whether money should be refunded. Some did nothing, arguing that it was best to wait for official confirmation. Somewhat predictably, the theatre reactions were determined by the class composition of the audience. In St Andrews Hall, the news was broken immediately, the orchestra played the Death March and the audience went home in a manner that was respectful, sombre, and silent. The Royalty, the Royal, the Grand, and the Metropole stopped the performance. The more down-market music halls, such as the Empire and the Britannia, stuck with the maxim that 'the show must go on', in spite of the fact that many of the performances were popular patriotic pieces like *Deeds that won the Empire* and *The Battle of Omdurman*.[2] The following morning the newspapers confirmed the story and announced that the theatres would remain closed throughout the period of mourning, although many opened the following

---

[1] C. A. Oakley, *The Second City* (Glasgow, 1946), pp. 238–9.
[2] Ibid.

Proceedings of the British Academy **128**, 17–34. © The British Academy 2005.

day.[3] Speaking at the General Assembly of the Church of Scotland some months later in May, the Scottish Secretary, Lord Balfour of Burleigh, told the audience that:

> We may speak of the magnitude of the loss not only to this country, but to the world at large in the death of our Queen. . . . Moderator, it is not too much to say that the name of Queen Victoria has become a synonym for all that is loftiest and noblest and purest in our age. She was so great that the more you saw of her the more irresistibly you were drawn within the sphere of her influence, and the more your reverence was increased. If I were to single out one attribute more than another for special notice, I would venture to lay stress upon the extraordinary faculty possessed by the Queen for inspiring at once love and respect.[4]

There was little doubt that the Scottish nation mourned the passing of Queen Victoria with great sincerity, all of which was a great testimony to her popularity.

The reason for Victoria's popularity is to be found in the way that Scotland's relationship with the British monarchy was transformed during her reign. This was done largely through her own efforts and, in particular, she publicly expressed deep affection for her northern kingdom. Without any sense of irony, Victoria took upon herself the heirdom of Jacobitism:

> Yes; and *I* feel a sort of reverence in going over all these scenes in this most beautiful country which I am glad to call my own, where there was much devoted loyalty to the family of my ancestors—for Stewart blood is in my veins, and I am now their representative, and the people are as devoted to me as they were to that unhappy race.[5]

As with the rest of the United Kingdom, the institution of monarchy increasingly took on a more symbolic and ceremonial role as its political power diminished during the second half of the nineteenth century. In an age of increased transportation and communication, the monarchy was increasingly adapted as an institution to reflect the grandeur and splendour of Britain and its expanding empire.[6] While mainstream British historians have noted this phenomenon, their Scottish colleagues have been less diligent. Indeed, more ink has been spilled on the abortive Jacobite attempts at a Stuart restoration

---

[3] *Glasgow Daily Mail*, 23 January 1901.

[4] *The Scotsman*, 15 May 1901.

[5] *Leaves from the Journal of Our Life in the Highlands* (1868, various editions); *More Leaves from the Journal of a Life in the Highlands* (1883, various editions) (hereafter *Journal*). *Journal*, 12 September 1875.

[6] F. Hardie, *The Political Influence of the British Monarchy, 1868–1952* (London, 1970); J. L. Lant, *Insubstantial Pageant: Ceremony and Confusion at Queen Victoria's Court* (London, 1979); David Cannadine, 'The context, performance and meaning of ritual: the British monarchy and the invention of tradition', in E. J. Hobsbawm and T. Ranger (eds), *The Invention of Tradition*

in the first half of the eighteenth century, than on the role of the institution of monarchy in Scotland and the important part played in cementing a sense of British identity north of the border in the period after 1707.[7] When attention does focus on the monarchy, it is usually to denounce the phoniness of 'Balmoralism' and its role in the construction of a sham Scottish identity.[8]

This state of affairs in Scottish historiography is unusual for the following reasons. Firstly, Victoria spent a lot of time in Scotland over a long period, and was probably seen in the flesh on her many tours by more Scots than any leading contemporary politician. For example, simply by virtue of the sheer number of annual visits north since the mid-nineteenth century, in all probability Victoria was seen by more Scots than William Gladstone, who was arguably the most popular politician north of the border in the second half of the nineteenth century. Secondly, the presence of the queen revived the use of a distinctive Scottish protocol for royal visits and reactivated the social circle associated with monarchy north of the border, which had lain dormant since the seventeenth century. Arguably, this was a factor in maintaining a distinctive sense of Scottish identity among Scotland's hierarchy, which was the social group most prone to Anglicisation. Thus at one society event, the marriage of Princess Louise to the Marquis of Lorne, her official adviser, Sir Henry Ponsonby, was given a telling off because 'Ponsonby speaks of his being [the Marquis of Lorne] a young Englishman, but he is *not*, he is a Scotsman and a Highlander.'[9] Finally, Queen Victoria presented the monarchy in Scotland in a recognisably Scottish guise and made repeated reference to the Scots' historic claim of joint ownership of the institution.[10]

It is the objective of this chapter to examine Scottish perceptions of the monarchy as part of a wider British identity in Scotland. It is well known that the Scots were said to have a 'holy trinity' of education, law, and church,

---

(Cambridge, 1983), pp. 120–39; W. M. Kuhn, 'Ceremony and politics: the British monarchy 1871–1872', *Journal of British Studies* 26 (April 1987), pp. 131–45; W. L. Arnstein, 'Queen Victoria opens Parliament: the disinvention of tradition', *Historical Research* 63 (1990), pp. 178–94.

[7] M. G. H. Pittock, *The Myth of the Jacobite Clans* (Edinburgh, 1995); M. G. H. Pittock, *Jacobitism* (Basingstoke, 1998); B. P. Lenman, *The Jacobite Risings in Britain, 1689–1746* (London, 1980); B. P. Lenman, *The Jacobite Clans of the Great Glen 1650–1784* (London, 1984); D. Szechi, *The Jacobites, Britain and Europe 1688–1788* (Manchester, 1994); F. McLynn, *The Jacobites* (London, 1985); E. Cruikshanks and J. Black (eds), *The Jacobite Challenge* (Edinburgh, 1988).

[8] G. Scott-Moncrieff, 'Balmorality', in D. C. Thomson (ed.), *Scotland in Quest of its Youth* (Edinburgh, 1932), pp. 17–24; O. Brown, *Hitlerism in the Highlands* (Glasgow, 1944); T. Nairn, *The Break-up of Britain* (London, 1987 edn); C. Craig, *Out of History* (Edinburgh, 1989).

[9] A. Ponsonby, *Henry Ponsonby, Queen Victoria's Private Secretary: his Life from Letters by his son Arthur Ponsonby* (London, 1942), p. 91.

[10] R. J. Finlay, 'Queen Victoria and the cult of Scottish monarchy', in E. J. Cowan and R. J. Finlay (eds), *Scottish History: The Power of the Past* (Edinburgh, 2002), pp. 209–25.

which acted as the main props of Scottish national identity that helped to keep it distinctive and separate from England. Yet, it can also be said that monarchy, the armed forces, and parliament acted as a comparable tripartite base of British identity in Scotland. The former trinity has been studied more intensely by historians of Scotland than the latter, in spite of the fact that British national identity in Scotland faced no serious challenge until the late twentieth century. The institution of monarchy was, it will be argued, an important factor in the promotion of this British identity in Scotland. Firstly, the chapter will briefly trace the ways in which Victoria re-established the notion of monarchy in Scottish society. This is important because Victoria set the template against which subsequent monarchs were judged. Secondly, the contrast between the popular perception of Victoria and her heir, Edward, will be examined to demonstrate how notions of Scottishness were important in determining attitudes towards the monarchy. This was especially the case as the celebrations in Scotland of his accession coincided with the tricentenary of the Union of the Crowns. Thirdly, the period surrounding the coronation of Queen Elizabeth will be examined as it took place in 1953, the 350th anniversary of the Union of the Crowns. Again, the incident will be analysed to chart ideas of Scottish identity in relationship to the British monarchy. Finally, the chapter will explore some of the reasons why the influence of monarchy as a unifying factor in British identity has declined in Scotland over the last twenty years.

Victoria—a Queen for Scotland

The subject of monarchy was highlighted in Linda Colley's path-breaking *Britons*.[11] Yet, the increasingly institutional and ceremonial use of the Crown as a symbol of Britishness in the later part of the eighteenth and early nineteenth centuries had little impact north of the border. The bad odour surrounding the 'Queen Caroline' controversy in 1820 was partially expunged with Sir Walter Scott's stage-managed visit of George IV in 1822.[12] With a good eye for pageantry and the importance of historic symbolism, Scott used the occasion to re-link the institution of monarchy with its Scottish antecedents, albeit in a heavily fabricated, tartanised, and highlandised guise. The 'Chief of Chiefs' was welcomed to Edinburgh in a manner that could have come straight from one of Scott's own novels; a 'plaided panorama', as

---

[11] L. Colley, *Britons: Forging the Nation 1707–1837* (New Haven, 1992), pp. 217–28.
[12] C. M. M. MacDonald, 'Their laurels wither'd and their name forgot: women and the Scottish radical tradition', in Cowan and Finlay (eds), *Scottish History*, pp. 234–42; J. Prebble, *The King's Jaunt: George IV in Scotland, 1822* (London, 1988).

his son-in-law, John Lockhart, described it. The year 1822 was important for a number of reasons. Firstly, it demonstrated that the Scottish past could be utilised as an important part in the construction of a more multi-faceted British identity that paid due deference to the historic nations of the United Kingdom. Secondly, it demonstrated the importance of the symbolic and ceremonial power of the monarchy in a Scottish guise. Finally, and arguably most important, it set the template of duality in the construction of a British identity that was based on a Scottish rendering of British institutions.

Yet, 1822 would have been a one-off event had it not been for Victoria. There is a danger in using the occasion of George IV's visit as the starting point for the subsequent development of a national identity in Scotland that lent many of its characteristics, such as tartan and Highlandism, to the creation of a wider British identity. The reality is that there was a gap of several decades before the monarchy would resurface in Scotland. It was the Victorian age that witnessed the incorporation of Highland symbolism as central to depictions of Scottish identity. Indeed, Victoria was largely responsible for much of this. Her glowing depictions of the Highlands in her *Journals* were much more influential than the visit of George IV. Victoria's Scottification of the monarchy was not a stage-managed event and was more of an organic development. Annual visits with many stopping off points allowed huge numbers of Scots to see the monarch and were usually marked with a plaque, fountain, or some such commemoration. Testament to her presence is to be found in the fact that these are littered throughout Scotland today. Royal visits acted as an important focal point in the construction of local civic identity and meant that local town or city officials had to reinvent traditional notions of royal protocol. The office of the Lord Lyon of Scotland came into its own once again as demand for knowledge about Scottish heraldry, pageantry, and royal symbols increased. Indeed, it is worth pointing out that the misuse of heraldic devices was one of the irritants that provoked nationalist discontent in nineteenth-century Scotland.[13] It is a fact worth stressing that the longevity of Victoria and her annual visits north of the border meant that there was a sustained royal presence in Scotland that had not been witnessed since the Union of the Crowns in 1603.

A key component of Victoria's success was the ability to reconnect with Scottish regal history. Victoria laid a great deal of emphasis on the fact that she was the heir of the Scottish line of succession. This manifested itself in a number of ways. In her *Journals* she referred to Scottish monarchs as her ancestors and even went so far as to claim that she had Jacobite blood in her veins.[14] For example, Mary, Queen of Scots was described as her 'poor

[13] H. J. Hanham, *Scottish Nationalism* (London, 1969), pp. 94–103.
[14] *Journal*, 12 September 1875.

ancestress' and at Cambuskenneth, near Stirling, the tomb of James III was restored by 'Victoria, a descendant'.[15] This was important because it suggested a line of continuity between her and the pre-union Scottish monarchy. By drawing attention to the Scottish antecedents of the British monarchy, Victoria enabled the Scots to claim part-ownership of the Crown by virtue of their history. This was best evidenced on a visit to Bannockburn, which she described as the place where her two ancestors, Edward I and Robert the Bruce, met in battle.[16] By claiming to represent the Scottish lineage of the Crown, as well as that of England, Victoria was able to present herself as the living embodiment of the union, in which the conflict of the past could be laid to rest, but the separate streams of that past were mutually respected.

Historians of Victorian Britain have drawn attention to the ways in which the symbolic and ceremonial power of the monarchy was built up during the nineteenth century. The monarchy was used as a focal point of British imperial prowess and a symbolic representation of the increasing power and splendour of the state.[17] This technique was also applied in the Raj, where a fusion of imperial and nativist traditions were re-invented to confer legitimacy on British imperial rule.[18] The same process can be observed in Scotland. Institutions such as the Order of the Thistle found themselves conspicuously revived on account of the greater presence of the monarchy in Scotland. The growth of 'Balmoralism' with its association of Highlandism and Tartanry can be viewed as a way in which to give the monarchy in Scotland a more conspicuous native identity. Victoria's endorsement of presbyterianism, likewise, reinforced the legitimacy of the national religion.[19] The pomp and splendour of the visit to Glasgow in 1858, for example, was the occasion to show the integrated role the Scots played within the Empire. By the time of the opening of Glasgow City Chambers in 1888, at which Victoria presided, the extent of the ceremonial role had been increased. It was an opportunity for all of Scotland's institutions and civic society to dress up in their finery and demonstrate to the world their distinctive national characteristics.[20]

The net effect of all this was to build up the popularity of Victoria in Scotland and give the monarchy a distinctive Scottish dimension north of the

[15] Ibid., 16 September 1873.

[16] Ibid., 23 August 1867.

[17] Cannadine, 'Context, performance and meaning'; K. Robbins, *Nineteenth-Century Britain: Integration and Diversity* (Oxford, 1988), pp. 172–4; B. Harrison, *The Transformation of British Politics, 1860–1995* (Oxford, 1996), pp. 90–1.

[18] B. S. Cohn, 'Representing authority in Victorian India', in Hobsbawm and Ranger (eds), *Invention of Tradition*, pp. 165–209.

[19] Queen Victoria, *Letters*, eds A. C. Benson and Viscount Esher, 3 vols (London, 1907), I, p. 381.

[20] *Hamilton Advertiser*, 'The Queen's Visit and Route Through Glasgow', August 1849; *Glasgow Herald*, 18 October 1859; ibid., 22 August 1888.

border. All the time this was reinforced by Victoria's continued presence, her open avowal of her love for 'the most intelligent part of the Kingdom', and her praise of Scots and Scottish characteristics.[21] Indeed, Victoria's popularity owed much to her willingness to defend the Scottish interest. In her reference to the Scottish monarchy, she never made the mistake of using the English numerals. Her open endorsement of presbyterianism and her willingness to oppose English ecclesiastical intrusions was warmly supported. Her portrayal of the supposed characteristics of the Scots as hard-working, well-educated, and moral was one that found favour with many in the population. Finally, her close relationship with her Highland regiments when she decorated soldiers at Balmoral reinforced the conception of Scotland as a martially gifted nation. The role of Victoria in cementing the affection of the Scottish people to the monarchy was pointed out half a century later by Andrew Dewar Gibb, Regius Professor of Law at Glasgow University:

> Possibly the long reign of Victoria, with its vague oriole of 'gloriousness', reconciled the people of Scotland to a royal house which had consistently ignored the existence of their country. That remarkable woman seems to have had a real kindness for Scotland. She built a house in the North Country, where she spent much of her time in her latter years. She professed great admiration for the Highlander, who seemed to have kept a chivalrous loyalty and devotion seen perhaps nowhere else in her day. She even sought the encouragement of the Gaelic language throughout the Highlands. She set her face against the episcopalising of the Church of Scotland, and put Archbishop Longley in his place when he tried it. Prince Albert thought Edinburgh the finest town which he had ever seen. The Queen was, of course, against what was called 'home rule' for Scotland, but her kindliness for the country should not be depreciated. The loyalty which was fostered by Victoria has been stimulated by the accession as queen consort of the daughter of a Scottish peer, who seems to care for Scotland and perhaps a little to understand it.[22]

Victoria was important because she was the first British monarch since the Glorious Revolution to recognise the distinctive national characteristics of her northern kingdom and, what is more, paid due deference to it. Furthermore, she encouraged a belief that the British monarchy was a composite Crown that owed its existence as much to Scottish history as to English history. Subsequent monarchs would be judged in Scotland on their ability to live up to this criterion.

---

[21] *Journal*, 1 September 1842; 12 September 1875.
[22] A. D. Gibb, *Scotland Resurgent* (Stirling, 1950), p. 287.

The Accession of Edward VII

The fact that Scotland was able to carve out a distinctive role for the monarchy was put in jeopardy on the accession of Edward. The 'playboy prince' did not have the same popularity as his mother and his antics were not approved of in presbyterian Scotland. Worse was to follow. Rather than use his own first name of Albert, he opted for Edward and chose to attach the numeral VII in accordance with the English line of the history of the British monarchy. This caused outrage north of the border, in that Victoria's hard work in giving the Scots a sense of ownership of the monarchy was completely undone by Edward's deference to English claims and indifference to Scottish ones. Furthermore, the issue of the numeral needs to be set in context. The incident was one of many at the turn of the century where a greater demand was made for due deference to be made to Scotland's claim as a historic mother nation of the empire. There had been a campaign from the 1880s against the use of 'England' and 'English' when referring to Britain and British.[23] The Scots took umbrage at the Arctic expedition and sent their own.[24] And tensions were increasing over the seemingly favourable treatment dished out to Ireland. While such incidents were wrapped up in the language of Scottish patriotism, they need not necessarily be construed as nationalist, because the principal reason for their manifestation was insensitivity to the fact that Scotland was not being treated as an equal with England in the union.

Edward's coronation was delayed because of illness and took place in 1902. His first official engagement in Scotland took place in the late spring of 1903, the tricentenary of the Union of the Crowns, although the family had come north for a holiday in the late summer of the previous year. The official coronation in 1902 did little to please the Scots. The English press made frequent reference to the new King of 'England', and the organisers of an exhibition in London to coincide with the event had the audacity to request the Scottish regalia be put on show. It was offensive to many Scots because it was treating the Scottish line of the monarchy as an aspect of minor interest, or even curiosity. Furthermore, as the Scottish Secretary of State, Balfour of Burleigh, pointed out, it was expressly forbidden by the Treaty of Union to remove the regalia from Edinburgh.[25] The incident was denounced as yet another example of English indifference to Scottish sensibilities. There was a

---

[23] See R. J. Finlay, *A Partnership for Good? Scottish Politics and the Union Since 1880* (Edinburgh, 1997), pp. 33–5.
[24] R. N. Rudmose Brown et al., *Voyage of the Scotia: The Story of Scotland's Forgotten Polar Heroes* (Edinburgh, 2004).
[25] Lady Frances Balfour, *Lord Balfour of Burleigh* (London, 1924), p. 95.

mobilisation of opinion against the use of the numeral VII. The Scottish Patriotic Association collected signatures of protest and for good measure put them on display in Glasgow's Kelvingrove Museum.[26] Letters appeared in most of the Scottish press, and the Loyal Addresses of the Church of Scotland and the Convention of Royal Burghs, arguably two of the most important institutions forming Scottish civil society, pointedly omitted the number VII.[27] The commemorative plaque to mark the visit of the king to Glasgow to lay the foundation stone of the Royal College of Technology (which became the University of Strathclyde) simply states 'laid by His Majesty, King Edward'. The king caused further ire when on a journey north he refused to leave his railway carriage when it stopped in Edinburgh, in spite of the fact that an official delegation from the city turned up to greet him.[28] All in all, it was a far cry from the attention paid to the northern kingdom by his mother.

The reaction of the south was mild amusement at the affront to Scotland's dignity. The comment from *The Times* summed up attitudes:

> The snub administered to them [the king and queen] by the Convention of Burghs, which is nothing if it is not truly and characteristically Scottish: their influence is no less unmistakable in the resolution of several public bodies to omit the 'numeral' from the inscription on their coronation medals, and in the untimely fits of economy that have overcome some authorities not as a rule averse to feasting.[29]

The fact that Edward failed to live up to his mother's ability to appease Scottish national sentiment is only one feature of the incident involving the numeral. A central aspect of public displeasure at the use of the VII was that it paid insufficient deference to Scotland's history and the fact that the nation had a legitimate claim of joint ownership of the British monarchy. Yet, what is strange is that there was little discussion of the origins of the Scots' claim to an independent system of monarchical numbering. After all, the occasion of the loyal addresses in Scotland was during the tricentenary of the Union of the Crowns, the key event in history that gave Scotland its legitimate claim to ownership of the monarchy. Yet, for all the furore and indignity, there was little mention of this event, nor was there any public celebration of the anniversary. The incident offers us a rare insight into Scottish historical mentality at this time. In most of the protests against English indifference to Scottish national sensitivity, it is the Treaty of Union (1707) that was used as the basis of Scottish claims to due recognition, not the Union of the Crowns

[26] *Scottish Patriot*, April 1902.
[27] *Glasgow Herald*, 15 May 1903.
[28] *The Scotsman*, 18 May 1903.
[29] *The Times*, 21 May 1903.

(1603). In part, this can be explained by the perceptions the Scots had of their history and the difficulties they had in reconciling themselves to the Stuart monarchy, upon which their claims under the Union of the Crowns for equal recognition would be based.

Of the four main popular icons in Scottish history in the nineteenth century, two relate to the Wars of Independence, Bruce and Wallace, and two to the nation's religious inheritance, John Knox and the Covenanters. By focusing attention on the Union of the Crowns, the awkward issue of the Stuarts' place in both Scottish and British history was raised and, ultimately, the problem would be traced back to Scotland. Much of nineteenth- and early twentieth-century Scottish identity focused on the nation's presbyterian inheritance. The anniversary of the signing of the National Covenant and the bicentenary of the Glorious Revolution, for example, were celebrated in Scotland. In populist history books, the conventional account of the Scottish past was that the nation's religious liberty was moulded in the struggle against the despotic Stuarts, and in particular the Catholic James VII, who persecuted the presbyterians during the 'Killing Times'. The years 1688 and 1690 were two important dates for Scots, as they marked the departure of James and the establishment of presbyterianism as the national religion of Scotland. The leader of the United Presbyterians, John Cairns, summed up the Scots' attitude to the relationship between church and state on the occasion of Victoria's Jubilee in 1887:

> Although we deny to a great and noble Queen like this any headship of any kind in the church of Christ, as our fathers denied it to the Stuarts, I as a Scotchman and a Presbyterian am thankful not only for her recognition of men like Norman Macleod and Principal Tulloch, but for her goodness to men like Thomas Guthrie and George Middleton [both eminent Free Churchmen] in their dying hours. In these things we see something deeper than womanly sympathy or native tolerance, even the Christianity which recognises everywhere the same divine image, and which, when it is set upon so lofty a throne, blesses both the country and the world.[30]

The historic episode of the Union of the Crowns could only be seen as an embarrassing and unhappy interlude in Anglo-Scottish relations because it led not only to an attempt to subvert Scottish liberties, but British ones as well.

The 'presbyterianisation' of Scottish history was especially marked in the nineteenth century. The effects of the Disruption of 1843 and the controversy of the union of the Free Church of Scotland and the United Presbyterian Church in 1900 demonstrated the ability of religion to stir the passions, and

---

[30] A. R. MacEwen, *The Life and Letters of John Cairns* (London, 1898), p. 774.

its divisive effect on Scottish society. Yet, it can equally be argued that the schisms and controversies were evidence of the powerful appeal of presbyterianism *per se*, and furthermore, the fact that all claimed to be representing the 'true historic national' church of Scotland that was moulded in the fire of seventeenth-century persecution meant that the presbyterians were unlikely to hold up the accession of a line of tyrants to the British throne in 1603 as something for the nation to be proud of. The Stuarts were largely written out of popular accounts of the nation's past. *Chambers' Dictionary of Eminent Scotsmen*, published throughout the nineteenth century, for example, features no prominent Jacobites and is none too flattering in its descriptions of James VI and Charles I. The former was described as having tyrannical tendencies and the latter was the author of most of his own misfortunes.[31] Statues were erected to Covenanting martyrs and popular literature perpetuated the myth of Scottish religious identity forged in the fire of Stuart persecution.[32]

For the Scots, it was the Treaty of Union in 1707 that marked the bedrock of the union and it was to the Treaty that the Scots made their appeals against English indifference. Evidence of this is to be found in the fact that although the anniversary of the Union of the Crowns passed in silence, the Union of the Parliaments was at least acknowledged.[33] Again, the importance of presbyterianism can be illustrated by the fact that for the coronation of George V, the head of the Scottish Episcopal Church was accidentally invited by the Herald's College, which once again called for the intervention of Lord Balfour of Burleigh to insist that due deference be given to the Church of Scotland as a national church in the ceremony.[34] At least with George, there was no issue with the numeral and his reign until 1935 was without event from the Scottish perspective.

The accession of Edward in 1936 and the use of the numeral VIII could have led to a repeat of the performance surrounding Edward VII, but his short reign was engulfed by the scandal of his involvement with Mrs Simpson, a divorcee, and an American to boot.[35] Furthermore, the period was one associated with heightening international tension and the after-effects of the Great Depression. Like the rest of the United Kingdom, most Scots were happy with his decision to abdicate within the year and with the accession of his brother George VI, who, as the Scottish press were pleased to point out,

---

[31] *A Biographical Dictionary of Eminent Scotsmen Originally Edited by Robert Chambers*, new edition by Thomas Thomson, 3 vols (Edinburgh, 1869), I, pp. 353–6, II, pp. 370–9.

[32] See E. J. Cowan, 'The Covenanting tradition in Scottish history', in Cowan and Finlay (eds), *Scottish History*, pp. 121–47.

[33] The *Glasgow Herald* ran a series of articles on the union during April and May of 1907. These were subsequently republished as *The Union of 1707* (Glasgow, 1907).

[34] Balfour, *Balfour of Burleigh*, p. 97.

[35] Not even the nationalist *Scots Independent* had much to say about it.

was married to a Scot.[36] The two Georges were popular in Scotland in the period after the First World War and maintained the symbolic and ceremonial role of the royal family in Scotland. The presence of the royal family for the launching of the *Queen Mary*, the Empire Exhibition of 1938, or on holiday at Balmoral was reported extensively in the press and the response of the crowds to royal visits remained enthusiastic, even though the Depression bit hard.[37] The advent of Scottish nationalism and the disquiet that began to emanate regarding Scottish treatment within the union led to calls for a more concerted policy of royal presence in Scotland in order to shore up British national identity. The importance of the royal family as important British figureheads who were above party politics was recognised by politicians. According to the Tory MP T. C. R. Moore, 'The royal residence should be occupied for three months by a representative of His Majesty. That would mean an enormous development in Scotland on the social side.'[38] One consequence of the clamour for more royal contact was the establishment of the annual garden party at Holyrood.

Queen Elizabeth—the Second?

The coronation of Queen Elizabeth in 1953 took place on the 350th anniversary of the Union of the Crowns and once again there was a furore about the numeral. Like the coronation of Edward, the event took place against a backdrop of increasing nationalist sentiment. The Scottish National Convention had mobilised some two million signatures in favour of Home Rule, and events such as the nationalisation of major industries had led many Tories to denounce the policy as one of shifting control away from Scotland to London. Sir Winston Churchill speaking in Edinburgh denounced the policy of the Labour government as one that would undermine Scotland's national status within the union:

> The principle of centralisation of government in Whitehall and Westminster is emphasised in a manner not hitherto experienced or contemplated in the Act of Union . . . If England became an absolute Socialist state, owning all the means of production, distribution, and exchange, ruled only by politicians and their officials in London offices, I personally cannot feel that Scotland would be bound to accept such a dispensation.[39]

[36] *Daily Record*, Special Edition, 12 May 1937.
[37] For example, the coverage given to the visit of George VI following the coronation was extensive and included the presentation of the Order of the Thistle to Queen Mary and the march past by the Royal Company of Archers at Holyroodhouse.
[38] Hansard, HC (series 4) vol. 272, col. 301 (22 November 1932).
[39] *The Scotsman*, 15 February 1950.

It was against this backdrop that the decision to use the numeral II caused discontent. As at the time of Edward, it was pointed out that there never had been a Queen Elizabeth in Scotland and that the use of II was inappropriate in Scotland. Again, there was a sense of confusion as to why this should so infuriate the Scots. Churchill suggested a compromise in that they would use the highest number from whichever line of the Scots and English monarchy, which in the case of Elizabeth would mean II, but should an heir named James be born, he would succeed as James VIII because the Scottish number was higher:

> Thus if a King Robert or King James came to the throne, they might be desig-
> nated to the appropriate Scottish succession, thereby emphasising that our
> royal family traces its descent through the English Royal Line from William the
> Conqueror and beyond, and through the Scottish Royal Line from Robert the
> Bruce and Malcolm Canmore and even further back.

It was not a commitment he bound his successors to, nor is there much evidence that he took the issue particularly seriously. Further pooh-poohing of the Scottish case was made by allusion to the fact that none of the Dominion nations had raised any objections to the numeral, even though they, likewise, had never had a Queen Elizabeth before.[40]

The issue of the coronation was also given an added impetus in that it occurred shortly after the removal or theft of the Stone of Destiny or Coronation Stone from Westminster Abbey. Taken on Christmas day 1950 by a group of nationalist Glasgow University students, the point was made that it was stolen from the Scots in the first place by Edward I during the Wars of Independence.[41] The theft caused outrage and sparked a widespread police hunt to recover the stone, whose disappearance was known to have upset the king. Roads into Scotland were checked by the police, as were the ports of the south of England, demonstrating how seriously the authorities took the inci-dent.[42] Events were ratcheted up when news broke that the king was ill, pro-voking a sympathetic backlash against the reivers, but though never explicitly stated, thoughts were turning as to what to do in the event of a succession without having the Coronation Stone. The stone was returned in the histori-cally significant Arbroath Abbey, with its allusion to the famous declaration, wrapped in a Saltire.

The incident was significant in two respects. Firstly, it exposed fault-lines in the idea of a shared British history and the contrasting views of the Scots and English regarding the Wars of Independence. Although many Scots were

[40] H. J. Paton, *The Claim of Scotland* (London, 1968), pp. 52–3.
[41] See Ian Hamilton, *No Stone Unturned* (London, 1954).
[42] *The Scotsman*, 12 January 1951.

appalled at the theft of the stone, many regarded the incident with a sense of amusement and there was a degree of nascent sympathy with the reivers. Furthermore, it highlighted the fact that an integral part of the English coronation ceremony involved placing the crown on the monarch's head while seated over the ancient Scottish coronation stone with its symbolic association of Scottish defeat and humiliation by Edward I, 'the Hammer of the Scots'. While the Scots regarded the Wars of Independence as perhaps the most heroic episode in the nation's history and Edward I as one of the greatest villains, the English view was not so charitable. As far as the view from the South was concerned, Edward was one of England's greatest kings, a view that has persisted down to this day. The theft of such an important English historical artefact which reflected the glory of the English Crown caused outrage. It was reported that the Archbishop of Canterbury said that 'there could be no simpler, more elementary illustration of the spiritual causes of the world's evil than the stealing from Westminster Abbey of the Coronation Stone.'[43] The English press regularly denounced the event as one of sacrilege and vandalism.

The decision to return the stone to Arbroath was dictated by the fact that security around St Giles in Edinburgh was tight, with the police keeping a watchful eye. By returning the stone to Arbroath Abbey, the reivers inadvertently tapped into an important seam of Scottish historical symbolism. The Treaty of Arbroath was a clear articulation of Scottish nationalism and was bound to turn minds to the heroic endeavours of Robert the Bruce, Scotland's most famous king. Also, the Declaration was significant because it articulated notions of contractual monarchy, in the sense that Robert was reminded that if he failed in his duty to safeguard independence he would be cast out and replaced by another.[44] The fact that the Burns Federation had sent a copy of the Declaration to every Scottish school in 1947 not only increased interest in the Wars of Independence, but also gave an unprecedented number of Scots access to the document itself. Though hard to prove empirically, the indirect attention focused on this aspect of Scottish monarchical history as a result of the theft of the stone must have had an impact on Scottish perceptions of the coronation barely two years later.

The event, however, was not associated with republicanism and once again showed evidence of a distinctive Scottish take on the question of the British monarchy. According to those who took the stone: 'His Majesty's petitioners, who have served him in peril and peace, pledge again their loyalty to him, saving always their right and duty to protest against the actions of his Ministers if such actions are contrary to the wishes or spirit of His Majesty's

[43] Quoted in Paton, *Claim of Scotland*, p. 59.
[44] E. J. Cowan, *For Freedom Alone: Scotland's Declaration of Independence* (East Linton, 2003).

Scottish people.'[45] In some respects, this was an echo of the Arbroath Declaration in that it was a reminder of the monarch's obligation to the community of the realm. For some it was only right that the stone was returned to Scotland, as it could then be returned under escort to Westminster for the coronation as a symbol of the 'free loyalty of the Scottish nation'. The event was one of many that indicated to the cabinet that Scottish nationalist sentiment was growing and led to the decision to inaugurate the Balfour Commission on Scottish administrative devolution.[46] In the General Election of 1951, the Conservative Party made good progress and a factor in this may have been that it was more adept at harnessing national sentiment to its cause than Labour.[47]

Perhaps most worrying for those connected with the monarchy was the fact that it was the Scottish middle class that seemed most upset about the issue of the numeral. Opinion poll evidence from the early 1950s shows that the working class in Glasgow felt more affinity with working-class people in other British cities than their middle-class co-nationals.[48] Certainly the types of protest, such as writing to the editors of *The Scotsman* and the *Glasgow Herald*, the stitching of 'ER I' into handkerchiefs and the like, were of a most genteel nature. The most serious issue was the blowing up of post-boxes bearing the offending ER II, events that led to the monogram's replacement with ER. A legal challenge to the use of the numeral was mounted by John MacCormick, leader of the Scottish Covenant Association and recently elected Lord Rector of Glasgow University. As with the numeral in 1903, MacCormick based his argument on an appeal to the Union of 1707, rather than that of 1603, and though he did not win his case was offered some solace by Lord Cooper, Lord President of the Court of Session, who endorsed the claim that the idea of parliamentary sovereignty had no basis in Scots law.[49] It may be suggested that it was in response to such discontent that it was decided that Elizabeth would visit St Giles in Edinburgh as part of the coronation celebration. The event was stage-managed to present a distinctive Scottish dimension. The Scottish crown was taken out for the Queen to hold and return as a symbolic acknowledgement of her Scottish line. It was presented by the three senior Scottish peers, all dressed in their traditional robes,

[45] Quoted in Paton, *Claim of Scotland*, p. 58.
[46] Cabinet Papers (50), 101, May 1950; Catto (Chairman), *Report on Scottish Financial and Trade Statistics*, Cmd. 8609 (Edinburgh, 1952).
[47] D. Seawright and J. Curtice, 'The decline of the Scottish Conservative and Unionist Party 1950–1992: religion, ideology or economics?', *Contemporary Record* 9:2 (1995), p. 332.
[48] S. B. Chrimes (ed.), *The General Election in Glasgow February 1950* (Glasgow, 1950), pp. 81, 182.
[49] J. M. MacCormick, *The Flag in the Wind: The Story of the National Movement in Scotland* (London, 1955), pp. 187–96, 215–19.

and the event was held in the historic location of St Giles. All in all, it was as close as it was possible to get to a separate Scottish coronation.[50] Yet, it back-fired. The Queen turned up wearing a two-piece suit, complete with handbag, and not the ceremonial robes that many had been expecting. Also, the fact that she simply held the crown of Scotland and did not wear it was a source of disappointment. The fact that the ceremonial robes were worn shortly afterwards at the opening of the Canadian parliament did not help ease the Scottish sense of frustration. Finally, her description of herself in the Christmas broadcast of 1953 as the first Queen of England to visit New Zealand did not help matters either.[51]

A further issue associated with the visit to St Giles was that, for the first time, it starkly illustrated in public the differences between the official posi-tions of the monarchy in England and Scotland on the basis of religion. Although the Church of Scotland gave up its 'national' status in 1929 on the occasion of its reunion with the United Free Church, to all intents and pur-poses it continued to act as if it remained a national church. Its history and standing in the community kept up the appearance of 'national' status. Church attendance in the 1950s was not decreasing, and indeed began to go up as a result of the Billy Graham 'Tell Scotland' campaign in 1955, and a furore about rumours of a plan to merge with the Church of England illus-trated how strong presbyterianism remained in Scottish society.[52] The coro-nation, however, threw into sharp relief the fact that the Queen was not head of the Church in Scotland and that in that Church she was an equal in the eyes of God. During the ceremony, no one acknowledged her as Queen by bowing or giving her recognition as being superior. The contrast with the cer-emony in Westminster could not have been greater. The extent to which this was a latent form of republicanism is debatable, but at the very least, it was yet another reminder of the awkward history of Scotland and the monarchy.

A Present and Future Role

Although there are notions of Scotland not having as much a sense of loy-alty to the monarchy in the period after 1945, this is not borne out by the evi-dence. The number of television licences more than doubled during 1953 as some 140,000 Scots families tuned in to watch the coronation on TV.[53] This

---

[50] *The Scotsman*, 24 June 1953.

[51] Paton, *Claim of Scotland*, p. 51.

[52] G. Walker and T. Gallagher (eds), *Battle Hymns and Sermons: Popular Protestantism in Modern Scotland* (Edinburgh, 1994).

[53] Scottish Statistical Office, *Digest of Scottish Statistics*, 11 (Edinburgh, 1958), p. 17.

rise was proportionate with the rest of the United Kingdom. The advent of the welfare state, far from displacing loyalty to the monarchy, arguably increased the royal presence in Scotland. The proliferation of state buildings, schools, municipal buildings, hospitals and the like meant that there was always something to be opened by and named after royalty, and this increased the monarchy's public profile north of the border. The tying together of the welfare state and monarchy in this ceremonial way was one method to ensure the survival of the popularity of the royal family and it cannot be concluded that greater state activity necessarily focused attention away from the Queen. Indeed, it might be argued that as a figurehead of the state, the popularity of the monarchy may have increased as a result of greater welfare intervention. The visit of the Queen to the University of Stirling in 1972 when students behaved in a drunken and raucous manner brought waves of condemnation from the Scottish press.[54] In the town itself, bus drivers, publicans, and other local businesses boycotted people with long hair on the basis that they might be the students who had insulted Her Majesty.[55] Public interest in the royal family was still great when it came to the marriage of the Prince of Wales to Lady Diana Spencer in 1981.

The reasons for decline in deference to the monarchy in Scotland are not dissimilar to those in England. There has been a steady decline in the number of Scots who served in the armed forces in the period after 1945. Though in itself not guaranteed to inculcate loyalty to the monarchy, it was, nevertheless, an institutional focus that has declined in relevance. The emergence of the counter-culture of the 1960s, likewise, helped in the decline of the deferential society, though it might be argued that, as this had less of an impact in Scotland, it might equally have been important in shoring up traditional attitudes. The key factor, however, was the twin aspect of the 'achieving society' of the 1980s, together with increased media intrusion into the private life of the royal family. The cultural history of the 1980s is dominated by the 'yuppie'. The advent of popular capitalism, deregulation, and privatisation, together with the espousal of the virtues of the free market, meant that many of the traditional assumptions regarding deference broke down. The 'sacred cows' of the past were fair game with the open encouragement of the young, ambitious, and talented to get on in life. Anti-establishmentism, according to one commentator, became part of the fabric of the new emerging generation of social leaders.[56] Obviously, this had an impact on popular perceptions of

---

[54] For example, see the coverage given to the event in the Scottish press throughout September 1972.
[55] *Stirling Observer*, 26 October 1972.
[56] A. Sampson, *Who Runs This Place? The Anatomy of Britain in the 21st Century* (London, 2004).

the royal family. Increasingly, wealth was promoted as the key criterion of social mobility. 'The grocer's daughter from Grantham' meant that less cachet was associated with noble birth. Together with an increasing cult of celebrity in which the lives of the rich and famous were subject to media intrusion, the royal family's domestic woes became tabloid fodder. The mystique went out of royalty.

Yet, as political scientists have pointed out, Scotland was largely immune to this change in culture that swept the south of England in the 1980s and 1990s. It can be argued that press intrusion would have the same impact north of the border, but given the Scots' predilection to hold on to the icons of the past, such as the welfare state, nationalised industry and the like, the question remains why the royal family did not maintain more support than it did. It may be the case that Scotland had historically been a less deferential society than England and in this case, the English were simply catching up with the Scots. Yet, comparisons with other predominantly left-of-centre nations such as the Netherlands, Norway, and Sweden, for example, show that there was no real decline in support for the monarchy there. One feature common to both Scotland and England was the inability of the royal family to update itself. In the Scottish context, little had changed from the time of Victoria. Balmoralism, Highland Games, and tartanry still characterised much of the royal family's image north of the border, almost to the point of caricature. The one event which did endeavour to keep pace with the changing nature of Scottish identity was the return of the Stone of Destiny. As a gesture towards Scotland's historic nationhood, it did little to change things. Indeed, one feature of the return of the stone was the fact that it could not be connected to the current monarchy; it was almost a tacit acceptance of the fact that the link was broken. Even with the opening of the Scottish Parliament, the presence of the Queen was counterpointed with the singing of the republican 'A Man's a Man for a' That'. The sending of Prince William to St Andrews University, the meeting between Prince Charles and Alex Salmond, then leader of the SNP, and the support of the Princess Royal for the Scottish rugby team, do indicate that there is a royal sensitivity to Scotland's national dimension, especially in the wake of devolution. One interesting aspect of the future will be the extent to which the royal family can disaggregate itself into British multinational components to take account of the changed political realities of devolution.

3

Re-inventing the Union: Dicey, Devolution, and the Union

JAMES MITCHELL

> Government requires make-believe. Make believe that the king is divine, make
> believe that he can do no wrong or make believe that the voice of the people is
> the voice of God. Make believe that the people have a voice or make believe
> that the representatives of the people are the people. Make believe that gover-
> nors are the servants of the people. Make believe that all men are equal or make
> believe that they are not.[1]

Introduction

AS EDMUND MORGAN MAINTAINED, the foundation of government requires
some fiction. He did not mean this in a pejorative way and noted that we
often call these fictions by some more exalted name, 'self-evident truths'. Fictions are necessary because 'we cannot live without them, we often take pains
to prevent their collapse by moving the facts to fit the fiction, by making our
world conform more closely to what we want it to be. We sometimes call it,
quite appropriately, reform or reformation, when the fiction takes command
and reshapes reality.'[2] Morgan's concern had been with the rise of popular
sovereignty in England and America. This chapter is concerned with the fictions and reshaping of the United Kingdom constitution over the twentieth
century. It attempts to explore the territorial nature of the UK, making use

---

[1] E. S. Morgan, *Inventing the People: The Rise of Popular Sovereignty in England and America*
(New York, 1988), p. 13.
[2] Ibid., p. 14.

Proceedings of the British Academy **128**, 35–49. © The British Academy 2005.

of the most significant contributor to the creation of fictions concerned with territorial politics.[3]

Albert Venn Dicey contributed to the creation of one fiction—that of parliamentary sovereignty. He contributed largely through popularising the notion. He was not its creator. Indeed, Edmund Morgan's most recent book, his biography of Benjamin Franklin, notes the way in which this fiction stymied efforts to reach a *modus vivendi* between the emerging American state and Britain, what Edmund Burke called 'devolution'. When parliament left duties on tea in 1770 in asserting its authority over the American colonies, Franklin had described the basis of its decision as the 'idle Notion of the Dignity and Sovereignty of Parliament, which they are so fond of, and imagine will be endanger'd by any farther Concessions'.[4]

But there were at least three Diceys. First, there was Dicey in caricature who is most familiar to us today, whose work is seldom read other than selective passages to be found repeatedly quoted to substantiate, whether dismissively or supportively, notions of parliamentary sovereignty. Second, there is Dicey the polemicist. This was Dicey true to himself. He was an inveterate opponent of Irish Home Rule and regarded this as more important than his legal theorising. Third, there was Dicey the novelist, in the sense meant above—as one who popularised a fiction. This Dicey had more to offer than has been appreciated. If we are looking for a new narrative both to make sense of territorial politics in the UK constitution during the twentieth century but also to outline principles with which we should operate, then this third Dicey has most to offer. Dicey's principles or, as he preferred, 'watchwords' have implications in an era which is not Dicey's. The nightwatchman state, which did not really exist even during his lifetime (this was part of another Diceyian fiction), has given way to a welfare interventionist state and this has important consequences. In the new era of devolved government, there are still further implications of applying Dicey's watchwords.

The Territorial Nature of the UK

The dominant paradigm that operated in political science and constitutional law for most of the twentieth century was that of the UK as a unitary state.

---

[3] Territorial politics was defined by Jim Bulpitt 'as that arena of political activity concerned with the relations between the central political institutions in the capital city and those interests, communities, political organisations and governmental bodies outside the central institutional complex, but within the accepted boundaries of the state, which possess, or are commonly perceived to possess, a significant geographical or local/regional character': Jim Bulpitt, *Territory and Power in the United Kingdom* (Manchester, 1983), p. 1.

[4] Quoted in E. S. Morgan, *Benjamin Franklin* (New Haven, 2003), p. 172.

This was rarely defined or exposed to critical examination. Central to this notion was parliamentary sovereignty or a particular understanding of parliamentary sovereignty. The Crown in parliament was sovereign and all other bodies were subordinate. In the twentieth century, Albert Venn Dicey was frequently quoted as the key figure who articulated this position. He was seen as the 'High Priest of Parliamentary sovereignty'.[5]

Allied to this was the notion of British territorial homogeneity. This was evident across a range of work. The key cleavage in electoral politics was class; 'all else is embellishment', as Peter Pulzer famously expressed it.[6] Studies of the organisation of British central government—both academic and official—stressed the functional basis of organisation. Haldane's study of the *Machinery of Government* at the end of the First World War[7] through to Sir Norman Chester's study of the *Organisation of British Central Government* focused on the functional,[8] though in both cases they acknowledged that there was a distinctive pattern of administration in Scotland and Ireland.

Simultaneously, there was an appreciation—at least outside England—that the UK was a multinational state and that there were patterns of politics and government that made the UK less than uniform. Works were produced focusing on distinctive politics which when read alongside the main body of texts that existed ought to have caused unease. Nonetheless, the homogeneity thesis, based on notions of the UK as a unitary state, operated in easy harmony with an appreciation that the UK was multinational. Scotland, (Northern) Ireland, and Wales were, at best, seen as exceptions to a general rule. Whenever some acknowledgement was given of evidence of something less than homogeneous it was presented as aberrant or ephemeral. There were exceptions but they were just that—exceptions to a general rule.

The absence of a formal entrenched written constitution was significant. These inconsistencies, which existed in apparent harmony, would have been difficult to reconcile in a formal written constitution. Different interpretations might exist but these were rarely tested in any meaningfully authoritative way. However, as students of new institutionalism are quick to remind us, institutions are not simply formal but also have an informal aspect. The rules of the game, conventions (with a small c as well as a capital C), and patterns of behaviour are at least as significant as more formal or concrete institutions—parliament, cabinet, and civil service.

[5] R. F. V. Heuston, *Essays in Constitutional Law* (London, 2nd edn 1964), p. 1.

[6] P. Pulzer, *Political Representation and Elections in Britain* (London, 1967), p. 98.

[7] Viscount Haldane, *The Machinery of Government*, HMSO, Cd. 9230 (London, 1918).

[8] Sir Norman Chester (ed.), *The Organisation of British Central Government, 1914–1964* (London, 1968).

Dicey's Contribution: Caricatures, Polemics, and Principles

Dicey's work, his thinking, and—even more notably—interpretations of Dicey have no official status in the UK constitution but have been influential in two related respects, though these two are often conflated. First, Dicey has been influential in informing how the constitution operated and operates, and secondly how it ought to operate: he has been both descriptively and prescriptively influential. It is significant and somewhat strange that though Dicey the student of government was largely discredited, Dicey the prescriber of how government and politics ought to operate remained very much alive. Complicating Dicey's contribution further is the distinction that has to be made between Dicey's work and interpretations of Dicey.

Indeed, the paradox of Dicey the discredited scholar with his enormous lasting influence may in part be explained by Dicey the sophisticated, if flawed and inconsistent, polemicist. Dicey was perhaps more than anything else a skilful polemicist. He himself regarded his political activities—campaigning against Irish Home Rule most notably—as by far his most important work in life and he was extremely talented in this regard. Even his opponents acknowledged this. John Morley wrote to Dicey after the publication of Dicey's first anti-Home Rule book admiringly:

> I must at once say that I am full of admiration, first at the exhaustive completeness with which you have handled the matter, and second at the faultlessness ... I don't know another instance when the subject of passionate and burning controversy has been so honestly dealt with ... Though it will be a great armoury for my opponents, I am still glad that you have written the book.[9]

At least, Morley noted, Home Rulers knew the worst they would face.

Although Dicey's views on parliamentary sovereignty are frequently mentioned, his views on the subject were not quite as straightforward as is often suggested. The common Scottish assumption that Dicey embodied parliamentary sovereignty as distinct from something peculiarly Scottish called 'popular' sovereignty is, in fact, Diceyian polemics turned on its head. This was, of course, most evident in recent times in the work of the Scottish Constitutional Convention. The Convention operated in the name of 'popular sovereignty'. The grandiosely entitled, 'A Claim of Right for Scotland', its founding document, invoked popular sovereignty in making its case for devolution. This picked up themes long present in nationalist discourse. That part of the opinion of Lord Cooper in *MacCormick* v. *Lord Advocate* is frequently referred to, in which the Lord President of the Court of Session

---

[9] Dicey Collection, Glasgow University Library, Ms. Gen. 508 (52–4).

questions the principle of the unlimited sovereignty of parliament. What is rarely acknowledged is that Cooper also noted that Dicey's views altered and that Cooper quoted from *Thoughts on the Scottish Union*, a work written in collaboration with Robert Rait. MacCormick himself was careful in including this excerpt in the appendix to his 1955 *Flag in the Wind*.[10]

But even in Dicey's work, frequently quoted as evidence of his support for parliamentary sovereignty, Dicey was more sophisticated than he is often presented. From many works citing Dicey as one who articulated an unlimited, absolutist notion of sovereignty, it would be difficult to believe that it was Dicey who wrote, 'If the doctrine of Parliamentary sovereignty involves the attribution of unrestricted power to Parliament, the dogma is no better than a legal fiction, and certainly is not worth the stress laid upon it.'[11]

He went on to note that the 'electorate in combination with the Lords and the Crown, is sure ultimately to prevail on all subjects to be determined by the British government . . . The electors can in the long run always enforce their will.'[12] Further, he discusses external and internal limits on the sovereign power of parliament. The external limit consists of the 'possibility or certainty that his subjects, or a large number of them, will disobey or resist his laws'.[13] The internal limit 'arises from the nature of the sovereign power itself',[14] by which he meant the self-imposed limits affected by character and circumstances. It was against this background discussion that Dicey observed, 'It would be rash of the Imperial Parliament to abolish the Scotch law Courts, and assimilate the law of Scotland to that of England. But no one can feel sure at what point Scotch resistance to such a change would become serious.'[15]

Representative government, he maintained, aimed to 'produce a coincidence, or at any rate diminish the divergence, between the external and the internal limitations on the exercise of sovereign power'.[16] Popular and parliamentary sovereignty, in Dicey's mind, are far less different than some would have us believe.

Dicey's own work on sovereignty may contain much that is inconsistent and confused, as Sir Ivor Jennings famously noted,[17] but Dicey was able to

---

[10] J. MacCormick, *The Flag in the Wind: The Story of the National Movement in Scotland* (London, 1955), p. 217.

[11] A. V. Dicey, *Introduction to the Study of the Law of the Constitution* (London, 8th edn 1923), p. 69.

[12] Ibid., p. 71.

[13] Ibid., p. 74.

[14] Ibid., p. 77.

[15] Ibid., p. 79.

[16] Ibid., p. 80.

[17] Sir Ivor Jennings, *The Law and the Constitution* (London, 5th edn 1959), pp. 144–92.

argue for a referendum on Home Rule without appearing entirely inconsistent, because of the frequency of reference to parliament's need to operate with the consent of the people. The fundamental problem Dicey had with his notion of parliamentary sovereignty is the same that all who choose to mix quasi-theological notions with the serious study of power must face. Sovereignty is an unhelpful concept, whether it comes in a parliamentary or popular form. The flaws in Dicey's articulation of parliamentary sovereignty are just as evident today amongst those who refer to Scottish popular sovereignty—that is the few who bother to do so now, as this does appear to have gone out of fashion. Students of government and politics should take heed of Harold Laski's warning to avoid talk of any kind of sovereignty.[18]

The caricature of Dicey as High Priest of parliamentary sovereignty was, of course, largely Dicey's own creation. But where it reaches absurd forms has been the portrayal of Dicey as having made only one contribution to debates on territorial politics. In this, Dicey probably shares blame with Gladstone. Gladstone had quoted Dicey when the Liberal Prime Minister had presented his first Home Rule Bill in 1886:

> I do not know how many gentlemen who hear me have read the valuable work of Professor Dicey on the *Law of the Constitution*. No work that I have ever read brings out in a more distinct and emphatic manner the peculiarity of the British Constitution in one point, to which, perhaps, we seldom have occasion to refer—namely, the absolute supremacy of Parliament. We have a Parliament to the power of which there are no limits whatever, except such as human nature in a divinely ordained condition of things imposes.[19]

Dicey appears to have been incensed by this reference and made frequent allusions to Gladstone's comments throughout his lifelong campaign against Home Rule. It could be contended that Gladstone—the convert to Home Rule—might equally be seen as the High Priest of parliamentary sovereignty.

What undoubtedly happened was that this notion of parliamentary sovereignty entered the debate on devolution a century later. Tam Dalyell is a case in point. For him devolution and a unitary state (built around parliamentary sovereignty) were 'mutually exclusive'. As he asked in a Parliamentary Question in 1977:

> Would it not be more honest to admit that it is impossible to have an Assembly—especially any kind of subordinate Parliament—that is part, though only part of a unitary state?[20]

[18] H. Laski, *The Grammar of Politics* (London, 5th edn 1948), p. 44.

[19] Hansard, vol. 304, col. 1048 (8 April 1886).

[20] Hansard, vol. 939, cols. 78–9 (14 November 1977).

The question is, of course, rhetorical. The problem with the question and with Dicey and Dalyell is that the premise is wrong.

Over a century after Gladstone, another British Prime Minister—resembling Gladstone in more ways than one, not least in a predilection for liberal imperialism or humanitarian intervention (depending on viewpoint)—was also to stress the protection of parliamentary sovereignty when he promised to deliver Home Rule. Tony Blair insisted in his interview with *The Scotsman* during the 1997 General Election that 'sovereignty rests with me as an English MP and that's the way it will stay'.[21] It was an unfortunate way of expressing it—he was presumably not intending to suggest he was the monarch—but the message was clear.

But Dicey had more, much more, to say about what political scientists would call territorial politics. Dicey was well aware of the multinational nature of the UK. He could be critical of those who failed to take account of the territorial diversity of the UK. In a 1901 article reviewing various books, mainly on Scottish history, Dicey noted the failure of many English historians to acknowledge national diversity. He noted that Hallam's *Constitutional History of England*, a work of 1,300 pages, included only seven on the constitution of Scotland. Macaulay's ignorance of the reasons behind the 1707 Treaty of Union was noted. Bagehot—author of the *English Constitution*—was criticised for paying scant attention to the Unions of 1603 and 1707.[22]

That did not make Dicey a great historian. He was, as noted earlier, at his best as a polemicist. Dicey the historian was Dicey the polemicist. Herbert Butterfield's notion of Whig history could have been invented to describe Albert Venn Dicey.[23] Indeed, many of those whom Dicey applauded were also distinctly Whiggish. His friend and sometime co-author, Robert Rait, belonged to that 'school'. Indeed, Rait's article on Dicey in the *Dictionary of National Biography* noted that Dicey and Rait had co-authored *Thoughts on the Union between England and Scotland* in 1920,[24] reviving an idea they had once considered, following discussion to develop a federal constitution for the UK after the First World War. It was a work motivated more by an objection to any fundamental alteration to the union rather than a desire to understand it. Nonetheless, leaving aside the historical problems with a book written with the aim of disabusing Home Rulers and federalists of their

---

[21] *The Scotsman*, 4 April 1997.
[22] A. V. Dicey, 'Thoughts on the Parliament of Scotland', *Quarterly Review* 225 (1916), pp. 438–55, at pp. 439–40.
[23] H. Butterfield, *The Whig Interpretation of History* (London, [1931] 1951).
[24] Albert Venn Dicey and Robert S. Rait, *Thoughts on the Union between England and Scotland* (London, 1920).

schemes, themes emerge in the book which had been propounded in previous books and many articles written by this most prolific campaigner.

However, before specifically mentioning the contents of *Thoughts on the Union between England and Scotland*, it is worth returning to Dicey's anti-Home Rule books. His first was his most significant work on the subject. Dicey wrote four books against Home Rule: *England's Case Against Home Rule*, 1886; *Letters on Unionist Delusions*, 1887; *A Leap in the Dark: A Criticism of the Principles of Home Rule as Illustrated by the Bill of 1893*, 1893; and *A Fool's Paradise: Being a Constitutionalist's Criticism on the Home Rule Bill of 1912*, 1913.[25] In addition, he wrote numerous articles. His second anti-Home Rule book was a collection of essays that had originally appeared in *The Spectator*. His third and fourth books were responses to Home Rule bills of the time. But each successive book added little that had not been written in his 1886 work though, of course, there were significant differences in each Home Rule bill, not least concerning representation in the sovereign parliament, that required Dicey's attention.

Dicey's Watchwords and their Implications

In *England's Case Against Home Rule*, Dicey spelt out his position with clarity. Dealings with Ireland should not be guided by 'equality, similarity and simultaneity', but by the 'watchwords', as he called them:

- unity of government
- equality of political rights
- diversity of institutions.[26]

These were the 'watchwords' that ran throughout his work. Whether extolling the virtues of the Anglo-Scottish union, arguing against Irish Home Rule, or attempting to describe the territorial politics of the United Kingdom, these three watchwords were present in much of Dicey's writings.

The form these watchwords took or should take was not always clear. Often, description and prescription were conflated. In his work on the Anglo-Scottish union, he was keen to show that it was 'at once a most revolutionary and a most conservative statute'.[27] Union had involved four 'revolutionary or

---

[25] A. V. Dicey, *England's Case Against Home Rule* (London, 1886); *Letters on Unionist Delusions* (Edinburgh, 1887); *A Leap in the Dark: A Criticism of the Principles of Home Rule as Illustrated by the Bill of 1893* (London, 1893); *A Fool's Paradise: Being a Constitutionalist's Criticism on the Home Rule Bill of 1912* (London, 1913).

[26] Dicey, *England's Case Against Home Rule*, pp. 30–1.

[27] Dicey and Rait, *Thoughts on the Union*, p. 238.

fundamental changes' in the constitutions of Scotland and England: 'Complete political union of the two Kingdoms';[28] 'Complete freedom of trade was established for all subjects of the United Kingdom throughout the United Kingdom, and all the Dominions and Plantations belonging thereto';[29] 'Complete security for the Church of Scotland with equal security for the Church of England';[30] 'The transference of the government of Scotland from a non-sovereign to a sovereign Parliament'.[31] But it was also conservative. While creating a new state, it also preserved English and Scottish 'nationalism'.[32]

This was a notable use of the term 'nationalism'. In parallel with this was Dicey's insistence that Ireland was not a nation but that the UK was. If there was one significant development in his thinking after *England's Case Against Home Rule*, then arguably it was his discovery of official or state nationalism.[33] It appears in his 1887 collection of essays initially published in *The Spectator*, and again and again thereafter. Indeed, Dicey's calls to allow the UK nation to determine the future of Ireland and Northern Ireland suggest he was the prototypical UK nationalist. Whether in his calls for a referendum or his demands that a General Election be fought on the issue before parliament determined (Northern) Ireland's fate—little place for parliamentary sovereignty then—Dicey fell back on popular sovereignty.

The real dispute in territorial politics in the UK has not really been about parliamentary versus popular sovereignty, but competing notions of which *people* should be consulted in the name of popular sovereignty. This may be excused. Many scholars today continue to use the term nationalism promiscuously, failing to distinguish between very different phenomena. State nationalism was related in Dicey's mind to popular sovereignty. But Dicey failed to reconcile his views on state and sub-state nationalisms, as is evident in his book on the Anglo-Scottish union. Less evidence can be found in *Thoughts on the Anglo-Scottish Union* of *equality of political rights*, but the underlying message was that Scots and English people, as individuals, enjoyed equality under the constitution. The 'watchwords' of *unity of government* and *diversity of institutions* were plain to see.

In an article written in 1881, Dicey had compared 'Two Acts of Union'—that with Ireland and the Union of 1707. The Anglo-Scottish union was a

---

[28] Ibid., p. 239.
[29] Ibid., p. 240.
[30] Ibid., p. 241.
[31] Ibid., p. 242.
[32] Ibid., pp. 321–49.
[33] James Kellas uses the term 'official nationalism' in *The Politics of Nationalism and Ethnicity* (Basingstoke, 1991), p. 3; and Michael Keating uses the term 'state nationalism' in *State and Regional Nationalism* (Hemel Hempstead, 1988) to refer to the nationalism of the state.

work of great statesmanship—'English policy has achieved no triumph so great as the union between England and Scotland.' But 'English policy has never more nearly failed of attaining any part of its objects than in the union with Ireland.'[34] The Irish union was incomplete compared to the Anglo-Scottish union. One instance was the continued existence of the Lord Lieutenancy. Only four years later, the establishment of the Scottish Office suggested that Dicey may have overstated how complete the Anglo-Scottish union had been.

A simple explanation for this inconsistency can be offered. Scottish nationalism was benign and not associated with demands for constitutional change, while its Irish counterpart was secessionist and deemed malign. Dicey would have been less relaxed about Scottish nationalism a century later. This gets to the heart of the dilemma facing state nationalists intent on maintaining the territorial integrity of the state. Do concessions meet or feed expectations? Many scholars have grappled with this question but it remains unresolved both theoretically and empirically. It is difficult to avoid the conclusion that, for Dicey, the Anglo-Scottish union worked because, at least when he was writing, it had public legitimacy across the state, whereas the Anglo-Irish union lacked consent; and Scottish nationalism was acceptable because it then posed no threat to the integrity of the state.

Two significant sets of questions follow from these observations: was it accurate? were the unions really the embodiment of these watchwords? was Dicey an historian or merely a polemicist? And what were the implications? indeed, what are the implications if we are to accept these watchwords today?

There was sufficient accuracy in Dicey's description to give it credibility. But it was seriously flawed. Administrative historians have been critical of Dicey's identification of three periods explaining the growth of government and administrative development in *Lectures on the Relation Between Law and Public Opinion during the Nineteenth Century*:[35] legislative quiescence, 1800–30; Benthamism or individualism, 1825–70; collectivism, 1865–1900. His notion of Benthamism as individualism was a partial account of Bentham's work, and the period 1825–70 was marked by a significant element of what he termed collectivism.

This is important in the context of Dicey's watchwords for territorial politics. The nature of government has had a major impact on the organisation of central government, including its territorial dimension. The interventionist welfare state—which Dicey did not support—has made government more

---

[34] A. V. Dicey, 'Two Acts of Union: a contrast', *Fortnightly Review* 36 (1881), pp. 168–78, at p. 168.
[35] A. V. Dicey, *Lectures on the Relation between Law and Public Opinion during the Nineteenth Century* (London, [1914] 2nd edn 1962).

complex. Trends which were already evident between 1825 and 1870 became obvious by the time of Dicey's death in 1922. These have become even more obvious in the period of the welfare state.

Unity of Government

Unity of government had been recognised in the form of the cabinet—an effective part of the constitution—by Bagehot, and there was a debate for much of the late twentieth century as to whether this still existed or whether the UK experienced prime ministerial government. More recently, the notion of a core executive has been discussed.[36] Defined as that part of central government responsible for co-ordinating and arbitrating, there has been debate as to which institutions might be included, though there is little doubt as to some of the key institutions. Whether it is cabinet, prime minister, Treasury, or some other core executive in some combination, there is agreement that complex decision-making involving decisions spilling over into other areas of public policy necessitates some unity at the centre. Public policy requires some modicum of unity of government at least to ensure co-ordination and arbitration.

Such unity of government was made difficult due to the nature of the interventionist welfare state: implementation, local government, departmentalism all tugged away at *unity of government* in the UK as elsewhere. But these challenges were, in fact, reasons for the need for unity of government. The danger of one policy undermining another and the need to maximise the impact of each, as well as decisions on scarce resources—be these money, expertise, time, or anything else, became even more pressing as the state's reach increased. The interventionist welfare state was complex and necessitated more co-ordination. Another reason for the importance of the centre which became significant in the era of the welfare state was the desire for equality. If equality of provision was to be achieved—or even attempted—across the state then some central mechanism was required to monitor and ensure this.

There can be no doubt that devolved government put pressure on government at the centre and has and will continue to undermine unity of government, but this pressure is not new, nor necessarily undesirable. Very little attention was paid to this in the long debates about devolution. Some new formal and informal institutions were set up—concordats, joint ministerial committees, sharing information, and so on, though much of this owes more

---

[36] R. Rhodes and P. Dunleavy (eds), *Prime Minister, Cabinet and Core Executive* (London, 1995).

to past practice than has generally been appreciated, and little, if anything, to the work of the Constitutional Convention.

Equality of Political Rights

Dicey's concern had been with equality of political rights, but as state intervention proceeded, more emphasis was placed on equality of citizenship rights, more broadly conceived. Dicey's demand for the 'Due Representation of England'[37] was made in terms of political equality. His call for more MPs for England was, of course, ignored but was consistent with his watchwords:

> The policy of redistribution [of Parliamentary seats] harmonises with the democratic spirit of the age. . . . The inequalities of our representative system may some of them be beneficial, but they are all opposed to democratic principle, and, what is of more consequence, to democratic sentiment.[38]

In the age of the welfare state, the issue becomes one of whether that principle should extend beyond political equality as understood by Dicey. The provisions of the Scotland Act, 1998 and the Electoral Commission recommendation that the number of Euro-constituencies in Scotland should be reduced to seven (instead of eight), accepted by the government, go some way towards meeting Dicey's watchword. But should this be extended to other aspects of citizenship?

If we conceive of citizenship as T. H. Marshall did as consisting of three inter-related sets of rights[39]—legal, political, and social—then we might ask whether modern Diceyians need to consider whether we should look again at public spending in the component parts of the state. For a variety of reasons, rights have differed between the component parts of the UK and even within each in some respects. Legal rights differ, though not in fundamental ways, between Scotland and England. Political rights, as already mentioned, have differed both in that there were detailed differences in the franchise north and south of the border, and also in the number of elected representatives. This followed from the nature of the union. As Dicey was well aware, the Anglo-Scottish union did not create uniformity and this diversity was evident in a number of forms. If Marshall's evolutionary account of citizenship is accepted, there should be no surprise that the absence of uniformity was transferred from one set of rights into the next. The final set of rights—social rights—coming with the establishment of the welfare state might have been introduced by a centralist Labour government (though, of course, the

---

[37] A. V. Dicey, 'The due representation of England', *National Review* 38 (1901), pp. 359–82.
[38] Ibid., p. 363.
[39] T. H. Marshall and T. Bottomore, *Citizenship and Social Class* (London, 1992).

roots of the welfare state long pre-date the Attlee government) but were not all imposed from the centre uniformly.

In one area of public policy the principle of equality of rights does exist and has long been accepted as fundamental. In *re*distributive policies few question that the same pension should be paid to old people in Perth as in Penrith (to adopt Tam Dalyell's style from the 1970s), that benefits to individuals should be the same in Bath as in Bathgate even if the cost of living differs in the various parts of the state. We have, however, been more willing to accept, even if not explicitly, that differences will exist in purely distributive policies—more spending on health in Helensburgh than in Hathersage. In part, this might be explained by an evolutionary understanding of citizenship rights as set out by Marshall. A more powerful explanation is the necessary consequence of the third of Dicey's watchwords—though it was not and could not have been foreseen by him.

Diversity of Institutions

Dicey's admiration for the 1707 Treaty of Union rested, as we have seen, on its being 'at once a most revolutionary and a most conservative statute'. It conserved many Scottish institutions and laid the foundations for others. But these were not, for the most part, what Dicey would have seen as political institutions but rather institutions of what today we would refer to as civil society (though admittedly Scots law and the Scottish courts are troublesome for purposes of categorising). Dicey's 'institutions' were civil institutions—most notably education—with functions which in time changed in two important respects: first, responsibility was transferred to the state, and, secondly, these responsibilities grew considerably. The problem for modern Diceyians is concerned with the first development. The state is now the main provider of education. Should education be treated as a *social right* analogous with political rights as part of modern citizenship, or should its provision be seen as unequal as an inevitable consequence of *diverse institutions*? In many respects this gets us to the heart of much of the debate on territorial politics and the constitution during the twentieth century.

The existence of the Scottish Office pre-devolution embodied Dicey's watchwords. *Unity of government* was provided for in that the Scottish Office was part of UK central government, with the Secretary of State sitting in the cabinet, appointed by the Prime Minister. *Diversity of institutions* was embodied in the Scottish Office, more than any other institution. This would also be true of the Welsh Office as well as Stormont and later the Northern Ireland Office. The Scottish Office did not seem to attract the attention of Dicey and, notwithstanding earlier comments, could conceivably have been supported by Dicey.

Political equality was, however, relatively less evident, though in many respects the existence of the territorial departments did not necessarily undermine this principle completely. MPs, though, were treated equally in the Commons regardless of the constituency represented (something that cannot be said of the Scottish Parliament whatever fiction we are expected to believe). There is no doubt that different levels of public spending across a range of distributive policies owes much to the existence of the Scottish Office. Dicey failed to account for the public policy impact of institutions. This may have been understandable in the context of institutions of civil society but when these institutions or their functions were transferred to the state there were clear implications in terms of developing differences across the state.

The situation has not changed post-devolution substantively. But there has been one significant change, as noted at the outset. Territorial politics has come forward—if not to the fore of UK politics consistently, then at least persistently. Anomalies that always existed have become more apparent and more salient.

Conclusion

Dicey was well aware of the inconsistencies and anomalies in the constitution:

> The constitution, it may be retorted, is full of anomalies. So be it. The idea that one unreasonable arrangement is justified by pointing to the existence of a hundred other equally unreasonable arrangements is characteristic of certain modes of thought. It is a notion which has found favour in turn with the opponents of every reform, but which has always lost its force from the moment that men became earnestly bent on the removal of some glaring abuse. Grant, however, to the apologist for things as they stand that an anomaly, though requiring defence, need not of necessity be an abuse.[40]

This allowed him to object to some inconsistencies while celebrating others. At the heart of Dicey's territorial constitution lay a major inconsistency. The three watchwords were themselves incompatible. Diverse institutions would inevitably lead to diverse policies and diminish the prospect for equality of rights even without very strenuous efforts to ensure unity of government. However, looked at another way, perhaps borrowing from fictions drawn from US constitutional tradition, these watchwords might each be seen as valid but in competition. The fifty-first Federalist Paper explained that

---

[40] Dicey, 'Due representation of England', p. 360.

'ambition must be made to counteract ambition' and in Federalist thirty-nine, Madison argued that the US Constitution was neither national nor federal 'but a composition of both'. In his classic account of the politics and ideas which made the Constitution, Jack Rakove refers to the 'untidy complexity' of this essay.[41] Public debate had, as Madison became well aware, 'reductionist tendencies',[42] and so too have Dicey's thoughts on the UK's territorial constitution.

Together, the three watchwords comprise a pluralist fiction which has informed constitutional debate. In the twentieth century, imbalances at the expense of diversity—whether in the establishment of centralised welfare after 1945 to create equality or centralised economic management after 1979 requiring unity of government (or even only perceptions of centralisation associated with these)—put pressure on the constitution. Over the century, concessions have been offered in the form of administrative and lately legislative devolution to counter-balance centralisation. In the new century, it now seems more likely that the threat to the state's integrity will come more from the new form that diverse institutions have taken. Diverse institutions do not exist in a vacuum separate from policies and rights. Dicey's three watchwords remain important but the balance has altered fundamentally.

Note. The author wishes to acknowledge the support of the Economic and Social Research Council (Grant no. L219252026).

[41] J. Rakove, *Original Meanings: Politics and Ideas in the Making of the Constitution* (New York, 1997), p. 161.
[42] Ibid.

4

After the Declaration of Perth: All Change!

JAMES G. KELLAS

A History of Sudden Changes

THE HISTORY OF SCOTLAND IS MARKED BY SUDDEN CHANGES, starting with the Union of the Crowns in 1603, and continuing through to and beyond the establishment of the Scottish Parliament in 1999. At the same time, there are long periods when nothing important apparently happens, despite predictions to the contrary (notably the failure to establish devolution from the first proposal for a Scottish legislature in the 1870s to 1997).

On top of that, people's attitudes unaccountably change. Politicians who once supported devolution became opponents, and vice versa. Voters who voted against devolution in 1979, voted for it in 1997. Parties which campaigned one way in one election or referendum campaigned another way at a later one.

This is also true of Scottish–English relations. In 1707, public opinion in Scotland opposed the union with England, but by the end of the eighteenth century the union was accepted by most. Even the name 'Scotland' was often replaced with 'North Britain' by the end of the nineteenth century. Yet by 1918, 'Scotland' came back and 'North Britain' disappeared officially, although it survived in names such as the North British Railway (which was itself abolished in 1923). In 1998, an opinion poll in *The Scotsman* (5 June) showed a majority (52 per cent) for independence. But when given the option of devolution, the electorate gave only 26 per cent support for independence (*The Scotsman*, 12 January 1999).

But there is no clear conflict between Scotland and England. Rather, the shifting conflicts mostly appear between the British parties (and between these and the SNP).

Proceedings of the British Academy **128**, 51–61. © The British Academy 2005.

Unionists as Scottish Nationalists

The great turning point in modern Scottish history was the establishment of the Scottish Office in 1885. But this was not a matter for Scottish–English hostility. The Scottish Office's appearance was sudden and gave no indication of its later significance. The Tories set it up, but were not really much in favour. The first incumbent was the Duke of Richmond and Gordon. When asked by the Prime Minister, Lord Salisbury, to take the post in August 1885, the Duke replied: 'You know my opinion of the office, and that it is quite unnecessary, but the Country and Parliament think otherwise—and the office has been created and someone must fill it. Under these circumstances I am quite ready to take it, and will do my best to make it a success (if this is possible!).'[1]

The attitude of the Conservatives towards the Scottish Office changed in the mid-twentieth century. They then saw it as a bulwark against nationalism and devolution. So it was that Tory Secretary of State for Scotland, Ian Lang, supported a strong Scottish Office, able to stand up for Scottish interests in London. He also thought that the Scottish Grand Committee could do 'virtually everything that Labour's devolved parliament would be able to do, except raise taxes'.[2] But the Tories had opposed the setting up of the Scottish Grand Committee in 1894, as the thin end of a wedge leading to devolution or even separation. Lang had continued the strategy of his predecessor, Malcolm Rifkind, who was a strong devolutionist in the 1970s, but a Thatcherite loyalist by the late 1980s: hence opposed to devolution. George Younger (Secretary of State for Scotland, 1979–86) similarly moved into line with Thatcher in 1979, although both he and Rifkind had voted Yes in the 1979 referendum.

Ian Lang's successor as Scottish Secretary was Michael Forsyth. Forsyth's Unionist-Scottish nationalism brought the Stone of Destiny back to Scotland in 1996. No greater contrast could be found to the occasion when the stone was 'stolen' from Westminster Abbey in 1950 (it was returned in 1951). The Tories were outraged, and the Scottish Secretary, Hector McNeil (Labour) was apoplectic at this effrontery to the UK establishment. George VI's death in 1952 was said to have been hastened by the event.

By 2003, the wheel had come full circle. After a steady growth in its functions from 1885, mostly brought in by Conservative governments, the Scottish Office was to all intents and purposes replaced by the Scottish

---

[1] Richmond to Salisbury, 9 August 1885. Salisbury Papers (Christ Church, Oxford): quoted by H. J. Hanham in 'The creation of the Scottish Office, 1881–87', *Juridical Review* n. s. 10:3 (1965), p. 229.
[2] I. Lang, *Blue Remembered Years: A Political Memoir* (London, 2002), p. 206.

Executive when devolution was established in 1999. The office of Secretary of State for Scotland persisted with a minuscule department (of around 100 civil servants), renamed the Scotland Office, and in 2003 it was made part of the Department of Constitutional Affairs, covering the Scotland Office, the Wales Office, and several English or British functions relating to constitutional reform. The offices of Secretary of State for Scotland and Secretary of State for Wales were made joint appointments with other cabinet appointments, in the case of Scotland, Transport, held by the Scot Alastair Darling. Around 10 to 15 per cent of his time was estimated to be spent on his Scottish duties.[3] Labour had adamantly insisted on retaining the Scottish and Welsh Offices when devolution was introduced in 1999, but by 2003 the rationale for these was gone. In effect, Labour abolished what the Conservatives had established.[4]

The same roundabout applies to the history of devolution. The Scottish Parliament and Executive were established by Labour, but only after a period of opposition to devolution from 1958 to 1974, and virtual denial before that.[5] The Conservatives until the 'Declaration of Perth' in 1968 never supported legislative devolution, but they were not averse to administrative devolution or even some form of federalism. It was Edward Heath, leader of the Conservative opposition, who made the Declaration of Perth, at the Scottish Conservative and Unionist conference. This appeared to be a momentous occasion in the history of Scotland, although its proposals were far from the devolution system we know today. The fact that they were made at all is still the subject of some mystery in the annals of Scottish political history.[6]

---

[3] 'The reshuffle in perspective', *Monitor* (The Constitution Unit, School of Public Policy, UCL), Bulletin Issue 24 (September 2003), p. 1.

[4] The Conservatives gave support to the Liberal bill to establish the Scottish Secretary, which was unlike their opposition to Labour's devolution proposals in the 1970s and 1990s. Party divisions were less firm in the 1880s than they became in the twentieth century. The 'voice of Scotland' in the cabinet continues through the large number of Scots who are members. But not of all these 'speak for Scotland', for their briefs are either British-wide or even English-only (John Reid became English Secretary of State for Health, although this department does not cover his constituency, Hamilton North and Bellshill).

[5] Some authorities claim that Labour was pledged to bring in devolution in 1945, and several Labour candidates in Scotland did support a Scottish parliament. The pledge is dismissed as 'window dressing' by Harvie and Jones, as it came only in the Scottish addition to the British manifesto. C. Harvie and P. Jones, *The Road to Home Rule: Images of Scotland's Cause* (Edinburgh, 2000), p. 58.

[6] Pressure came from within the Scottish party, and a study group was set up in 1967. Sir William McEwan Younger, a party grandee (Hon. Sec. of the Scottish Unionist Association, 1955–64 and Chairman of the Conservative Party in Scotland, 1971–4), and Dundee University academic and party activist John Berridge pressed the case for devolution. Heath and the Scottish party accepted their opinions. Heath was probably convinced by the argument for

Nationalists as Unionists

The SNP began as a devolutionist or federalist party but by 1945 was shaping up to be only an independentist one. A strong faction, however, supported devolution through the Scottish Convention movement, climaxing in the Scottish Covenant of 1949, which pledged its signatories to support the establishment of a Scottish Parliament 'within the framework of the United Kingdom'. Such devolutionism was rejected by the SNP, but the party was not clearly 'separatist' until the 1960s. In 1979 the SNP withdrew its support from the Labour government in a vote of no confidence over Labour's devolution tactics, opening the door to Thatcher and Thatcherism.

The SNP sought the setting up of a Constitutional Convention, but when one was set up in 1989, it refused to take part. The reason was apparently Labour's dominating role, and the fact that independence could not be expected to emerge from such a body.

Yet the SNP was not opposed to devolution, if that was all that was available. So in 1997 it joined Labour and the Liberal Democrats in the Scotland Forward referendum campaign for Yes votes. Even so, Donald Dewar, the Labour Scottish Secretary, suspected and disliked the SNP so much that he later refused to give Sean Connery (an SNP supporter) his expected knighthood, although he had appeared with him on the same platform in 1997. Connery was later knighted under the governments of Henry McLeish (Scottish First Minister) and Tony Blair.

Federalists as Devolutionists

The Liberal Democrats changed stance on two counts. They had long supported federalism, but settled for devolution when that was offered by Labour in the late 1970s. In 1999 they joined Labour in a Scottish Executive coalition government. The Liberals were in favour of proportional representation in the form of the Single Transferable Vote (STV), but settled for the Additional Member System (AMS) when Labour in 1995 proposed that for the Scottish Parliament. By 2003, STV was being canvassed by Labour, but now the Liberal Democrats were suspicious (rightly) that Labour was not so much converted to STV as opposed to the results of the List system of election, which had allowed Tommy Sheridan's Scottish Socialist Party to gain

---

devolution, for he kept to his support for a Scottish Parliament through the Thatcher and Major years when such an opinion was anathema. But to him Thatcher and Major were also anathema, so anything they supported would be unlikely to appeal to Heath—and conversely.

representation at the expense of Labour (it also gave the Greens representation). So, paradoxically, it seemed for a time that the Liberal Democrats could be the party supporting AMS, with Labour supporting STV.

Socialists as Nationalists

The Labour Party started as a Home Rule (that is, nationalist) party. In 1888 Keir Hardie established the first socialist party in Britain, the Scottish Labour Party. It stood for both socialism and Home Rule. The communist John MacLean went further and sought independence, as did C. M. Grieve (Hugh MacDiarmid). In the 1970s, Jim Sillars led another Scottish Labour Party, which stood for 'maximalist' devolution. In the 1990s Tommy Sheridan's Scottish Socialist Party supported Scottish independence, as it still does.

Labour officially condemns nationalism of all kinds, and Scottish nationalism in particular is the object of some venom (British nationalism is let off lightly, for example over the EU and the euro). Nevertheless, the case for devolution depends on nationalism in Scotland (regional devolution is rejected for Scotland, although it makes some sense for Orkney and Shetland and the Western Isles). The opening ceremony of the Scottish Parliament on 1 July 1999 was marked by nationalism almost beyond the dreams of the SNP, although it was masterminded by the anti-nationalist Donald Dewar. So socialism and nationalism were combined here in the service of the Scottish Labour Party.

Explaining the Changes and Paradoxes

These changes and paradoxes in Scottish politics have to be explained. Two methods of explanation are apparent. The first is structural, the second ideological.

The Structural Explanation

The structural approach is essentially based on the context of institutions and events, which shape the 'rational choices' of parties and politicians. These choices in theory benefit them electorally, and they behave in certain ways because of the structure of politics in which they find themselves. However, their perception of this structure may be faulty, or the result of ideological predispositions.

Edward Heath made the Declaration of Perth in favour of a Scottish Assembly because it appeared that the electoral position of the Scottish Conservatives was threatened by the SNP's electoral advances, notably in by-elections. To counteract this advance, the Conservatives felt that they had to satisfy the demand for some form of Home Rule.

They were also in opposition at the time, so did not have to implement the promise of a Scottish Assembly immediately. By 1970, they were in power and the Declaration was reneged on at the Scottish conference in May 1973. Yet it was resurrected the following year (May 1974), after the February election had shown a strong SNP advance to seven seats and 22 per cent of the vote, mainly at the expense of the Tories.

Margaret Thatcher replaced Heath as leader in 1975, and at first she continued Heath's devolution policy. By 1976, however, she had changed to anti-devolution. The explanation seems to be that the structure of parliamentary government requires oppositions to oppose, and after 1974 Labour was the devolution party (another conversion brought about by the threat of lost seats to the SNP). The Conservative opposition to devolution continued right up to late 1997 (after the referendum had shown a big majority for a Scottish Parliament). When the structure changed to a devolution system, the Scottish Tories accepted devolution as a political imperative, and indeed became more enthusiastic than Labour about establishing a separate Scottish political base with maximalist powers (for example, over fiscal matters). That was because there was no reason to join the sinking ship of the English Conservatives, when there was a chance of some power in the Scottish Parliament (the Scottish Tories lost all their Westminster seats, but won eighteen in the Scottish Parliament, all on the List).

To summarise, on this explanation the changes of policy and behaviour in Scottish politics derive from 'rational' choices based on the situation determined by voting behaviour and the institutional structure. A party has to be elected, and to play a role in a legislature either as government or opposition. These determine what is done.

The Ideological Explanation

A completely different explanation is one that sees political actions as the result of beliefs. In this mode, politicians are constrained by their long-term ideologies, and the continuities in their parties' principles. They cannot easily change from one position to another.

In this explanation, parties are either nationalist or anti-nationalist, devolutionist or anti-devolutionist, and this determines their policies through the years.

There is some truth in this approach, but not a great deal. Conservatives have not espoused Scottish independence, but they have not ruled it out either, as John Major showed in his preface to the 'Taking Stock' White Paper (1993).[7] The SNP has not endorsed the union, at least not in principle, even if the 1949 Scottish Covenant did. Labour officially retains its belief in the union, but individual mavericks such as Denis Canavan and John McAllion have said that they do not oppose independence in principle. George Galloway is the most recent example. But all have now left the Labour Party. Jim Sillars went all the way from anti-devolutionist Labour in the 1960s to membership of the SNP in the 1980s (then out of that in the 1990s, but still independentist). Donald Dewar did not rule out independence if a majority of Scots wanted it, and called devolution 'a process'. Henry McLeish, former First Minister and successor to Dewar, in bitter retirement wrote in his memoirs of the need for the Scottish Parliament and Executive to act more independently of London.[8]

The Liberal Democrats believe in federalism and STV, but they have settled for devolution and the AMS, apparently consistent with their beliefs. By March 2004, however, the Scottish Liberal Democrat leader and Deputy First Minister, Jim Wallace, was calling for the Scottish Constitutional Convention to be reconvened to discuss greater powers for the Scottish Parliament.[9] The party conference went further and voted on 27 March in favour of all tax powers being devolved.[10]

Does ideology thus determine politics? The unionists in Scotland cannot easily cease to be unionists, and Labour cannot abandon its belief in the class (?) struggle in the British state, even if devolution, in Neil Kinnock's words, divides the British working class along lines of nationality (he was a vehement opponent of devolution in the 1970s, but came round to supporting it in the 1980s).

The Liberal Democrats have no deep-seated objection to independence, as Gladstone proclaimed the rights of nations to self-government, with the Irish in particular to be granted Home Rule (but not independence) in his 1886 conversion. But Gladstone never extended this to Scotland and Wales. In this he resembled John Stuart Mill, and even Karl Marx, whose sympathies for Irish nationalism did not include any other form of nationalism in Britain. Some of today's Liberal Democrats have toyed with the idea of independence.

---

[7] Cm. 2225.
[8] H. McLeish, *Scotland First: Truth and Consequences* (Edinburgh, 2004).
[9] *The Herald*, 25 March 2004.
[10] *Sunday Herald*, 28 March 2004.

Conclusion

In the final analysis, it looks as if the structural analysis carries more weight than the ideological one. Politicians and parties move over the years as the structure of politics determines, particularly electoral advantage and the 'adversary' parliamentary system. They are not consistent in their partisan beliefs, even if they are constrained at the outer edges by ideology. They can go so far to change, but no further.

Scotland is not for them a 'zero-sum game'. If Scotland has devolution, it is not a total loss for unionists or nationalists, although it is not an optimum choice. Moreover, English–Scottish relations are friendly. Public opinion in England is not hostile to devolution or even independence for Scotland, and Scotland is not hostile to England in constitutional matters, or even social relations. There are too many 'cross-cutting cleavages' for that, one of which is party support. Even some (for example, Alex Salmond and Andrew Wilson) in the SNP now talk of a 'British society' in conjunction with a Scottish state.

Independence is more problematic than devolution. Some Tories claimed in the 1990s that independence made more sense than devolution and, as mentioned previously, some erstwhile Labour politicians have moved closer to the independence option. But on the whole unionists remain British, whether Conservative or Labour. Liberal Democrats are European before they are British, and see Scotland as part of a 'Europe of the Nations and Regions'. The SNP is for independence, even if it is 'gradualist' on that.

An assessment of the future of Anglo-Scottish relations must be optimistic. England is permeated by 'British' values, including its leading politicians, whose Scottishness is clearly evident. But all politicians accept that if Scotland votes for independence it should have it. Scots for their part are benign towards the British state and England. Intermarriage between Scots and English is very common, to the point where it is often difficult to distinguish between the two nations. No great ethnic, religious, or political divide exists between them. The constitutional options for Scotland are relatively neutral in this regard. It is difficult to imagine an independent Scotland pursuing an anti-English policy, any more than Norway pursued an anti-Swedish policy after 1905. Membership of the EU keeps nations in line with each other, and nationalism is moderated. This is the result, not so much of the Union of 1603, as of the later Union of 1707 and how it came to operate, and most recently of the EU. The democratic ideology of the late twentieth century legitimised the sovereignty of the voting public, and with it the right of national self-determination. Whatever the Scots determine by their votes they will have. All parties and politicians seem to be agreed on that.

Appendix: The Parties and the Constitutional Options for Scotland

1. The Scottish Conservative and Unionist Party

Before 1968: Anti-Home Rule.

1968: Pro-Assembly (Declaration of Perth).

1976: Anti-devolution (Thatcher).

1979: Referendum—party recommends a No vote, but Lord Home said 'Vote No for something better' (implying an Assembly with tax powers?). After the vote, Home drops support for an Assembly.

1993: 'Taking Stock' White Paper (Cm. 2225) promises reforms of Scottish Office and Scottish Grand Committee. In preface, John Major concedes the claim of Scottish nationalists that 'no nation could be held irrevocably in a Union against its will' (p. 5).

1997: General election and double referendum (on the principle of a Scottish Parliament, and on tax-raising powers). Conservatives recommend a double 'No-No' vote in the referendum.

1999: First Scottish Parliament election—Conservatives anti-devolution, anti-PR, but emerge as stronger in the Scottish Parliament (nineteen seats, eighteen of which on PR Lists) than in the British Parliament (no seats).

After 2000: Scottish Conservatives switch to strengthening Scottish Home Rule with tax powers, and more independence from British/English Conservative policies (e.g. on student fees and personal care for the elderly). Now support PR.

2. The Labour Party

Before 1958: Pro-Home Rule.

1958–74: Anti-devolution.

After 1974: Pro-devolution.

1979: Referendum—Labour officially recommends a Yes vote, but 'Labour vote No' campaign, headed by Brian Wilson (Chairman), Robin Cook, and Tam Dalyell (Vice-Chairmen) splits party.

1988: Labour MPs (with the exception of Dalyell) subscribe to the Claim of Right for Scotland, a highly nationalist document which 'acknowledges the sovereign right of the Scottish people to determine the form of Government best suited to their needs' and pledges its adherents to fight for the establishment of a Scottish Assembly through a Constitutional Convention.

1989: Labour joins the Scottish Constitutional Convention, which agrees to the name 'Parliament', not 'Assembly', with tax powers and proportional representation.

1997: Blair springs a two-question referendum on devolution, causing the resignation of the Convention co-chairman, Lord Ewing (Harry Ewing, former Labour MP). The other co-chairman, David Steel (Liberal Democrat), stays on.

After 1999: Scottish Labour ministers (with Liberal Democrat coalition colleagues) in Scottish Executive introduce policies not supported by Labour in England (e.g. abolition of student fees, personal care for the elderly).

2004: Former First Minister, Henry McLeish, writes in his memoirs of the need for greater independence for Scottish Parliament and Executive.

3. The Liberals/Liberal Democats

1918: Liberals support a federal system for Britain with PR (by single transferable vote).

1977–8: Liberals join 'Lib-Lab Pact' to support Labour's devolution legislation.

1981: SDP formed, which includes some well-known anti-devolutionists. Makes Lib-SDP Alliance (1982) uneasy on this question. Soon anti-devolutionists change to pro-devolution.

1989: Scottish Liberal Democrats join Scottish Constitutional Convention, but fail to win Single Transferable Vote system or federalism. Also discontent over number of MSPs and mandatory equality in numbers of women MSPs.

1995: After compromises, SLDs committed to Labour proposals.

1996: SLD attacks Labour's proposal for a referendum, but in 1997 joins Labour and SNP in Scotland Forward campaign (advocating Yes-Yes votes).

1999: SLD joins Labour in Scottish Executive coalition (while remaining in opposition at Westminster).

2003: SLD opposes Labour candidates in Scottish Parliament and local elections, but resumes coalition after election.

2004: SLD leader calls for Scottish Constitutional Convention to be reconvened to discuss greater powers for Scottish Parliament, and the SLD conference votes for all tax powers to be devolved.

4. The Scottish National Party

To 1960s: Not clearly committed to independence, although certainly in favour of a Scottish Parliament. Split between 'gradualists' (who accept devolution as first step to independence) and 'fundamentalists' (who accept only independence). This split continues to the present.

1978–9: Further split on tactics towards Labour's Scotland Bill. While supporting a Yes vote in the 1979 referendum, all eleven SNP MPs voted against Labour in the vote of confidence on 28 March 1979, thereby causing the downfall of the Labour government, the election of Thatcher and the end of any prospect of devolution for twenty years.

1988: Members of the SNP were involved in drawing up the Claim of Right for Scotland, with its proposal for a Scottish Constitutional Convention (discussed in the SNP from 1980, and explicitly supported in 1988).

1989: The SNP decides not to join the Scottish Constitutional Convention—why is not very clear.

1997: The SNP is not at first committed to supporting devolution, but is not prepared to campaign against it. Joins the Scotland Forward campaign, and SNP supporter Sean Connery appears on the platform with Donald Dewar (but Dewar later opposed a knighthood for Connery).

After 1999: Former SNP MP Margo MacDonald attacks devolution (while taking a seat in the Scottish Parliament), and in 2003 leaves the SNP (her husband, former SNP MP Jim Sillars, had advocated abstention in the 1997 referendum, and had effectively left the party after 1992, when he was defeated in Govan by the defection to Labour of (as he said) 'ninety-minute patriots'. Sillars himself had been a

Labour activist in the 1960s and early 1970s, and had led Labour's attack on the SNP (*Don't Butcher Scotland's Future*, etc.).

2003: SNP loses seats in the Scottish Parliament elections, and leader John Swinney faces leadership challenge at conference, but wins easily. Nevertheless, SNP split between Swinney supporters (gradualists) and Alex Neil's fundamentalists continues. Swinney resigns in 2004.

5

What has the Scottish Parliament achieved, and what can it teach Westminster?

BARRY K. WINETROBE AND ROBERT HAZELL

TO UNDERSTAND THE SCOTTISH PARLIAMENT AS WE SEE IT NOW ON THE MOUND,[1] and to provide some context, we need a little history and background. For most people in the UK, and, significantly, for the media in particular, when they think of a parliament at all, they almost certainly think of Westminster, and the House of Commons. The United Kingdom Parliament is the 'default' parliament, and this has inevitably had an impact not just on how any other parliament in the UK is perceived, but on how any new parliament was created.

Under the British constitution—largely unwritten, with its doctrine of parliamentary sovereignty—any new parliament within the UK would be a creation of the UK government and parliament, rather than being the product of some form of fundamental constitutional process. As such, it would be, under UK constitutional law, a subsidiary or second-level parliament, no different in strictly legal terms to any body created by a UK Act of Parliament. If you think that this is just a dry theoretical legal point, look westwards across the water to Northern Ireland, and how a fully fledged parliament created in the early 1920s and functioning for half a century, was suspended and then abolished by Westminster. And look at the various bodies, up to and including the devolved Assembly, which have been created, activated, suspended, or abolished there since the 1970s.

If a devolved parliament is 'made in London' then it is not surprising to find that it is something that is both familiar to, and convenient for, its creators. This was certainly the case for the Scottish Assembly devised

[1] This chapter is based substantially on the paper delivered at the Conference on Anglo-Scottish Relations Since 1914, a Symposium organised by the British Academy and the Royal Society of Edinburgh in November 2003. As such, notes have been kept to a minimum, and only the most essential updating to the time of writing (April 2004) has been included.

Proceedings of the British Academy **128**, 63–77. © The British Academy 2005.

under the ill-fated Scotland Act 1978, which was rejected in the March 1979 referendum. It was very much a product not just of its political times—a minority Labour Government, anxious to appease growing nationalist sentiment in Scotland, facing stiff opposition from its own side as well as its political opponents—and was, rightly, seen in Scotland as a 'hand-me-down' from London rather than something tailored to fit Scottish circumstances.

There is no need to repeat the well-known story of the campaign for devolution during the eighteen years of unsympathetic Conservative government in the 1980s and 1990s. For present purposes, what is relevant was the widespread determination that any devolution scheme in the future would be the result of a home-grown process, devising something that would genuinely be appropriate for Scotland and would be modern and innovative. Most important, it would be 'not like Westminster', not some mini-Westminster or a pale imitation of the House of Commons. This constant refrain applied to all aspects of a parliament, from its structures and environment, through its procedures and practices, to its very culture.

The Labour and Liberal Democrat opposition parties involved themselves fully in this process, regarding devolution as a proper policy response in Scotland to the prevailing political situation, and also as part of a wider package of constitutional reform. Yet, for a party that wished to be the government in the future, Labour in particular was well aware that any devolution scheme should be in tune with the UK government's general ability to govern and to deliver its manifesto. Their close involvement in the Scottish Constitutional Convention ensured that any proposed scheme would be politically deliverable, and this was entrenched when they came to power in 1997 and produced a detailed policy in the July 1997 White Paper, and in the Scotland Bill at the end of that year. Massive public endorsement in the September 1997 referendum, remarkably smooth passage of the bill through both Houses of Parliament in 1998, and all-party involvement in the Consultative Steering Group all helped to create the idea that, though Scottish devolution was created by UK government, devolution and the new parliament were essentially 'made in Scotland'.

So what we have had since 1999 has been a system of devolved governance, and a parliament that comes with a lot of baggage, much of it potentially conflicting and contradictory. It was devised to fit Scottish circumstances, but created at Westminster as part of a wider package of constitutional change. It was to be 'not like Westminster', yet Westminster was the obvious primary parliamentary model. It was to embody a 'new politics' emphasising consensus rather than confrontation, yet its structures retained the essential elements, and much of the existing personnel, of British party-driven governance which made that culture shift very difficult to implement.

For 'new politics' to succeed, well-entrenched 'old governance' notions would have to be surmounted.[2]

And how to measure and assess the performance of a new parliament, with all these various pressures and aspirations? By how different it is from Westminster? By how much it appears to be a 'real' parliament, which may be, from a public and media perspective, how much it actually resembles the more familiar Westminster? Is its performance to be measured more by what it does or how it does it? What quantitative and qualitative measures are relevant and appropriate? How much is its performance due to its own endeavours, or to the new voting system, or to the role of the Scottish Executive, or to the policies of the British government?

For present purposes, the main assessment criteria are those adopted by the parliament itself, namely the four key principles of the Consultative Steering Group report:[3]

- power-sharing
- accountability
- openness and accessibility
- equal opportunities.

There is no generally accepted inclusive list of functions that a parliament is expected to carry out. However, any list would include these core functions:

- representing the people
- making the law
- providing, sustaining, and scrutinising the executive
- controlling the budget
- providing an avenue for the redress of grievances
- managing itself effectively to carry out the above five functions.

How the Scottish Parliament has carried out these functions while adhering to its ambitious 'key principles' underlies any meaningful assessment of its performance. The Procedures Committee published the results of just such an exercise in a major report in March, just before the General Election.[4] Many of these issues are relevant to parliaments across the world and we come back to this at the end.

---

[2] See further, B. Winetrobe, *Realising the Vision: A Parliament with a Purpose* (London, 2001).
[3] *Shaping Scotland's Parliament: Report of the Consultative Steering Group* (Edinburgh, 1999).
[4] Scottish Parliament Procedures Committee, *The Founding Principles of the Scottish Parliament*, 3rd report 2003, SP Paper 818, March 2003. This massive report, published at the very end of the parliament's first session, was debated by the new parliament (SP OR 26 November 2003, cols 3599–652).

Early Days and Growing Maturity

So, in May 1999, the Scottish people voted in, by a new mixed-member system, a brand-new parliament. Its operating procedures had been devised by the Scottish Office, based on the report of the Scottish Office's Consultative Steering Group (CSG), and promulgated by UK delegated legislation just a few weeks before. Many of its leading lights on the political and administrative side were old UK hands—being Westminster MPs or peers, or senior Scottish Office staff—many of whom were closely involved in creating the parliament. On the other hand, many of the MSPs, other than those from a local council background, were new to representative politics on this exposed national scale, and many expected to be involved in a 'new politics' type of governance. The novelty of a formal coalition government meant that there was a premium on traditional party discipline and whipping.

The parliament's activities would be reported by a Scottish media well-versed in political journalism, but relative novices at the more specialised environment of parliamentary reporting. Calm, consensual parliamentary deliberation does not make as good copy as inter-party and intra-party arguments, personality clashes, 'who's up, who's down', rebellions, government defeats and so on. The new-born parliament was a sitting duck for critical media coverage of how the high-flown rhetoric of the last fifteen years was working out in practice. The more experienced Scottish Executive machine was more adept than the parliament at deflecting much of this critical flak away from it and towards the parliament.

The crucial weeks between the election and first meeting of the parliament in early May and the assumption of the parliament's and Executive's full powers on 1 July (symbolised by the formal opening ceremony by the Queen) were marked by much housekeeping activity within the parliament. However necessary this was, such a far from flying start laid the parliament open to hostile comment, and this was compounded when the debate on levels of MSPs' allowances in early June descended into a messy, acrimonious and rather inarticulate argument over the relative representative roles of constituency and regional list MSPs. That the British media habitually turns on those people and institutions that it has helped to build up is a commonplace. Yet the unexpected ferocity of its devolution coverage had a crucial negative impact on the perception (and self-perception) of the young parliament, and of devolution itself.

Within this challenging environment, the parliament set about gearing up operationally. Presiding Officers were to be elected; committees appointed and resourced; a code of conduct for MSPs devised, and detailed procedures for handling questions, motions, petitions, and all the other parliamentary paraphernalia worked out. And all this while the parliament was actually working, and while the UK government was handing over to it the poisoned chalice of responsibility for the building of the new parliamentary complex at Holyrood. The implementation period of eight months or so between election and full operation that was originally conceived by the British government had been cut to a matter of days or weeks. There would be no luxury of 'test runs' for all the novel procedures and practices of a new parliament.

Added to this were the early pressures, both external and internal, for the parliament to adopt familiar—that is, Westminster—ways of working. These ranged from demands from some MSPs for daily prayers at the start of sittings to the spontaneous establishment of all-party groups of MSPs and interest groups on a wide range of policy issues. The most visible, and perhaps most significant, example was the early adoption of a First Minister's Question Time, which did not exist in the original rules, but has become so entrenched in the parliament's ways of working, that in September 2003 it was extended from twenty minutes to half an hour.

A major influence on the parliament was that of the Executive, the devolved Scottish government, which, in a Westminster-model parliament, is both an external and internal influence. As the July 1997 White Paper made clear, it was the government's expectation that the Executive–parliament relationship would be very much like that between government and parliament in London.[5] Governments in the UK are used to regarding parliaments as instruments of government, a place where their legislation is enacted and their policies announced and approved. If this sort of 'executive dominance' model became entrenched at Holyrood, it would undermine the aspirations for a different style of parliamentary politics.

We can now look at four interlocking aspects of the parliament in operation over its first four-year session, as examples of how it has performed and how it may have lessons for Westminster.

Arrangement of Parliamentary Business

Emblematic of the differences between Holyrood and Westminster is the way in which parliamentary business is arranged. The House of Commons[6] system, where the government of the day has the formal and actual initiative and control over the parliamentary schedule and the content of its business,

---

[5] *Scotland's Parliament*, Cm. 3658, July 1997, para 2.6.

[6] This chapter, unless stated otherwise, concentrates on the House of Commons as the appropriate comparator at Westminster for the Scottish Parliament. However, it should be recognised that the House of Lords betrays some Holyrood-like characteristics in its procedures and practices, though this less adversarial and executive-dominant culture is probably due more to its unelected, secondary status than to any conscious 'new politics' thesis.

demonstrates executive dominance and the relative lack of parliamentary autonomy. Business is arranged through private, secret 'usual channels' of government and opposition business managers, and announced to parliament by the (significantly named) Leader of the House, without any formal means of the House to amend or reject it.[7]

In the Scottish Parliament, there is a Parliamentary Bureau, which is the business committee comprising the Presiding Officer and a business manager from each of the parties with five or more MSPs. It proposes the forward business programme, including the sitting times, to the plenary, where it can be debated, amended, and voted upon. It also decides the committee system, including the number, remits, memberships, and convenerships. Minutes of the Bureau's meetings are published. On the face of it, therefore, it is a very different and much more open, transparent, inclusive, and democratic system than that of the House of Commons.

In practice, the picture is not quite so rosy. The Bureau meets in private, and the published minutes are brief and uninformative. Its meetings are often short and formal, because the real negotiations between business managers and with the parliamentary authorities have often taken place informally in advance. Committee memberships are in practice a matter for the parties themselves. The qualification requirements for Bureau representation exclude small parties or independent MSPs, whose only option is to form a group of five or more members if they can and thereby gain a representative. As a collection of representatives of the party leaderships (with the business managers of the two coalition parties being Executive ministers), it is a very 'front-bench' body, and as such is a convenient mechanism for all sorts of parliamentary matters beyond its strict business management remit to be discussed. It also has an Executive majority, because each representative wields a vote equivalent to the size of their parliamentary party, and, in practice, this is exercised as a 'block vote'. In short, what exists in Scotland is a form of institutionalised 'usual channels', a step forward from Westminster, but not as much as it could be.

The Procedures Committee has examined the structure and work of the Bureau, seeking ways of making the process more open and transparent while retaining the perceived efficiencies of the current arrangements. This is a very sensitive area, as it impinges on the jealously guarded rights and interests not just of the Executive, but also of the party groups and of the parliamentary authorities, often at the expense of backbenchers, small parties and, worst of all, the public. Nevertheless, there are obvious lessons for Westminster, if it is genuine in wanting to be a more autonomous and

[7] M. Rush and C. Ettinghausen, *Opening Up the Usual Channels* (London, 2002).

responsible parliament. Various reform proposals for the arrangement of parliamentary business have been made from within Westminster and from external commentators, but all have foundered on the fundamental issue of executive and party control. Genuine reform of business management arrangements, and of committee selection, can only come as part of a wider cultural and structural shift of power from the government towards parliament itself. The Constitution Unit is preparing a paper, as part of its proposed Strengthening Parliaments research programme, on how business arrangements in Holyrood and in selected Commonwealth countries can be relevant to the UK parliament, taking into account these wider issues and constraints.

Legislation

A key function of a parliament is to make laws, and primary legislative power was seen as an essential element of a powerful and effective devolved Scottish Parliament. Yet this area of parliamentary activity is traditionally one where the executive has a leading role, and so its operation can be a significant factor in shaping the culture and style of the parliament. In addition, given the subsidiary nature of the Scottish Parliament in UK constitutional terms, the scope and nature of the parliament's legislative responsibilities are tightly prescribed in UK statute, even to minimum requirements of the legislative process.

The right of legislative initiative does not belong solely to the Executive. As at Westminster, individual members can introduce bills, and, further, so can committees. In the parliament's first session, some of the most controversial and noteworthy legislation has come from non-Executive initiative, the most famous successful examples being the Tommy Sheridan warrant sales bill and the Mike Watson anti-hunting bill. MSPs are each allowed to introduce two bills in each four-year session, which may not sound much in relation to individual MSPs, but in aggregate could amount to more than two hundred bills. This raises serious issues of time and resources for non-Executive bills, as, unlike Westminster, Standing Orders do not provide for dedicated or guaranteed parliamentary time for their consideration. This gives much discretion on the progress of such bills to the Executive-dominated Parliamentary Bureau. Also, unlike the Executive, MSPs and committees did not initially have access to statute law drafting specialists, although this has been partly remedied by the creation of a Non-Executive Bills Unit (NEBU) within the parliament. In practice, non-Executive bills tend to be much like those at Westminster, their subjects being either controversial matters which may give the issue an airing but are unlikely to be enacted, or small, technical issues that are supported by the Executive and so have a decent chance of making progress. One interesting by-product of these mechanisms has been the *de facto* development of 'opposition party initiative', where proposals for bills notionally come from individual MSPs but in practice represent party policy. Perhaps this is an area both Westminster and Holyrood could develop in formally recognising 'Opposition Bills' as they do 'Opposition Debates'.[8]

The legislative process for bills in the parliament follows a three-stage process, as required by the Scotland Act, which very roughly equates to the Westminster process of second reading, committee stage, and report/third reading. It also has to take into account two fundamental aspects, that of the parliament being unicameral, with no 'other house' to review or tidy up legislation prior to enactment, and the need for legislation to be within the parliament's legislative competence. This latter aspect is dealt with at both ends of the process, with a statement of legislative competence by the Presiding Officer on a bill's introduction, and mechanisms for UK government interventions after a bill is passed but before Royal Assent.

The main procedural innovation in the parliament's legislative process is at Stage 1, which is a two-part stage, involving a committee examination on the principles of a bill *before* a general plenary debate. This is different from the standard Westminster arrangement of a bill's scrutiny beginning with a general debate in the chamber at second reading,[9] and has some resemblance to the little-used 'special standing committee' process at Westminster. Stage 2, which is the detailed line-by-line committee scrutiny stage, is normally conducted by the same committee as took Stage 1, which helps in the continuity of scrutiny, but can cause problems where, as with the anti-hunting bill, a committee which has unsuccessfully recommended that a bill be rejected by the parliament at Stage 1 may have to deal with it at Stage 2.

As well as the 'lead committee', legislative scrutiny will also be conducted by other relevant committees, such as the Finance and Subordinate Legislation committees. All committees can take evidence and conduct consultations as part of their scrutiny. Indeed, the lead committee may well have earlier conducted some form of pre-legislative scrutiny on the legislative proposals, such as on a draft bill or a White Paper. This emphasises not just scrutiny continuity, but also the potential for what some outside bodies have complained of as 'consultation overload', where the parliament and the Executive

---

[8] At the time of writing, the parliament's Procedures Committee is examining the non-Executive bills process, and whether and how they should be prioritised to take account of the parliament's limited time and resources. While in part a technical matter of parliamentary procedure, this issue has raised many more fundamental questions about the nature and purpose of the parliament, and its relationship with the Executive.

[9] Though the practice of committee examination of draft legislation is becoming more common at Westminster.

may conduct consultation exercises a number of times on the same policy issue at different stages in the process.

The Executive has tended to adhere to an annual legislative cycle, notwithstanding the parliament's four-year session arrangement, where there is no equivalent of the Westminster practice of bills not passed within the annual session being lost. Perhaps this is because of a hangover from Westminster practice within the administration, or because the volume of legislation has been greater than originally expected. This pace puts pressure on parliamentary time and resources, and highlights the tensions between proper and fully participative scrutiny and the Executive 'getting its business'. It also raises the question of what constitutes good scrutiny and good parliamentary legislative practice, when the initiative and timing is largely in Executive hands. The parliament regularly cites the number of bills examined and passed as evidence of its performance, and media and public pressure also tends towards assessment of Executive success in terms of legislative output.

But there is evidence from external evaluation that the Scottish Parliament is more effective than Westminster in its scrutiny of legislation. Mark Shephard of Strathclyde University has attempted systematically to evaluate the impact of the Scottish Parliament on all Executive legislation in its first term, 1999–2003. At first blush, he found that the Executive seems to dominate the process, much as at Westminster. But when he analysed the different types of amendments and allowed for Executive adoption of the policy behind opposition and backbench amendments, he found evidence that the parliament makes more of an impact, and concluded that 'expectations of power sharing between the Executive and Parliament are being realised'.[10]

The Westminster legislative process has long been criticised as inefficient and ineffective, with little genuine engagement by MPs and the public in government legislation. The standing committee stage, where bills are supposed to be subjected to intensive line-by-line scrutiny, is more of a standing joke. Legislation has been a central focus of Commons 'modernisation' over the last seven years, with routine programming (i.e. timetabling) of legislative business and more scrutiny of draft legislation the centrepieces. However, there is a long way to go,[11] and Holyrood could provide some useful pointers.

[10] M. Shephard and P. Cairney, 'Does the Scottish Parliament matter?', paper presented to American Political Science Association conference, September 2002.
[11] The current House of Lords Constitution Committee inquiry into the legislative process may provide some guidance for further reforms.

Committees

The committee system of the Scottish Parliament was intended to be its powerhouse, the place where much of its important business would be transacted. Whereas Westminster committees are often seen as secondary to what happens in the chamber, working away 'upstairs' generally out of public sight, the Scottish parliamentary committees were seen to be as important as the plenary, to be open and accessible, and a key means of delivering the parliament's 'new politics' culture of transparency and public participation, and to provide a worthwhile career alternative to ministerial office. To maintain this co-equal status between committee and plenary, Standing Orders generally forbid sittings of each to take place at the same time, unlike Westminster practice.

The main structural distinction between the Holyrood and Westminster committee system is that, in Edinburgh, the committees are multi-purpose, dealing with legislative and policy scrutiny, as well as with relevant petitions and budgetary issues. In particular, there is no Westminster-style division between

- select committees, scrutinising government policy and administration
- standing committees, examining the detailed provisions of bills.

The idea behind multi-purpose committees was that committee members would gain expertise in the area of public policy within their committee remit, by examining that policy in all its manifestations, whether in legislation, administrative policy, financial administration or otherwise. In addition, it was hoped that the more collegiate, less partisan approach of Westminster select committee practice, as compared with the trench warfare of standing committees, would apply to all areas of a committee's work, including the scrutiny of Executive bills. Conversely, there were fears that the opposite might occur, where a more adversarial culture would infect the inquiry and scrutiny work of committees.

Generally, the end-of-session verdict on committees is 'good, but could do better'. The fears of a loss of necessary culture of collegiality have largely been unfounded, as committees have developed their own style and personality. However this has been tempered by greater than expected turnover of membership (including 'promotion' of conveners to ministerial office), which has diluted the potential for acquiring subject expertise. The overall workload has been much heavier than was envisaged by the initial fortnightly meeting cycle, and much of this has been due to the legislative work given to them by the Parliamentary Bureau. This focus on legislation—mainly but not exclusively that initiated by the Executive—has put pressure on the committees' ability to set their own work programmes and agendas, and to conduct general policy inquiries. It also has led to frequent complaints that even legislative scrutiny has been compressed by Bureau-imposed timetables for completion of the various legislative stages. These pressures have also inhibited scope for committees to develop more innovative ways of working and of engaging the wider public in their activities.

On the plus side, committees have been a focus for some innovations which should be relevant to Westminster, in addition to their holistic structure and approach. They have been far more proactive than their London counterparts in, for example:

- *openness and transparency*, including holding more than evidence-taking meetings in public session; publishing agendas and background briefing papers on their websites in advance of meetings, and publishing detailed procedural guides on committee operation;
- *participation*, including the public petitions system; different forms of consultation, through IT methods and by the holding of public seminars and meetings, and by meeting all around Scotland;
- *information-gathering*, through use of commissioned external research and use of members as 'reporters' (a variant of the continental 'rapporteur' system).

In terms of their public policy impact and in holding the Executive to account, any verdict must be more subjective and tentative.

There are instances, most notably over the famous Tommy Sheridan member's bill abolishing poindings and warrant sales, where the collegial structure and style of committee operation have led to Executive retreats on policy. Ministers and officials are regularly called before committees, and there is a genuine effort by committees to hear from a wider range of potential witnesses, beyond the 'usual suspects'. The in-built Executive majorities on committees have not prevented committees from conducting inquiries into sensitive policy areas, such as the current enterprise committee inquiry on the impact of policy south of the border on university finance in Scotland. The use of specialised committees such as finance, equal opportunities, and subordinate legislation, acting in conjunction with the subject committees, should provide a more comprehensive and rounded examination of policy.

However, there is still a sense of a ritualistic engagement between committees and government, much as is seen at Westminster, due mainly to the Executive's adherence to traditional UK notions of ministerial responsibility and control of the policy development process. The Procedures Committee has proposed that the Civil Service should not regard itself as working exclusively for ministers, but should be willing and able to assist MSPs generally in their parliamentary work.[12] The experience of the National Assembly for Wales shows the unrealism of this aspiration. That started as a formal body corporate, with officials serving everyone, but quickly found the need to establish an Executive/Assembly split and to demarcate that group of officials who work for the Assembly and its members, leaving a (much larger) separate cadre of officials who work for the Executive.[13]

Several Westminster structures and practices have been adopted or considered at Holyrood, such as the development of the Conveners Group as a version of the transformed Liaison Committee of Commons select committee chairs. There is even pressure for the First Minister to be subject to a regular questioning session before it, much as the Prime Minister has done before the Liaison Committee. Where Westminster processes are seen as effective, they are generally adopted at Holyrood, such as the Audit Committee being a devolved version of the Public Accounts Committee. More generally, there has been less formal co-operation and joint activity between committees in London and Edinburgh than some had originally hoped (mainly for technical, procedural reasons), though informal co-operation between staffs and individual committee members has flourished, both bilaterally and as part of wider inter-parliamentary relations.[14] On specialised internal matters, such as procedural reforms or standards regulation, both parliaments face similar challenges and problems and sharing of experiences is mutually beneficial.

Accountability and Representation

The final area examined here is that of the more general democratic functions of parliament, of holding government to account for their policies and actions, and of representing the interests and views of the wider public. Much of this work is done within the legislative process and in committees, examined already, but no account of the Scottish Parliament can ignore areas of formal proceedings such as parliamentary questions, debates, petitions, and of more informal work such as constituency casework and cross-party groups.

---

[12] Scottish Parliament Procedures Committee, *The Founding Principles of the Scottish Parliament*, paras 513–48.

[13] See generally, R. Rawlings, *Delineating Wales* (Cardiff, 2003) and *Report of the Commission on the Powers and Electoral Arrangements of the National Assembly for Wales*, published 31 March 2004: http://www.richardcommission.gov.uk/content/finalreport/report-e.pdf. Though our chapter considers what Holyrood can 'teach' Westminster, the Richard Commission report demonstrates that devolved Wales has been keen to learn from, and, in many ways, emulate, the devolved parliament in Scotland.

[14] House of Lords Constitution Committee, *Devolution: Inter-institutional Relations in the United Kingdom*, 2nd report, 2002–3, HL Paper 28, January 2003.

One serious criticism of the CSG Report analysis, which set the early tone for the parliament's operation, was not just its failure to take proper account of the role of party, but also of the importance of 'extra-parliamentary activity', that is, the wider role of a parliament and its members outwith the formal proceedings of plenary and committee meetings or of Parliamentary Questions. Because the constituency representation role of elected members is so entrenched in British politics and governance, the new MSPs slipped naturally into the Burkean representation of their local constituents' interests and grievances. Regular local surgeries were held, meetings of local groups were attended, and motions and questions were lodged on matters of constituency interest. The procedure for lodging motions in the parliament's Business Bulletin rapidly became used for the same purposes as 'Early Day Motions' in the Commons, even including the messages of congratulations on local sporting achievements. Members business debates at the end of each sitting were very much like the daily Commons adjournment debates, with the important proviso that they have tended to be more like genuine debates, with six or more speakers, rather than the formalistic exercises in the Commons Chamber involving little more than the main speaker and the minister replying.

Public engagement, which is such a key parliamentary strategy at Holyrood,[15] brings with it risks of improper lobbying and unequal access. Standards regulation has always been strict, partly because of the recent history of parliamentary sleaze at Westminster, and early scandals like 'Lobbygate' and 'Officegate' have kept this aspect on the front burner. The growth of cross-party groups has caused problems of lobbying, despite a rather innovative and detailed regulatory system, intended to be very different from the 'all-party group' system at Westminster. These arrangements are currently under review by the parliament's Standards Committee, and demonstrate, along with the similar problems of the Scottish Parliament and Business Exchange scheme,[16] the potential dangers of a more open and interactive parliament than is traditional at Westminster.

The most visibly innovative mechanism in the parliament is the public petitions system, operated through a dedicated Public Petitions Committee. This has been a great success, in terms of symbolising the parliament's principles in action, with over 600 petitions submitted and examined in the

---

[15] For a very recent example of Westminster looking at Holyrood experience in this area, see the evidence taken from two Holyrood officials by the Commons Modernisation Committee on 24 March 2004, as part of its inquiry into improving public engagement (uncorrected transcript: http://www.publications.parliament.uk/pa/cm200304/cmselect/cmmodern/uc368–ii/uc36802.htm). It should be borne in mind that the Modernisation Committee is chaired by a cabinet minister, the appropriately named Leader of the House of Commons.

[16] This scheme is a variant of the long-running Industry and Parliament Trust scheme at Westminster.

first session. Various achievements have been claimed for the process, in generating wider policy debate on matters such as a Borders rail link, hospital closures, and chronic pain. Interest groups have learned to use the public petitions system as one strand of their campaign strategy alongside more traditional techniques. The Procedures Committee has recommended that the system be given greater resources to allow it to develop further, and it has attracted much admiring attention at Westminster and beyond. It remains to be seen whether the system will become fully entrenched as a meaningful parliamentary process, or whether the novelty value of the process will wear off, as petitioners come to regard it as better for publicity than for the opportunity to influence policy.

Plenary procedures for holding the Executive to account are generally less innovative than other areas of the parliament's activity. Oral questions, ministerial statements and general debates are substantially similar to Westminster processes, and often as formalistic. In fact, through mechanisms such as the parallel chamber of Westminster Hall, and 'unstarred question' short debates in the Lords, the UK parliament may be ahead of Holyrood in providing opportunities for plenary scrutiny.

Conclusions and Prospects

The Scottish Parliament can be described as more of a 'working parliament' by comparison with the classic Westminster model of a 'debating parliament'. That is one reason why it has received a bad press. The media like political theatre, which makes for good reporting, and have been too ready to dismiss Holyrood as a 'numpty parliament'. This is a great shame, because it means that the committees, where most of the parliament's work is done, go relatively unreported, and thus operate largely out of the public eye. The Scots have a better parliament than their media allow, and benefit more from the solid scrutiny of a working parliament, plodding though that may sometimes be, than the sound and fury of a debating parliament.

The committees are probably the Scottish Parliament's greatest single practical achievement. They have been more innovative and outward looking than their counterpart committees at Westminster, in travelling round Scotland, using reporters to extend their reach, and commissioning external research. They invite evidence on a bill as part of the standard process of legislative scrutiny, unlike the closed legislative process at Westminster; and they bring greater expertise to bear, because bills are scrutinised by the relevant subject committee. They all scrutinise departmental spending plans as part of the Scottish Parliament's more systematic approach to scrutinising the overall budget. And through the process of public petitions they are open to suggestions from the public about topics which merit parliamentary investigation.

The other main feature of the parliament by comparison with Westminster is its greater institutional autonomy in relation to the Executive. The Presiding Officer chairs the Parliamentary Bureau which arranges the forthcoming business, and which proposes it to the parliament for its approval. Although not perfect, it is a great deal more transparent and inclusive of minor parties than are the 'usual channels' of the Chief Whips of the major parties doing a deal in secret at Westminster, and a government minister announcing it to the House as a *fait accompli*. Another feature of the parliament's greater autonomy is that in Scotland it is the parliament that recruits independent 'Officers of Parliament' such as the Ombudsman and the Information Commissioner, rather than relying on the Executive to do so.[17] This relative autonomy is both a cause and consequence of its unique culture and ethos, which has been built upon its four key principles.

Finally, the Scottish Parliament has shown a determination to be a learning parliament. Before the end of its first term, the subject committees were invited to prepare 'legacy reports' to hand on to their successor committees in the new parliament, so they should not start again from scratch. The Procedures Committee undertook a comprehensive review of the operation of the parliament against its founding principles. The parliament seems keen to improve its own performance, and to learn from best practice elsewhere. It has a more coherent conception of what it is and what it is for than does Westminster, and that is a necessary foundation for a democratic institution that genuinely wishes to improve itself for the benefit of its people.

How can academics help? In all the academic writing about parliaments, there is a surprising dearth of studies of the performance of the institution as a whole. To fill this gap the Constitution Unit is hoping to launch a collaborative project on Strengthening Parliaments with partners in Australia, Canada, and New Zealand. The intention is to involve initially just one or two parliaments in each country, with a strong team of academics working with each parliament. With their help we hope to develop an agreed conceptual framework for defining the role and functions of Westminster-style parliaments, and then to develop more systematic means of evaluating their performance against each of those functions. In time we hope to develop a toolkit which will enable parliaments to monitor and evaluate their own performance. If it comes off, the project should help to ensure that the Scottish Parliament will not be alone when it comes to future reviews of its own performance, but could draw on expert help and advice from a network of like-minded parliaments from around the Commonwealth.

[17] O. Gay and B. Winetrobe, *Officers of Parliament: Transforming the Role* (London, 2003).

FINANCE

6

Financing the Union: Goschen, Barnett, and Beyond

IAIN McLEAN

Goschen

THE UNITED KINGDOM IS NOT A UNITARY STATE, but a union state as defined by Stein Rokkan and Derek Urwin:

> The *union state* [is] not the result of straightforward dynastic conquest. Incorporation of at least parts of its territory has been achieved through personal dynastic union, for example by treaty, marriage or inheritance. Integration is less than perfect. While administrative standardization prevails over most of the territory, the consequences of personal union entail the survival in some areas of pre-union rights and institutional infrastructures which preserve some degree of regional autonomy.[1]

Rokkan and Urwin, a Norwegian and a Scot, may have been thinking of the Maid of Norway who died in 1290 on her way to becoming Queen of Scotland. But Great Britain fits their description perfectly. England and Scotland were dynastically incorporated in 1603. When the dynastic union was threatened by the childlessness of Queen Anne, English ministers offered the Scots a treaty of union. What emerged was codified in the Acts of Union of 1707.[2] The Acts and Treaty of Union guarantee the continuation of some separate Scottish institutions. The administration of Scotland was never assimilated with that of England.

The union with Ireland was more unequal because King George III vetoed Catholic emancipation in 1801. The leaders of Catholic Ireland never

---

[1] S. Rokkan and D. Urwin (eds), *The Politics of Territorial Identity: Studies in European Regionalism* (London, 1982), p. 11.
[2] The plural is important: see N. MacCormick, 'The English constitution, the British state, and the Scottish anomaly', *Proceedings of the British Academy* 101 (1998), pp. 289–306 and N. MacCormick, Chapter 16 of this volume.

Proceedings of the British Academy **128**, 81–94. © The British Academy 2005.

regarded the union as legitimate. As with Scotland, the administrative integration of Ireland was less than perfect. In contrast to Scotland, however, neither was its political integration. The election of a bloc of MPs from the Irish Party, beginning in 1874, meant that devolution to Ireland would be forced on to the UK political agenda as soon as the Irish Party came to hold the balance of power. That first happened at the General Election of 1885. Immediately afterwards, W. E. Gladstone announced his momentous conversion to Home Rule. However, the pivotal position of the Irish Party meant that whoever governed the UK would have to consider loosening the tie with Ireland.

Gladstone drafted the entire 1886 Home Rule Bill himself. This may have been magnificent but it was not wise. There were three glaring defects in his bill. One concerned Ulster, where he did not recognise the unwillingness of Protestants to be ruled by a Home Rule Irish government. A second concerned Irish representation in the House of Commons after devolution. The bill proposed to remove it; but that would have entailed taxation without representation. The third was public finance. The arrangements in the bill were neither equitable nor economically efficient. Ireland was given no power to tax and the fiscal transfers from the UK government to the government of Ireland would have been quite inadequate. Gladstone's three problems are with us yet.

Gladstone's bill was defeated when ninety-three Liberals joined the Conservatives in voting against it. In the ensuing 1886 General Election the Conservatives swept to power with their new Liberal Unionist allies, including Joseph Chamberlain and George Goschen. After getting rid of the mercurial Lord Randolph Churchill, Lord Salisbury appointed Goschen as Chancellor of the Exchequer later in 1886. Goschen announced his 'equivalent' or 'proportion' in his 1888 Budget. It represented the first block grant to the semi-integrated Scottish and Irish administrations. A proportion of tax receipts was earmarked to the three territories in the proportions 80:11:9 to England (and Wales), Scotland, and Ireland. The ratio was arbitrary, being neither the population ratio nor the ratio of tax receipts of the three countries. But it served unionist statecraft for the succeeding eighty years.

Unionism is about preserving the union of the United Kingdom (and the Empire). Ireland was a reluctant member of the union, so Unionists must try to head off Ireland's threat to public order. Doing so by coercion alone was plainly not working. After 1886, the Unionists embarked on 'killing Home Rule by kindness'. By 1905 they had ended Ireland's land grievances by buying out the Irish landowners with (mostly British) taxpayers' money. They failed to kill Home Rule.

In Scotland, there was no equivalent to the Irish Party. But the parliament of 1885 contained five Highland Liberals who became known as the Crofters'

Party. Like the Irish Party they were pivotal in that classically hung parliament. They secured the revolutionary Crofters' Act 1886, which gave crofters security of tenure (better than that offered to Irish peasants in the 1881 Land Act) and established a Crofters' Commission (still in existence) to protect crofting tenure.

Like the Irish and Scots land legislation, the Goschen proportion aimed to kill Home Rule with kindness. It became a device for quiet redistribution—enough (in Scotland) to contain separatism but too inconspicuous for the English to notice.

Over the decades, Scotland's relative population and relative GDP per head both fell, although its relative needs probably rose. But the Goschen formula was a convenient way of avoiding arguments. In 1923 Stanley Baldwin, then Chancellor, accepted that although the Scotland–England population ratio had dropped below 11:80, the Goschen formula should be retained for its 'rough justice'. As Prime Minister, Baldwin allowed public spending in Scotland to rise above the Goschen proportion—on the grounds that 'political unrest was [not] in the interests of the Union'[3]. This tactic was polished to its finest by Tom Johnston, the forceful Secretary of State for Scotland from 1941 to 1945. Herbert Morrison called Johnston

> [o]ne of the most able men in the technique of getting his own way at cabinet committees. . . . He would impress on the committee that there was a strong nationalist movement in Scotland and it could be a potential danger if it grew through lack of attention to Scottish interests.[4]

Willie Ross (Labour, 1964–70 and 1974–6), Ian Lang (Conservative, 1990–5), and Michael Forsyth (Conservative, 1995–7) all repeated the Johnston threat to good effect.[5] That is why Scottish identifiable public spending per head is now 20 per cent or so higher than English. It depends on the Scottish nationalists being a credible threat to the union—and on UK politicians caring about preserving the union as an end in itself. Therefore, it is not surprising that the UK's present arrangements were codified in 1978–9, when the Scottish nationalist threat, as seen from Westminster and Whitehall, was last at its peak.

---

[3] I. Levitt, 'The Scottish Secretary, the Treasury, and the Scottish Grant Equivalent, 1888–1970', *Scottish Affairs* 28 (1999), pp. 93–116, at pp. 100–1.

[4] H. Morrison, *Herbert Morrison: An Autobiography* (London, 1960), p. 199.

[5] I. Lang, *Blue Remembered Years* (London, 2002); J. Mitchell, 'Spectators and audiences: the politics of UK territorial finance', *Regional and Federal Studies* 13:4 (2003), pp. 7–21.

Barnett

The Barnett formula is described elsewhere.[6] I discuss the politics of its origins, and its implications for public finance since 1997.

The Labour Party entered the February 1974 General Election opposed to devolution, thanks largely to Willie Ross. It entered the October 1974 General Election pledged to devolution, thanks to Lord Crowther-Hunt and a misinterpreted opinion poll.[7] Labour was as unionist as the Conservatives, but for a different reason. It needed to protect the over-representation of Scotland and Wales,[8] because it needed its many Scottish and Welsh seats in order to govern the UK. Most left-wing governments since 1886 have held a minority of seats in England. The Liberal government of 1906 and the Labour governments of 1945, 1966, 1997, and 2001 have been the only ones to have an English seat majority.

Therefore, when the SNP won seven seats and 22 per cent of the Scottish vote in February 1974, Labour took fright. They knew that on 22 per cent a party with dispersed support, such as the SNP, was penalised by the electoral system. But at somewhere between 30 per cent and 35 per cent, the system flips from penalising to rewarding dispersed parties. With 35 per cent of the Scottish vote, the SNP would win more than half the seats in Scotland and would demand independence. Harold Wilson's constitutional adviser, the Oxford academic Lord Crowther-Hunt, had served on the (until then ignored) Kilbrandon Commission on the Constitution. He persuaded Wilson to swing around to supporting devolution. They had to impose this turn-around on their own, undevolved, Scottish Executive. They commissioned private polls in the summer which appeared to show that there was a groundswell of demand for devolution in Scotland. Analysed more carefully, they show only that there was a groundswell of demand for more public spending.[9]

The Scotland and Wales Bill of the ensuing Labour government was therefore designed to grant devolution while preserving Labour's capacity to govern the UK. Therefore it retained seventy-one seats for Scotland and thirty-six for Wales in the House of Commons, whereas the number propor-

---

[6] D. Heald and A. McLeod, Chapter 7 of this volume; I. McLean and A. McMillan, 'The distribution of public expenditure across the UK regions', *Fiscal Studies* 24 (2003), pp. 45–71; T. Edmonds, 'The Barnett Formula', House of Commons Library Research Paper 01/108: http://www.parliament.uk/commons/lib/research/rp2001/rp01–108.pdf .

[7] I. McLean and A. McMillan, *State of the Union* (Oxford, 2005), ch. 8.

[8] I. McLean, 'Are Scotland and Wales overrepresented in the House of Commons?', *Political Quarterly* 66 (1995), pp. 250–68.

[9] The polls did not ask whether the Scots would like to pay more tax: McLean and McMillan, *State of the Union*, ch. 8.

tionate to population would be about fifty-seven and thirty-one. If the Scotland and Wales Bill had followed the lines of the Government of Ireland Act 1920, their seats would have been cut further, to about forty and twenty-five, in exchange for a devolved assembly. In finance the bill did not propose any alteration to the block grant arrangements that still echoed Goschen, notably in higher public spending per head. In 1979, the Treasury's Needs Assessment attempted to measure the needs per head in each of the UK's four territories for the services that the bill would have devolved, and the actual spending (Table 6.1).

Table 6.1. HM Treasury, 'Needs Assessment 1979' (data for 1976–7). England = 100.

	England	Scotland	Wales	Northern Ireland
Needs	100	116	109	131
Spending per head	100	122	106	135

Source: HM Treasury.

These and similar numbers[10] stoked up an English backlash against the devolution bill. It was strongest in the North-East, with its long border with Scotland, similar social and economic problems, but less public spending per head than Scotland. A Labour government seemed to be punishing the Geordies for voting Labour and rewarding the Scots for voting SNP. Furthermore, devolution as proposed might entrench Scotland's advantage, with seventy-one continuing MPs and a Secretary of State in addition to a devolved assembly.

A Geordie-led guillotine revolt killed the Scotland and Wales Bill in February 1977. The government then reintroduced two separate bills for devolution to Scotland and to Wales (which were enacted but, in effect, fell at the change of government in 1979) and looked for ways to dampen the English backlash. Treasury officials had long believed, along with 'all Departments other than the Scottish Office and all MPs other than Scottish ones that the Scots had been getting away with financial murder',[11] in the words of a Scottish Office civil servant in charge of devolution policy at the time. They therefore proposed a new formula for block grant to Scotland. It would award money to fund domestic services in a single block, rather than programme by programme; and it would award all *increments*, although not the base amount per head, in proportion to the relative population of

[10] See especially Northern Region Strategy Team, *Public Expenditure in the Northern Region and Other British Regions*, Technical Report no. 12 (Newcastle upon Tyne, 1976).
[11] J. Ross, letter to Prof. James Mitchell, 1985, cited in paper to ESRC Devolution Conference, Birmingham, January 2002.

Scotland and the rest of Great Britain. The formula was introduced by Joel
Barnett, Chief Secretary to the Treasury. Its existence was first acknowledged
in 1980, by which time it had been extended to cover block grants to Wales
and Northern Ireland as well. David Heald first named it the 'Barnett formula', and predicted: 'Perhaps, some day, this will make Joel Barnett as
famous as Lord Goschen!'[12]

The Barnett formula was never intended to be permanent. Lord Barnett
has told the Treasury Committee that he did not expect it to last 'a year or
even twenty minutes'.[13] He has become a vociferous critic of his eponymous
formula. Had devolution come into force in 1979, the Barnett formula would
have given way to a needs-based formula, for which the Treasury Needs
Assessment was preparing the ground. However, Barnett has survived, to be
embedded in the White Papers (although not the Acts) offering devolution to
Scotland and Wales. The Treasury's operational manual shows how 'Barnett
consequentials' are now calculated for funding devolved services in the three
territories. The Treasury line remains that 'there are no plans to change the
Barnett formula'. When Deputy Prime Minister John Prescott suggested
otherwise in an interview with *The Guardian* during the 2001 General Election campaign, he was slapped down brutally by the Prime Minister's official
spokesman, Alastair Campbell, the following day. But in March 2004
Prescott's deputy Nick Raynsford repeated to *The Journal*, the Newcastle
daily that is the bitterest enemy of Barnett, that 'the case for reconsidering
the basis of funding is getting stronger all the time'.[14]

If it ain't broke, don't fix it. But Barnett is broke. It now has no defenders
outside Scotland—who are perceived in the rest of the UK to be defending
the indefensible. I now explain why Barnett is broke, propose an alternative
block grant mechanism, and examine the growing demand for 'fiscal
autonomy' for Scotland.

Barnett was a new Goschen for modern unionists. Margaret Thatcher was
described by one of her cabinet ministers as 'the most Unionist politician in
Downing Street since the war'.[15] She curtly rejected past Conservative policy

---

[12] D. Heald, *Territorial Equity and Public Finances: Concepts and Confusion*, Centre for the
Study of Public Policy, University of Strathclyde, Studies in Public Policy no. 75 (Glasgow,
1980).

[13] In oral evidence to the Treasury Committee, HC Select Committee on the Barnett Formula
2nd Report (HC Paper (1997–98) no. 341).

[14] HM Treasury, *Funding the Scottish Parliament, National Assembly for Wales and Northern
Ireland Assembly: A Statement of Funding Policy*, 3rd edn, 2002 http://www.hm-treasury.
gov.uk/mediastore/otherfiles/funding_devolved.pdf ; P. Hetherington, 'Scots and Welsh face subsidy axe', *The Guardian*, 24 April 2001; J. Mitchell and F. Nelson, 'Barnett and the 2001 General
Election', *British Elections and Parties Review* 12 (2002), pp. 171–89; P. Linford, 'It's all to play
for', *The Journal*, 3 March 2004, p. 1.

[15] H. Young, *One of Us: A Biography of Margaret Thatcher* (London, 1990), p. 465.

of devolution to Scotland on taking office in 1979 (see Chapter 4, Kellas). She was lucky as well as determined. If devolution had been more salient to the Scottish people, her curt rejection might have led to disorder. But the pro-devolution forces did not regroup until the Scottish Constitutional Convention in 1989, after Scotland had been used as the first laboratory for the Poll Tax.

Without devolution Mrs Thatcher, like Lord Salisbury, must kill Home Rule by kindness. But public spending was supposed to be a bad thing: so how could it be presented as a good thing in Scotland and Wales? For if it were not so presented, the Scots and Welsh would not know that their government was killing Home Rule by kindness, and might therefore return in force to Home Rule or separatism. Furthermore, the Barnett formula should have led over time to convergence on to equal public spending per head. That would represent (relatively at least) a sharp cut in public spending within Scotland.

The virtues of public spending were trumpeted by three territorial Secretaries of State under the Conservatives: the ultra-wet Peter Walker in Wales (1987–90), and the dry Ian Lang and even drier Michael Forsyth, the last two Conservative Secretaries of State for Scotland (1990–7). Intellectually it was easy for Walker but harder for the other two. Lang initiated the series *Government Expenditure and Revenue in Scotland (GERS)* in order to show what a good deal Scotland got from the union, and how any fiscal autonomy would lead to either reduced services or higher taxation, because of Scotland's structural deficit. In a leaked letter to Prime Minister John Major, Lang wrote:

> I am disappointed that both you and the Chancellor have reservations about publishing the booklet I have prepared and printed setting out the details of the government's expenditure and revenue in Scotland. I judge that it is just what is needed at present in our campaign to maintain the initiative and undermine the other parties.[16]

Michael Forsyth was forced into more dangerous contortions, publishing a consultants' report on local government spending in Scotland which showed that Scottish local authorities spent more per head and raised less per head in tax revenue than English ones. That might go down well in Duns, but awfully in Alnwick.

Why, though, did the higher spending per head persist, given that Barnett was supposed to lead to convergence? Because killing Home Rule by kindness was incompatible with the convergence properties of Barnett. One of them

---

[16] I. Lang to J. Major, 1992, quoted by Mitchell, 'Spectators and audiences', p. 14.

had to go. Barnett was bypassed whenever an expensive pay settlement might have brought its convergence properties to public attention.

And Beyond

The Labour victory in 1997 brought devolution but solved none of Mr Gladstone's questions. The Ulster question continues to rankle. The representation question has been reborn as the West Lothian Question (WLQ). After the next boundary review, the number of Westminster seats in Scotland will be reduced to (but not below) its population share; the number of seats in Wales is to stay untouched. That satisfies nobody. It riles the Scots because the number of MSPs is linked to the number of MPs. Therefore, although Westminster representation is a 'reserved' matter, it knocks on to the internal arrangements for the Scottish Parliament. But it riles (some of) the English too. Because the territories are not reduced below their population share of Westminster seats, the West Lothian Question remains as unanswered as it was when Tam Dalyell asked it in 1977, or Joseph Chamberlain in 1886. Reduced representation is probably the best answer to the WLQ. It is certainly the only one that does not lead to severe contradictions.

The finance question is easier than Ulster but harder than the WLQ. There are two main alternatives to Barnett. One is a regime of greater fiscal autonomy and a smaller vertical fiscal imbalance; the other is a reformed needs assessment.

But first it might be asked, *Why can the government not sustain its line that there are no plans to alter the Barnett formula?* The answer is that since 1999, Barnett has started to bite. Politicians in all parts of the UK are nursing sore hands, and blaming it on Barnett.

As Barnett is a convergence formula, it is a mathematical necessity that the faster public spending rises in England, the faster it will converge in the three territories towards equal spending per head. Until 1999, Chancellor Gordon Brown held public spending at the outgoing Conservatives' planned level. Then there were sharp real increases in the overlapping Spending Reviews in 2000 and 2002 (SR 2000/2002). But if plans to spend on a devolved service (education, say) increase in real terms by 6 per cent per annum in England, as in SR 2002, the real increase in Wales and Northern Ireland is only about 5 per cent, and in Scotland less than 5 per cent because of Scotland's declining population. The territories still get a real increase, but they are on a convergent glide path.

In 2002, Northern Ireland Finance Minister Sean Farren called for Barnett to be replaced by a needs-based formula. Officials believe that, although currently spending per head on devolved services remains high, it will have dropped below Northern Ireland's relative needs during the lifetime of SR 2002. In Wales, the opposition to Barnett was curiously muted until the 2003 National Assembly election, although Plaid Cymru argued for replacing it by a needs formula.[17] Labour politicians in Wales knew that Barnett did Wales no favours, but any criticism could damage their own party colleagues and would play into the hands of Plaid Cymru. They also doubted whether they had enough robust allies in other parts of the UK. Both of these constraints have now gone, after the poor performance of Plaid Cymru and the SNP in the 2003 elections and the prospect of some elected English assemblies.

In the English regions, a search on newspaper databases for the string 'iniquitous AND Barnett AND formula' produces many hits, mostly from Newcastle but also from Plymouth. Strictly speaking, the Barnett formula has got nothing to do with England, where regional expenditure is governed by a different (and also broke) set of formulae.[18] But politically, it does. The call for Barnett reform is spreading from its original home in Newcastle to other regions of England. Five of the twelve written submissions to the recent Treasury Sub-Committee inquiry into regional expenditure patterns came from English regional organisations (as well as one each from Plaid Cymru and Alex Salmond MP). Of those seven, six explicitly called for Barnett reform and the seventh, from London, did so implicitly.[19] The voters of the North-East of England voted down an elected assembly in late 2004. That kills the idea outside London. But unelected regional bodies will keep the politics of regional public expenditure on the agenda. Two powerful ministers—Chancellor Gordon Brown and Deputy Prime Minister John Prescott—have also signalled their interest in reforming regional policy. It was the first thing Brown mentioned in his speech to the 2003 Labour Party Conference.

Even in Scotland, three of the four main parties have called for Barnett reform. Scotland's glide path is gentler than that in the other two territories. If present policies continue, Scotland will not be reduced to equal public spending per head with England for perhaps fifteen or twenty years. But Barnett is biting already. Not so much on the total public expenditure available to Scotland, which is not yet a constraint, but in the policy restrictions it imposes. A notable example is the English Higher Education White Paper

---

[17] Plaid Cymru, 'The case for replacing the Barnett Formula', submission to House of Commons Treasury Sub-Committee inquiry into Regional Spending, HC 234-ii, 2002–03 (2003), Ev.13–Ev.18.

[18] McLean and McMillan, 'Distribution of public expenditure', *passim*, esp. p. 61; I. McLean et al., *Identifying the Flow of Domestic and European Expenditure into the English Regions*, DTLR Contract no. LGR 65/12/75 (Oxford: Nuffield College and London: ODPM, 2003). At http://www.nuff.ox.ac.uk/projects/odpm/ .

[19] House of Commons Treasury Committee, *Regional Spending: Memoranda* (2003) HC 234-ii.

of January 2003.[20] Written by Ministers who are *de facto* ministers for England and a department that is almost entirely a department for England, it has huge knock-on consequences about which nobody consulted the devolved administrations in advance.[21]

A telling detail for anoraks: the White Paper proposed a large increase in university funding through three streams. One (student funding) has received huge publicity; the other two almost none. But the second stream is direct grants to English universities for teaching and research via the funding council HEFCE. The third stream is a steep increase in research grant money from the research councils. HEFCE comes on the Vote of the education department DfES, and the increase in the first two funding streams therefore carries a Barnett consequential for the three devolved administrations. But the research councils come under the Department of Trade and Industry (DTI), and that increase carries no Barnett consequential because the DTI is deemed to be a UK-wide department. Research Council funds go by the councils' judgement of where the best research is—disproportionately to South-East England. The authors of the White Paper appeared to be unaware of this several-hundred-million-pound wrinkle. The story calls to mind the visit of Scotland's leading public intellectual, John Stuart Blackie, to his Oxford counterpart, Benjamin Jowett, in 1866. 'I hope you in Oxford don't think we hate you,' said Blackie. 'We don't think about you,' replied Jowett.[22]

It is thus in the interests of Scotland as well as those of all eleven other regions of the UK that Barnett should go. In favour of what? The two games in town are 'fiscal autonomy' and 'needs assessment'.

Fiscal Autonomy

SNP and some Liberal Democrat and Conservative politicians have called for 'fiscal autonomy'. A little digging shows that they mean quite different things by the same phrase. The SNP version is optimistic, but worth a try in 2007 if the Scots vote for it. The Conservative version could be implemented sooner than that, and it is backed by good arguments in public finance.

The SNP version of fiscal autonomy is Scottish independence within the European Union. *GERS* suggests that tax rates would have to go up or public spending down if Scotland left the UK.[23] Nationalist sums due to Alex

[20] Department for Education and Skills, *The Future of Higher Education*, White Paper, Cm. 5735 (London, 2003). http://www.dfes.gov.uk/hestudents/hestrategy/pdfs/DfES-HigherEducation.pdf.
[21] I. McLean, 'Devolution bites', *Prospect* 84 (March 2003).
[22] Quoted in C. Harvie, *Scotland and Nationalism* (London 1977), p. 121.
[23] A. Goudie, '*GERS* and fiscal autonomy', *Scottish Affairs* 41 (2002), pp. 56–85.

Salmond MP show the opposite. The Nationalist sums are ingenious smoke and mirrors but they do not add up. They require that Scotland gets all the oil revenue; that the price of oil is high; and that Scotland's oil does not run out. Relax any one of the three, and the smoke evaporates.

In the 1970s, the UK government made it clear that in no circumstances would it cede control of oil revenues to Scotland. In its view, to do so would be to enact Scottish independence. This was unduly strident. The governments of Australia and Canada, for instance, give the power to tax mineral resources to their states and provinces. But it became clear that It's *not all* Scotland's Oil. Any arbitration would set a boundary running out to sea north-east, not due east, from Berwick and would therefore assign some UK North Sea oil revenue to England. An independent Scotland would also have to decide how much autonomy and control over oil revenue to give Shetland, a matter on which the SNP MPs in the 1974–9 parliament contradicted one another. Alex Salmond now contends that Scotland's share of oil revenues should be in the range between 66 per cent and 90 per cent; others might think those numbers optimistic.[24]

But the real trouble with SNP economics lies in the second and third assumptions. The oil price will not always be high; and one day the oil will run out. Fiscal autonomy based on a stream of natural resources revenue would be precarious. The SNP version of fiscal autonomy is a gamble. A much better argument is that an independent Scotland could repeat Ireland's spectacular performance as an Anglophone entry point for inward investment to the European Union, and accordingly see very rapid growth after independence. But there seem to be fewer nostalgic Scots-American capitalists than nostalgic Irish-American capitalists.[25]

The Conservative argument for fiscal autonomy is one that a Canadian or Australian public finance specialist would be at home with. I summarise the Conservative fiscal autonomists' position, not necessarily in language they would use.

The UK has one of the largest *vertical fiscal gaps* (also known as vertical fiscal imbalances—VFI) in the democratic world. VFI exists when one tier of government has the power to tax and another has the power to spend. The Scottish Executive could vary the standard rate of income tax by up to 3p in the pound. But even if levied at the top rate it would cover only maybe 5 or 10 per cent of the *difference* in public spending per head between Scotland and England, let alone of the baseline. The Welsh and Northern Irish

---

[24] J. P. Grant (ed.), *Independence and Devolution: The Legal Implications for Scotland* (Edinburgh, 1976); A. Salmond, submission to House of Commons Treasury Sub-Committee inquiry into Regional Spending, HC 234-ii, 2002–03 (2003), Ev.9–Ev.10.
[25] See further *Scottish Affairs* 41 (2002), a special issue on fiscal autonomy.

assemblies have no power to tax, and none is proposed for the proposed English regional assemblies either.

VFI reduces the incentives for both central and local government to tax efficiently, and it encourages politicians to play blame games against one another. If citizens are unclear who provides which service then each tier of government can blame the other. Scots politicians can turn from the difficult task of providing good public services to the easier task of blaming their problems on the English. That is admittedly harder for the Executive than for the opposition, as it would involve Labour blaming Labour. But Jack McConnell's refuge from fiscal reality takes the form of defending Barnett when it has no other friends in the world. When, as it must, it disappears, his successors will face a tougher world. If the Scottish Executive raised more of what it spent, say the fiscal autonomists, it would face the tougher world immediately, to maybe short-term pain but long-term gain. Scots politicians and Scots citizens would face the true costs and the true trade-offs between public services and tax savings. Fiscal autonomy would require radical change:

- The three devolved authorities must each have the same power to tax. If it was right for Labour to argue in 1997 that the Scottish Executive should have the power to tax (and I believe that it was), then the power should have been given to Wales and Northern Ireland as well.
- The UK must 'vacate some tax points' (in Canadian terminology)— that is, allow a certain proportion of, say, VAT and income tax receipts to be kept by the devolved administrations.
- The taxation of real estate must become more progressive and more comprehensive. That old Liberal favourite, a land value tax, is the best way. It would take time to introduce, but the target for introducing it should be 2009, the centenary year of Lloyd George's People's Budget, of which land taxation was intended to be the culmination.[26]

A Needs Assessment

The above may be too strong for many. If fiscal autonomy, once stripped of comfort blankets, is naked, the other viable alternative to Barnett is a needs assessment regime. But every location in the UK would claim that what it

---

[26] For a full version of this argument, see I. McLean and A. McMillan, *New Localism, New Finance* (London, 2003).

happened to lack, it needed. Where needs formulae already exist, in local government and health funding, decades of lobbying are embedded in the needs formulae. The Scottish local government needs-formula includes a weighting for miles of roads built on peat. The English school needs-formula includes a weighting for ethnic minority pupils. If you have a lot of roads built on peat and a lot of ethnic minority pupils, you can readily see why you need more public spending per head. If you do not, you may not.

In England, the present needs-formulae work reasonably well in the Health Service. They work badly for local government services (education, housing, personal social services, police, fire, environmental services). This is for two main reasons: regression on past spending, and political interference.

Regression on past spending may be explained as follows. The formula used to assign grant to local authorities uses multiple regression. This involves predicting a dependent variable (here grant per head to each of 150 councils) from a range of independent variables such as indicators of poverty, remoteness, proportion of elderly people, proportion of school-age children (and within that the proportion of ethnic minority children), and so on. For some services, the values of the independent variables for each council area can be got from the Census or similar external sources. This is true of data for children and pensioners for example. But for some services you cannot do this. Ideally, you should be measuring outcomes—say, how happy people are. If you can't do that, you should at least measure outputs—say, the number of people seen by social services departments per annum. When you cannot even do that, you have to measure inputs—say, the amount that each council has spent on social services. If you can only measure inputs, you are regressing against past spending. If a council has spent unusually highly in the past, it will get an unusually high grant in the future. But its high past spending may be due to high need, or low efficiency, or high costs, or a political decision to give priority to that service. Multiple regression cannot tell those apart. It is at severe risk of rewarding councils for past inefficiency.

Political interference is easier to understand. When the government proposes to revise the formulae, it publishes 'exemplifications'. These show how each authority would fare under each of the grant regimes proposed. Politicians like exemplifications. All they need do is choose their favourite authority, run through the exemplifications, see under which regime their favourite does best, and choose that regime.

These examples[27] suffice to show why the English local government grant system is broke. It sits alongside Barnett, which is also broke. And the conjunction of the two is more broke still (if that is possible). It is the yawning

---

[27] There are more in McLean and McMillan, *New Localism*, pp. 26–7.

gap between expenditure per schoolchild in Duns and per schoolchild in
Alnwick, per patient in Dunbar and per patient in Berwick, that generates all
those 'iniquitous Barnett formula' stories in the Newcastle press and leads
Lord Barnett to denounce his own formula.

So a future territorial needs-formula must follow lines different to both
Barnett and the English regime. It must ensure that each comparable citizen of the UK is treated equally wherever she lives; and it must be compatible with economic efficiency. The second criterion requires that there
be no incentives to politicians to make their territory appear 'needy'—
something for which the present English regime and the present EU regime
are notorious.[28]

McLean and McMillan have proposed a regime that meets these criteria.
There would be a Territorial Grants Commission, modelled on the highly
successful Commonwealth Grants Commission of Australia. It would be an
arms-length body like the Electoral Commission or the Committee on Standards in Public Life—appointed by politicians, but thereafter unable to be
intimidated. Its commissioners would be appointed by agreement between
the UK government and all the territorial governments, including those of
London and any other self-governing English regions. Its staff would be public servants drawn or seconded from the relevant agencies including the
devolved administrations. Each territory with elected government would have
one vote at meetings; those English regions without elected assemblies would
also get one vote each.

There would be two, mutually dependent, ground rules. The first is that
decisions on block grant must be taken by unanimity. This is to give each
region the same bargaining power, and avoid the Scots, or anyone else, playing the Johnston card. But, to avoid deadlock, if agreement is not reached by
the known deadline for decision, then the additional grant to each territory
for the following year will be inversely proportional to the GDP of that territory. This 'inverse GDP rule' is both fairer and more efficient than Barnett.
It would lead in the long run not to equal spending per head, which cannot
be the right target, but to spending proportional to the need of each region.
But regions would not have an incentive to be, or remain, poor. As public
spending per head is less than GDP per head, a regional government which
raises its region's GDP per head will always gain more from that than it
would lose in public spending.

Where Mr Gladstone failed, I modestly offer that route to success.

---

[28] McLean and McMillan, 'Distribution of public expenditure', pp. 59–60; McLean and
McMillan, *New Localism*, pp. 17–19.

7

Scotland's Fiscal Relationships with England and the United Kingdom

DAVID HEALD AND ALASDAIR McLEOD

Introduction

THIS VOLUME ACKNOWLEDGES THE UNION OF THE CROWNS ON THE DEATH OF ELIZABETH OF ENGLAND IN 1603, 104 years before the Union of the Parliaments. The intervening century was one in which much happened, including a period when Scotland was incorporated into a full union with England and Wales. However, in terms of fiscal relationships, the Union of the Parliaments was a much more significant event than the Union of the Crowns. Prior to that, leaving aside the period of the Commonwealth, there were two independent countries sharing a common monarch. After that, there was a single government. Even without the asymmetry that has been such a feature of this union, it is exceptionally difficult to run fully self-financing units within a single polity. Moreover, data on relative fiscal 'contributions' usually do not exist, whether through conscious political or administrative choice or because of poor data collection systems.

The distinction drawn by Rokkan and Urwin[1] between 'unitary states' and 'union states' has been frequently applied to Scotland.[2] Whether the imperfect integration of Scotland into the union is something to be celebrated or deplored depends upon the perspective adopted, but important consequences follow, as are discussed below.

---

[1] S. Rokkan and D. Urwin, 'Introduction: centres and peripheries in Western Europe', in S. Rokkan and D. Urwin (eds), *The Politics of Territorial Identity: Studies in European Regionalism* (London, 1982), pp. 1–17.

[2] See, for example, M. Keating, *Plurinational Democracy* (Oxford, 2001), pp. 20–1; and J. Mitchell, *Governing Scotland: The Invention of Administrative Devolution* (Basingstoke, 2003), pp. 2–3.

Proceedings of the British Academy **128**, 95–112. © The British Academy 2005.

The magnetic pull of London and the South-East of England within the single economy is a most striking phenomenon. The relative demographic trends that are presently much discussed were established long ago, as evidenced since the 1801 Census by Scotland's declining proportion of UK population.[3] This context is bound to affect debates about parliamentary representation and about public money, with explicitly and implicitly conflicting views being held as to whether Scotland's counterpart is England or a region of England of comparable size. Intriguingly, there has been a considerable amount of historical accident in determining both representational and expenditure proportions.

Longevity of Formulae

Both the Goschen formula and the Barnett formula have had lives far beyond that originally envisaged. The Goschen formula lasted for nearly three-quarters of a century, having been announced in 1888 as a means of allocating assigned revenues in connection with local government.[4] The Barnett formula, now twenty-five years old, was originally a temporary measure for the initial funding of the proposed (but never established) Scottish Assembly,[5] pending the introduction of a more permanent arrangement,[6] but has proved more durable. The fact of the matter is that, where a devolved level of government has some power over the allocation of resources amongst the different services for which it is responsible, there has to be some means of deciding the overall allocation, with the minimum of disturbance, within the timescale of the public expenditure system operated by the Treasury. This is true whether the devolution in question is merely adminis-

---

[3] See D. A. Heald, *Formula-Based Territorial Public Expenditure in the United Kingdom*, Aberdeen Papers in Accountancy, no. W7 (Aberdeen, 1992), p. 29.

[4] G. McCrone, 'Scotland's public finances from Goschen to Barnett', *Fraser of Allander Institute Quarterly Economic Commentary* 24:2 (1999), pp. 30–46.

[5] The Scottish Assembly was to be set up under the Scotland Act 1978; however, following the failure to achieve sufficient support in a referendum, it did not proceed. By that time, the still-to-be named Barnett formula had been used to determine the expenditure the Assembly would have had in its first year, and that amount became the relevant part of the budget of the Scottish Office in that year. The use of the formula was continued by the incoming Conservative government; see D. A. Heald and A. McLeod, 'Fiscal autonomy under devolution: introduction to Symposium', *Scottish Affairs* 41 (2002), pp. 5–25.

[6] McCrone, 'Scotland's public finances from Goschen to Barnett', pp. 35–6.

trative or whether it is political; both the Goschen and Barnett formulae were used in circumstances of administrative devolution.[7]

Provided they are not, or do not become, too controversial, formulae of this sort can be a convenient device to smooth the process. Both the Goschen formula and the Barnett formula became at various times something for the Scottish Office to defend as a means of protecting its policy space and the perceived expenditure advantage they protected.[8] Moreover, there is an advantage to the UK government in not having to devote disproportionate resources, at a time when it can least afford them, to protracted and difficult negotiations over a relatively small part of total UK public expenditure.[9]

Attitudes to the Barnett Formula

Attitudes to formulae such as Goschen and Barnett are conditioned, partly at least, by the perceptions of the extent to which the arrangements are favourable. These perceptions are not always based on reality. At the moment there is the bizarre situation whereby everyone thinks they are losing from the Barnett formula: the Scots, Welsh, and Northern Irish because of convergence;[10] and the English, especially in the North-East and London, because

[7] While the formal ability of the then Scottish Office to allocate within an overall envelope was greatly increased in 1979, there was some discretion, particularly within individual services, prior to that; see D. A. Heald and A. McLeod, 'Public expenditure', in *The Laws of Scotland: Stair Memorial Encyclopaedia* (Edinburgh, 2002), ch. 10, paras 480–551, esp. para. 535.

[8] Mitchell, *Governing Scotland*, p. 150, shows how opportunistic were the arguments of both the Treasury and the Scottish Office, with regard to the application of the Goschen formula, supporting it or condemning it according to circumstance. In contrast, the protection of the Barnett formula has been a consistent theme of the Scottish Office and its successor Scottish Executive.

[9] See C. Thain and M. Wright, *The Treasury and Whitehall: The Planning and Control of Public Expenditure, 1976–1993* (Oxford, 1995), p. 326; A. Midwinter, 'The Barnett formula and Scotland's public expenditure needs', in Treasury Committee, HC Select Committee on the Barnett Formula 2nd Report (HC Paper (1997–98) no. 341), pp. 29–32; and D. A. Heald and A. McLeod, 'Beyond Barnett? Funding devolution', in P. Robinson and J. Adams (eds), *Devolution in Practice*, Institute for Public Policy Research (London, 2002), pp. 147–75.

[10] In Scotland, the difference between the actual formula consequences and the amount by which the Assigned Budget would have increased if Scotland received the same percentage increase as England has become known as the 'Barnett squeeze'. This has been quantified by N. Kay and by J. and M. Cuthbert: N. Kay, 'The Scottish Parliament and the Barnett Formula', *Fraser of Allander Institute Quarterly Economic Commentary* 24:1 (1998), pp. 32–48; J. Cuthbert and M. Cuthbert, 'The Barnett squeeze in Spending Review 2000', *Fraser of Allander Institute Quarterly Economic Commentary* 26:2 (2001), pp. 27–33. In the Scottish media, this lower percentage growth rate than in England has often been portrayed as unjust, as though equal percentage increases were an entitlement, irrespective of the base.

they see it as preserving an unfair advantage. McLean has denounced the Barnett formula as unjust,[11] a view to which Lord Barnett himself now subscribes.[12] It is, indeed, 'nobody's child'.[13]

To some extent, this confusion is understandable. Prior to devolution, the details were little understood beyond a small group of civil servants and academic commentators, mostly in Scotland. These were transactions within a single government and generally regarded as boring and abstruse. For years the Scottish media regularly reported that Scotland obtained 10/85ths of English expenditure (that is, absolute expenditure, not the annual increment) and continued to report the 10/85ths proportion long after it had been superseded in 1992. Since these were internal transactions, governments felt little need to explain the details, or even to make much effort to correct misapprehensions. With devolution in place since 1999, the mechanics are now much better understood: for example, no one now makes the mistake of thinking the Barnett formula applies on absolute expenditure. However, there are still gaps in available data, as explained below. Presumably, more information will become available over time, particularly when politically opposed devolved administrations demand more information of the UK government.

How the Arrangements have Worked under Devolution

The transition to devolved government seemed to go smoothly. There was no obvious disruption of public services due to transitional funding problems. The Scottish Executive and Parliament have coped well with the business of allocations, though many in single interest pressure groups would disagree with that. No doubt the existence of a bureaucracy already versed in these matters was a major factor, as was the continuity in the arrangements for determining, and to a large extent providing, funding. Added to that, the transition was lubricated by the large increases since 1999 in Departmental

---

[11] I. McLean, 'Previous convictions', *Prospect* 19 (1997), p. 80; and I. McLean, 'Memorandum', in House of Lords Select Committee on the Constitution (HL Paper (2001–02) no. 147): *Devolution: Inter-Institutional Relations in the United Kingdom. Evidence Complete to 10 July 2002*, pp. 422–7.

[12] Lord Barnett, oral evidence, in Treasury Committee, HC Select Committee on the Barnett Formula 2nd Report (HC Paper (1997–98) no. 341); Lord Barnett, Speech in House of Lords Debate on the Barnett Formula, Hansard HL (series 5) vol. 628, cols 225–9 (7 November 2001); and Lord Barnett, Oral Parliamentary Question on the Barnett Formula, Hansard HL (series 5) vol. 643, col. 913 (27 January 2003).

[13] See D. Bell and A. Christie, 'Finance—the Barnett Formula: nobody's child?', in A. Trench (ed.), *The State of the Nations 2001: The Second Year of Devolution in the United Kingdom* (Thorverton, 2001), pp. 135–51.

Expenditure Limits (DEL), and the consequential (in the Barnett sense) increases in provision for the Scottish Parliament. Devolution was therefore implemented at a time of relative plenty, not in the conditions of relative famine that had been expected.[14]

The processes are now much better understood. Prior to devolution the operation of the Barnett formula was explained only in general terms, with the 'block rules' unpublished. The detailed operating rules are now in the public domain; the Treasury published them in its *Statement of Funding Policy*, originally issued just before the 1999 elections, and updated at each Spending Review.[15] There is also information in the public domain on what happens to DELs between Spending Reviews. It can be shown that the process is much more complex than simply applying the formula proportion, reflecting the way in which devolution finance is embedded within the Treasury's public expenditure control system.[16]

There are still gaps in the data: there is no publication of the precise operation of the formula, and no explanation of how the additions at each stage were arrived at; in some ways it is surprising that the Scottish Parliament has never demanded a full reconciliation of successive expenditure figures. It is also extremely difficult, if not impossible, to tie up the numbers published by the Scottish Executive with those published by the Treasury. No doubt timing differences have much to do with that, but these are capable of explanation. Crucially, there is no published information on comparable provision in England, beyond some unsatisfactory information in successive issues of the *Statement of Funding Policy*.[17] Such information is vital for the assessment of the vexed question of whether or not there has been convergence and, if so, how much, because otherwise the relevant expenditure aggregate cannot be analysed. The Westminster Scottish Affairs Committee has repeatedly

[14] See D. A. Heald, N. Geaughan, and C. Robb, 'Financial arrangements for UK devolution', *Regional and Federal Studies* 8:4 (1998), pp. 23–52.

[15] HM Treasury, *Funding the Scottish Parliament, National Assembly for Wales and Northern Ireland Assembly: A Statement of Funding Policy* (London, 1999, 2nd edn 2000, 3rd edn 2002, 4th edn 2004).

[16] Heald and McLeod have provided for Scotland, Wales, and Northern Ireland a reconciliation between the respective Assigned Budget DELs in Spending Reviews 2000, 2002 and 2004. They demonstrate why it is inappropriate to attempt to see the workings of the Barnett formula in successive public expenditure announcements, in the absence of data showing the size of changes arising from other sources (e.g. changes in measurement conventions, such as the switch in 2001–2 from cash to resource). D. A. Heald and A. McLeod, 'Embeddedness of UK devolution finance within the Public Expenditure System', *Regional Studies* 39 (2005), pp. 495–518.

[17] Appendix C of the Treasury's 2002 *Statement of Funding Policy* does give figures for provision for comparable sub-programmes for 2002–3. It is not clear, however, to what stage of the process these relate (original plans, plans supplemented by in-year adjustments, or estimated outturn); and they do not separate English and Welsh expenditure in England and Wales programmes. It is therefore not possible, even if the run were long enough, to construct a meaningful time series.

attempted to elicit this information, but the UK government has simply pretended not to understand the request.[18]

Of course, there has been controversy. In Scotland there have been arguments about convergence—the so-called 'Barnett squeeze'; about the role of tax-varying powers in economic policy; and generally about fiscal autonomy. In England, particularly the North-East and London, there are continuing mutterings about Scotland occupying a privileged position. Much of this is ill-informed, partly, but not wholly, because of the lack of hard information on convergence. It is difficult to gauge the political importance of this controversy, though we do not accept McLean's proposition (in Chapter 6 of this volume) that the extent of controversy is such that the Barnett formula is 'broke'. Whatever the fiscal relationships within the United Kingdom, the various asymmetries guarantee that there will be controversies. Their salience probably depends on political context, in particular on the size of Westminster majorities, the state of the UK and regional economies, and the public expenditure climate. Thus far the controversies on Barnett have been sporadic and have operated on different time frames in different countries/regions.

Although the figures are not ideal for the purpose, some evidence of convergence can be detected in the identifiable public expenditure series in the annual publication *Public Expenditure: Statistical Analyses*, eliminating Social Security and Agriculture etc. spending. Using this method, Goudie calculated that expenditure per head in Scotland had reduced from 30 per cent above that in England in 1987–8 to 20 per cent above in 1999–2000, notwithstanding the offsetting effect of further falls in Scotland's relative population.[19] Although there is no definitive evidence in regard to the relevant 'comparable expenditure',[20] it seems more than likely that there has been some convergence in recent years.

There are a number of reasons for this. Two features of the system that had a major role in limiting the amount of convergence have been eliminated. Originally the Barnett formula was operated in a volume-planning environment, and therefore only operated on the increment after inflation had been taken into account. Volume planning was replaced by cash-planning in the early 1980s, but echoes lived on until the public expenditure reforms of 1992.[21]

[18] HC Scottish Affairs Committee, Minutes of Evidence Taken before the Scottish Affairs Committee, 7 November 2001, HC 345-i (2001–02); HC Scottish Affairs Committee, Scotland Office Expenditure, 1st Special Report, HC 198 (2002–03); and HC Scottish Affairs Committee, Scotland Office Departmental Report: Minutes of Evidence, Tuesday 17 June 2003, HC 815-i (2002–03).
[19] A. Goudie, 'GERS and fiscal autonomy', *Scottish Affairs* 41 (2002), pp. 56–85.
[20] Because the functional coverage of devolved expenditures differs among Scotland, Wales, and Northern Ireland, three separate series for comparable expenditure in England are required.
[21] In the period from the end of volume planning to 1992, baselines, including that of the Scottish Office, for the 'new' year in each Public Expenditure Survey were set at the level of the

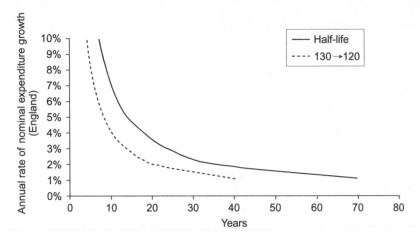

Figure 7.1. The convergence effect of the Barnett formula.

Added to that, the previous procedure, whereby in-year additions to provision were granted to departments responsible for funding public sector pay awards, such as for nurses and the police, was ended. Departments are now expected to cope with pay within the provision agreed in Surveys and Spending Reviews (with, arguably, more realistic provision being made in the first place). The point is that the in-year increases for Scotland were formerly determined on the basis of actual 'impacts', not by the Barnett formula (which would have produced a lower result). The primary reason for these reforms in public expenditure control was not to bring about faster convergence. That was merely an incidental consequence, though one that would have nonetheless been welcome to the Treasury, of actions taken for much wider reasons.

These factors will have made the rate of convergence through the 1990s higher than it would otherwise have been. However, given the low growth in nominal public expenditure, convergence would still not have been particularly great. One of the features of Barnett is that the rate of convergence increases with the rate of growth of nominal expenditure on comparable services in England. The relationship is not linear. Figure 7.1 shows how the rate of nominal growth affects the 'half-life'.[22] At a rate of growth of comparable nominal expenditure in England of 2 per cent, the half-life (shown by the solid line) is thirty-five years. Thus it would take thirty-five years for expenditure per head

---

previous year's provision plus an enhancement largely compensating for inflation; see Thain and Wright, *The Treasury and Whitehall*, p. 48. The abolition of this arrangement in 1992 was not publicly announced until December 1997; see 'Supplementary Memorandum Submitted by HM Treasury on Tuesday 16 December 1997', in Treasury Committee, HC Select Committee on the Barnett Formula 2nd Report (HC Paper (1997–98) no. 341), pp. 36–9.

[22] The 'half-life' is a concept borrowed from nuclear physics, where it is used in connection with the rate of decay of particles. It is the time taken for a quantity to reduce to half its original value.

20 per cent above that in England to reduce to 10 per cent above. In contrast, at a rate of growth of nominal expenditure of 8 per cent, the half-life is nine years. The dotted line in Figure 7.1 shows the years taken for an expenditure per head differential of 30 per cent to reduce to one of 20 per cent. In both cases, it will be seen that the rate of convergence is very sensitive to growth rates of nominal public expenditure in England.[23]

The public expenditure climate has changed and the significant increases in DEL since 1999 seem bound to have led to faster convergence. Paradoxically, this has not been noticed, particularly since the Scottish Executive, in common with departments in England, has had difficulty spending budgeted amounts. This context provided opportunities to adopt policies involving higher expenditure (such as on tuition fees, personal care, and concessionary fares), including those with no parallels in England to generate future formula consequences. Such commitments may cause future difficulties in a harsher expenditure climate.

Possible Institutional Developments

Although there are few systems with sub-national governments where the sub-national units all have precisely the same powers and responsibilities, and where all are of a comparable size, the asymmetries in the United Kingdom are particularly marked. This must raise the possibility of some convergence in terms of powers. The Richard Commission,[24] set up by the National Assembly for Wales, has recommended that the Assembly should acquire primary legislative powers, and that a tax-varying power is desirable, but not essential, in the event of that happening. The Northern Ireland Economic Council commissioned a review of funding arrangements for the Northern Ireland Assembly,[25] one of the issues being greater alignment with Scotland. In England there have been developments with the establishment of the Greater London Authority and the publication of the White Paper on

[23] The calculations underlying this illustration assume that the formula is operated on the entire increment (as it now is) and there is no by-pass. They also assume, for simplicity, that the relative populations remain constant. The effect of relative population change on the operation of the formula has been modelled by Cuthbert. See J. Cuthbert, 'The effect of relative population growth on the Barnett squeeze', *Fraser of Allander Institute Quarterly Economic Commentary* 26:2 (2001), pp. 34–7. This does not affect the overall conclusion, though relative population decline reduces the speed of convergence for Scotland, as the index is calculated on a per capita basis.

[24] Lord Richard (chair), *Report of the Commission on the Powers and Electoral Arrangements of the National Assembly for Wales* (Cardiff, 2004), http://www.richardcommission.gov.uk/content/finalreport/report-e.pdf.

[25] D. A. Heald, *Funding the Northern Ireland Assembly: Assessing the Options*, Northern Ireland Economic Council Research Monograph 10 (Belfast, 2003).

English regional devolution.[26] It has to be said, however, that substantial devolution to the regions of powers over health and education, for example, would be far more radical than in the devolved countries, where there had already been long histories of administrative devolution and separate health and education departments. Expenditure-switching powers at the level of English regions would challenge the functional role of Whitehall departments, now predominantly responsible for England.

Perhaps it would be unwise to expect that changes, if they happen at all, will come quickly. The gestation period of devolution to Scotland and Wales was very long indeed, with protracted activity in the 1970s followed by an interlude of virtually an entire generation when the issue was, to all intents and purposes, off the UK agenda. Further movement, especially in England, would run counter to the clear centralist instincts and the impatience of the current government, parts of which may be inclined to view calls for more regional control with some scepticism. All of this, of course, is speculation: the future may well turn out differently. It remains unsettled whether the counterpart to the devolved countries is to be England or individual English regions.

Funding: Options for the Future

There are two questions to consider: how expenditure is to be determined; and how it is to be funded. Obviously these two questions can be closely linked, but they would only be one and the same if there were to be a separate taxation system under the control of the Scottish Parliament and—crucially—if there were no needs equalisation. Where there is needs equalisation, it is the details of the equalisation system that determine the base amount of expenditure.[27] The base amount may be supplemented, positively or negatively, by tax-varying powers, but that does not alter the basic point.

Determining Expenditure Levels

The first option would be to continue with the present system. At some stage, this would result in provision in the devolved countries falling *below*

---

[26] Office of the Deputy Prime Minister, *Your Region, Your Choice: Revitalising the English Regions*, Cm. 5511 (London, 2002). The 2004 referendum in the North-East region removed the possibility of *elected* regional government in the foreseeable future.

[27] It is possible to devise equalisation schemes (equalisation of fiscal potential) that allow the lower-tier government to freely chose its level of expenditure; see D. N. King, *Fiscal Tiers: The Economics of Multi-Level Government* (London, 1984), pp. 168–70. This used to be a characteristic of revenue support grant systems for local authorities, but was suppressed because this involved (a) marginal incentives to higher expenditure and (b) either an open-ended budgetary commitment by central government or offsetting reductions in resource standard.

a needs-related index. Determining when that happens could only be done after a fresh UK-wide needs assessment (see below). While it never has been the intention that convergence should continue to that stage, it has to be noted that equalisation on the basis of equal expenditure, or revenue, per head is relatively common in other jurisdictions. That, for example, is broadly what happens in Canada and Germany.

On the other hand, if the view is taken that provision in the devolved countries should be broadly based on need, then the question arises as to what happens when convergence goes below that. This is likely to happen in Wales before it does in Scotland or Northern Ireland. There is, however, no means at present of determining when that is likely to happen. It is not just a case of lacking meaningful data on convergence, though that is a major factor. There is no up-to-date assessment of need; the last published material appeared in 1979,[28] and that was not universally agreed. While there is reason to believe that the Treasury has updated internally the 1979 assessment from time to time, nothing has been published. Nor has recent work co-ordinated in Northern Ireland by the Department of Finance and Personnel reached the public domain, though, paradoxically, a commentary on that work has been published.[29] A needs assessment produced in isolation by the Treasury would command no credibility in the devolved countries and some new 'independent' institutional machinery would need to be established.[30]

A needs assessment would not be a straightforward task: it requires subjective judgements on the extent to which particular indicators of need lead to different spending requirements; and there will have to be decisions as to the extent to which differential demand, for example because of different take-up rates of private provision, should be allowed for. Above all, it has to be understood that a needs assessment cannot come up with any absolute definition of need and the associated spending requirement. Need, in this context, is a political judgement. All that a needs assessment can hope to do is to arrive at some estimate of the extent to which providing the same level

---

[28] HM Treasury, *Needs Assessment Study: Report* (London, 1979).

[29] A. Midwinter, *Northern Ireland's Expenditure Needs: A Preliminary Assessment*, Northern Ireland Assembly Research Paper 81/02 (Belfast, 2002).

[30] Two arguments have regularly been used against such machinery. The first is that such a transfer of public functions into a new quango would be undemocratic and lacking in accountability. Provided that the role is advisory, as is the case with the Commonwealth Grants Commission in Australia, this objection now appears weak, especially since executive functions over monetary policy have been transferred by the Treasury to the Bank of England. The second is that of cost: any arrangement of this kind, both in terms of the operating costs of the body and costs imposed on governments and other bodies, would certainly be more expensive than either the present system or a needs assessment conducted entirely within governments. These additional costs would have to be justified on the basis of accountability benefits flowing from greater transparency and the possibility of the arrangements commanding a reasonable measure of consent.

of specified services in different areas will lead to different spending require-ments.[31] The predominance of England in terms of relative size may lead to the English configuration of, for example, services and charging policies becoming the 'standard' that is costed.

A second option would be to replace population with some other proxy indicator of needs. Inverse GDP has been suggested,[32] as has social security.[33] The problem here is that there is no evidence that either of these indicators would serve as a satisfactory proxy for need to spend on devolved services and, in the absence of a needs assessment, there is not going to be such evi-dence. On the face of it, neither seems particularly plausible. The major expenditure responsibilities of the Scottish Parliament are health, education, and social work services—not obviously directly related to either of these suggestions.

If a needs assessment has to be carried out in order to validate proxy indi-cators, it would seem to make more sense to use the results more directly. The results of such an assessment could be used to amend the Barnett formula, substituting needs-weighted population for population. When the expendi-ture index is initially higher than the needs index, this modification would prevent 'overshooting'. Figure 7.2 shows that, instead of convergence being towards equal expenditure per head ($E = 100$), it would be towards a needs index (N); this is the line B^{nw}. Heald and McLeod also demonstrated the pos-sibility of smoothing the transition, in order to ensure that the needs index is not reached in an abrupt fashion.[34] In that case, convergence switches, at a threshold value T above N, from being towards $E = 100$ to being towards $E = N$. Accordingly, the convergence line B_z^{nw} is identical with the normal Barnett convergence line B until reaching the threshold at Z, and then converges on $E = N$.

A third option that has been suggested is the complete financial re-integration of the devolved countries into the United Kingdom, in particular imposing the same distribution systems for health and for local government UK-wide. Leaving aside the fact that the systems in England have come

[31] See Heald and McLeod, 'Beyond Barnett? Funding devolution', pp. 159–62. Whereas McLean is convinced that Scotland is currently over-funded relative to needs (McLean, 'Memorandum'), Midwinter disputes that conclusion: A. Midwinter, 'Devolution and public spending: arguments and evidence', *Fraser of Allander Institute Quarterly Economic Commentary* 25:4 (2000), pp. 38–48). These arguments are a prologue to the debates that would accompany a needs assessment.

[32] See I. McLean, 'Financing the union: Goschen, Barnett, and Beyond', Chapter 6 of this vol-ume; and I. McLean and A. McMillan, 'The distribution of public expenditure across the UK regions', *Fiscal Studies* 24:1 (2003), pp. 45–71.

[33] See R. R. MacKay, 'Regional taxing and spending: the search for balance', *Regional Studies* 35 (2001), pp. 563–75.

[34] Heald and McLeod, 'Beyond Barnett? Funding devolution', p. 161.

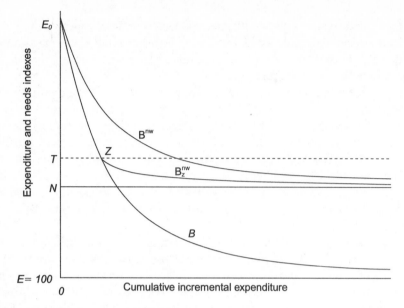

Figure 7.2. Convergence on a needs index.

under fierce criticism, this would be portrayed as the turning of the parliament and Assemblies into a sort of super local and health authority, in fundamental conflict with the notion of devolution. It seems more likely that, if this option ever really sees the light of day, it would be as a Treasury negotiating position rather than as a serious proposition.

A fourth option, which has in various guises received a lot of publicity, is that of greater fiscal powers for the Scottish Parliament.[35] At one level, the suggestion that the parliament should seek more fiscal powers when it has made little use of the powers it already has—and looks unlikely to use the 'tartan tax' power in the foreseeable future—seems surprising.

The markedly changed public expenditure climate, with rapid increases in both nominal and real devolved expenditure and a significant level of under-spending, has diverted attention away from the upward use of the tartan tax. However, there has been a considerable amount of political and media atten-tion on the downward use of the tartan tax power.[36] It seems likely that min-isters and civil servants in the Scottish Executive view this option with caution since they would expect the Treasury to react by initiating a needs assessment. In the absence of a recent needs assessment, such a downward

---

[35] See the symposium on fiscal autonomy in *Scottish Affairs* 41 (2002).
[36] See, for example, A. Bruce and T. Miers, *Scotland's Hidden Tax Cutting Powers*, Policy Institute Series: Economy no. 3 (Edinburgh, 2003).

use might be regarded as evidence that the expenditure index was higher than the needs index. From a public finance perspective, it is a matter of legitimate political choice for a high-needs political entity to trade off lower expenditure for lower taxes, without its needs-based entitlements being challenged. However, the political repercussions are unpredictable, especially given the fiscal centralism characteristic of the United Kingdom.

It is also not true that the Scottish Parliament is particularly out of line with the mainstream of sub-national assemblies in its fiscal powers, especially when compared to others in Europe. It has, for example, more powers than the German *Länder*, arising not only from its explicit tax-varying power but also from its legislative and financial control over local authority functions and taxation. Nevertheless, the idea of greater tax powers has acquired considerable momentum, drawing support from across the ideological and constitutional spectra.

On the face of it, many of the calls for 'fiscal autonomy' would mean a move from an expenditure-based system of allocation to one where the amount of revenue raised is the main determinant. This would only be true, however, if there were no equalisation. The effect of an equalisation system can be to change a nominally revenue-based system into one that is, in reality, expenditure-based,[37] as illustrated by the 1921–72 experience of the Stormont Parliament where that reality was obscured. Moreover, the existence, perhaps even the absence, of equalisation gives politicians an avenue to blame shortcomings not on their mismanagement but on the iniquities (or absence) of equalisation. Thus, while it is clearly true that the current funding system does not put as much responsibility as would be ideal on devolved politicians, the ability of a revenue-based system to change that can be overstated.

There are also practical constraints on tax variation *within* the United Kingdom,[38] particularly arising from the effects of globalisation and the existence of EU rules, that are often simply ignored in public debates. This is not to say that a move towards a revenue-based system of devolution finance would be impossible. But those putting forward such systems for serious consideration must address the questions of equalisation and practicality. Arguments, implicitly based on Laffer curves, that lower business taxes would, through increased growth, be self-financing ought to provoke scepticism, as they are too convenient. Moreover, it is never advisable to ignore the views of the UK Treasury. There are indications in one of the evaluation reports of the 'five euro tests' that the Treasury envisages that a more activist

---

[37] See Kilbrandon Royal Commission on the Constitution, *Royal Commission on the Constitution, 1969–1973: Report*, Cmnd. 5460, 5460–i (London, 1973).
[38] See Heald, Geaughan, and Robb, 'Financial arrangements for UK devolution', p. 30.

role for fiscal policy would be a consequence of the loss of discretion over interest rates inherent in euro membership.[39] This type of consideration would reinforce the Treasury's traditional centralist rein on the UK fiscal system; a lower business tax strategy within the United Kingdom is extremely unlikely to be tolerated by UK governments. It is a matter of judgement whether an independent Scotland could imitate the post-1988 economic development strategy of Ireland, though matters of timing suggest not.[40]

Funding

Although it is not the case, as is sometimes suggested, that the Scottish Parliament receives all its funding from central government, it does receive by far the greatest element from this source.[41] Clearly there are other options.

One would be separate taxation, as discussed above. Another possibility is a system of assigned revenues, widely used in some federations. In such systems, all or part of the revenues from particular taxes are allocated to sub-national governments. Such a system could be used for any tax, though in some cases some proxy (such as population) for the actual revenues generated in particular areas would have to be used for practical reasons. It is important to understand that a system of assigned revenues confers no fiscal power on sub-national governments. It is not a form of fiscal autonomy, and in reality it does nothing to alter the vertical fiscal imbalance. (It may be supplemented by tax-varying powers, but that is a different point.) The judgement on whether or not it would be worth pursuing a system of assigned revenues turns on whether or not this would increase the perception of the responsibility of devolved politicians.

Charges are a source of potential funding, an option stressed by Bailey and Fingland.[42] However, the most probable trajectory—with some exceptions—is for the charge-financed percentage to fall through time and for political decision-makers in Scotland, Wales, and Northern Ireland to be less enthusiastic about charges than their counterparts (at present UK governments) for England.

---

[39] HM Treasury, *Fiscal Stabilisation and EMU: A Discussion Paper* (London, 2003).

[40] The US economist Paul Krugman expressed the view that the window used by Ireland is now closed; see S. Bain, 'Scots "too late" to copy Ireland', *The Herald*, 29 October 2003. For the view that Scotland's fiscal advantages would better take the form of lower taxes, especially business taxes, see J. Cuthbert and M. Cuthbert, 'Can fiscal autonomy improve a devolved Scotland's economic prospects?', *Scottish Affairs* 41 (2002), pp. 86–101.

[41] See Heald and McLeod, 'Fiscal autonomy under devolution', p. 11.

[42] S. J. Bailey and L. Fingland, 'The tartan tax versus other revenue-raising options: economic perspectives', *Fraser of Allander Institute Quarterly Economic Commentary* 28:3 (2003), pp. 30–7.

Other Current Developments

There is much going on at present in England with implications for the funding of the devolved administrations. The possibility of extra revenue for services in England from congestion charging and from tuition fees in higher education would mean proportionately less coming through the Barnett formula.[43]

The 'Balance of Funding' review (of local government in England) is raising the possibility of the replacement of the council tax, a discussion that has its parallels in Scotland.[44] There are superficial attractions in replacing council tax with some sort of income-based tax, but property taxes have their advantages. Specifically, they are extremely difficult either to avoid or evade; have clear visibility; and could be made less regressive, for example, by introducing more bands and varying the multipliers that apply relative to the standard (band D) charge. They are suitable as a financing source for sub-national governments and form part of the portfolio of taxes that finance a modern welfare state. In addition, any sort of income tax would be subject to much tighter Treasury control than has been applied to property taxes, with the yield being sensitive to Treasury decisions on tax base and rate structure.

Taken together, these two points raise the question as to how much policy divergence from England there can be in practice, and how much the devolved administrations will, willingly or not, be forced to follow policy leads. Devolved administrations cannot be 'more generous' across the board than the UK government for England, unless there is a funding advantage and/or above-UK-average fiscal effort. Priorities might be different, but only within a budget envelope. Another relevant point is that the dynamics of the current system imply that the proportion of self-financed funding of the Scottish Parliament will fall over time, a circumstance hastened by the rapid increases in centrally funded public expenditure since 1999.

Conclusion

The first thing that needs to be said is that fundamental changes cannot be undertaken overnight. In-depth consideration is needed, not just for Scotland, of the implications of proposed changes. This will involve consultation with

[43] Extra revenue generated by charging schemes will not attract the operation of the formula, and if the extra revenue is used in substitution for direct funding, with a consequent reduction of provision in England, there would be negative formula consequences.

[44] See M. Danson and G. Whittam, *Paying for Local Government Water and Sewerage Charges Fairly: The Case for a Scottish Service Tax and a Scottish Water Charge*, Department of Economics and Enterprise, University of Paisley (Paisley, 2003, mimeo).

interested parties, perhaps requiring a formal process such as an Inquiry or Commission of some kind. Transitional arrangements need to be worked out, again in consultation. The change cannot be so abrupt as to cause serious management and political problems. Apart from that, it does not seem right to implement fundamental changes now, only six years into a new system.

For these reasons, it seems more likely that any change in the short term will have to be incremental—building on rather than upsetting the current arrangements. This conclusion might, however, have to be revisited if there were some sort of constitutional crisis, for example if conflict between a UK government and one or more of the devolved administrations were to become particularly intense, or if Scotland seemed to be heading towards independence. Otherwise, what is likely to produce modifications to the current framework is that the tacit assumption behind the Barnett formula—that some convergence is desirable—will be rendered untenable by more rapid convergence than might have been foreseen, pushing one or more of the devolved administrations below what they perceive as their 'N' in Figure 7.2.

In any event, as convergence bites, one of the devolved administrations will at some stage feel that it has an unanswerable case that expenditure per head has converged towards that in England to such an extent that it is close to, or even below, that which would be justified on the basis of relative need. At that stage it might call for a new needs assessment. That would not be without its difficulties and would only have a chance of wide acceptance if it was supervised by an independent Commission. However, the reception of the recommendations of such a Commission can be expected to be highly politicised.

While some sort of tidiness is always attractive, it can be an illusion. There will always be difficulties at the edges, and the extent to which UK government seeks to influence, formally or informally, policy developments is always going to be contentious. Nor can it be assumed that there can ever be a solution that will be immune to criticism and controversy. There are always going to be deep disagreements about such fundamental matters as money and the operation of power. Of course, the particularly asymmetric structure of the United Kingdom, in terms of relative population and relative economic growth rates, compounds the problem. In these circumstances, the issue might be more about finding an acceptable level of self-financed expenditure, and finding ways of ensuring that self-financing as a proportion of the total does not diminish with time, than about major changes.

At the same time, we will need to keep alert to the effects of the evolution of the overall public expenditure system. Changes such as to the *details* of public expenditure control affected the operation of Barnett prior to devolution, and such things as resource accounting, the greater use of private finance, and the extension of user charging will have had their effects since devolution. To some extent the recent effects will not be noticeable now because of the amount of money currently going through the system. The devolved administrations need to ensure that they have well-equipped and resourced finance departments, as well as active parliamentary scrutiny: one is not a substitute for the other. An unknown factor that has now been removed is the implications of elected regional bodies in (some) English regions taking on expenditure responsibilities.

The Barnett formula may be under some stress, but it is not 'broke'. It must be delivering some convergence—probably at as fast a rate as could be managed without creating severe difficulty, both in terms of budgetary pressure and macroeconomic impact.[45] Indeed, the Treasury may be getting more than it expected. Radical changes to the system would require transitional arrangements to minimise such problems, and the effect of these could well be very similar to that of the current situation. Indeed, the Barnett formula itself started life as a transitional arrangement.

Tension about financial arrangements, whatever they are, is an inevitable consequence of the asymmetrical structure of the United Kingdom. The only way to remove this would be full integration (implausible, and likely to generate pressure for constitutional change) or independence (a political choice). Otherwise, there is a choice between mechanisms that are simple in principle, like Goschen and Barnett, or Australian-type formalised mechanisms that might provide the basis for much more detailed central intervention in policy and expenditure priorities. Achieving political devolution, whilst keeping the expenditure-switching discretion evolved by successive Secretaries of State for Scotland, was a highly significant feature of the devolution funding settlement.

In such a setting, it is easy but unproductive to write Armageddon scenarios. There might be intense political conflict between Edinburgh and London over the constitutional status of Scotland. Or there might open up a wide ideological gulf between the devolved administrations and the UK government as to the proper range of public functions. In the latter context, it would be remarkably easy for a hostile UK government to undermine the finances of the devolved administrations in the following way. Taxpayers in England could be allowed to offset 60 per cent of the costs they incur on private hospital treatment against their income tax liabilities, with the resulting cost being deducted from National Health Service spending in England. If

[45] On the potential macroeconomic impact on the Scottish economy of lower-than-England growth rates of public expenditure, see L. Ferguson, D. Learmonth, P. G. McGregor et al., *The Impact of the Barnett Formula on the Scottish Economy: Endogenous Population and the Darling Amendment*, Department of Economics, University of Strathclyde (Glasgow, 2003, mimeo).

there were substantial take-up of this option, there would be large negative formula consequences for the devolved administrations that would seriously disrupt their planning and discharge of devolved functions.

The above example illustrates the obvious point that a UK government that wished to make the union unworkable could do so. However, that union has demonstrated a remarkable resilience and its future is properly a political choice. If there is the political will to make devolution work, funding mechanisms can be found that, however imperfect and exposed to more public glare, can be evolved to meet changing circumstances. Although, at some future time, the name of Barnett may disappear, some similar kind of mechanism might well be in place.

8

Devolution, Social Citizenship, and Territorial Culture: Equity and Diversity in the Anglo-Scottish Relationship

CHARLIE JEFFERY

Introduction

NO OTHER SET OF SIGNIFICANT DECENTRALISATION REFORMS have been conceived and implemented with such little conscious attention to their statewide implications as devolution in the UK. Devolution is a project of the parts, not the whole. Its logic is piecemeal; different UK ministries have introduced different kinds of institutional reform for different reasons in each part of the UK. In Northern Ireland devolution is about peace-building. In Scotland it is about giving expression to a strong sense of national identity, but also buying off separatist pressures. In northern England it is about economic regeneration, in southern England at most about better regional-level co-ordination of central government activity. The rationale in Wales lies somewhere between Scotland and northern England, mixing identity and economic factors.

All these may be good grounds for devolution in each of the UK's territories. But all of them also cause spillovers beyond those territories. All impact on the nature of the union that makes up the UK. These spillover effects of reform in the parts on the nature of the whole have been neglected. Strikingly, there have been no systematic articulations of what the UK as a whole in its post-devolution format is for, what the role of the centre should be, how the centre should relate to the territories, how the parts now add up to make a whole. That neglect reflects a mixture of parochialism and complacency. Because devolution is asymmetrical, establishing different relationships of each of the territories to the centre, the devolved administrations have no particular incentive to think UK-wide. And the instinct of the centre is, as tradition would have it, to muddle through the new complexities of UK-devolved relationships on a pragmatic and ad hoc basis. This means that

Proceedings of the British Academy **128**, 113–129. © The British Academy 2005.

most central-devolved interactions are on a one-to-one, bilateral basis. The main institutional innovation for UK-wide, multilateral coordination—the Joint Ministerial Committee—is rarely used. The absence of systematic, UK-wide inter-governmental co-ordination between centre and parts appears increasingly problematic to devolution commentators.[1] There have been strong calls for better thought-through co-ordination mechanisms to link the activities of central and devolved governments and to contain the potential for conflict between them that is set to emerge at the latest when the pan-British hegemony of the Labour Party comes to an end.[2] The Whitehall reshuffle which brought the Scotland and Wales Offices loosely within the ambit of the new Department of Constitutional Affairs, though poorly organised, was at least a sign of incipient acceptance on the part of central government that more systematic UK-devolved relationships need to be created.[3]

However, little attention has yet been thrown on another, equally vital aspect of the relationship of centre and parts: the impact of devolution on UK citizenship. For devolution changes the content of UK citizenship. Being a citizen post-devolution can mean that the state—UK-level or in its devolved incarnations—carries out different functions for you to different standards in different places. Of course it also did before devolution, but to a lesser degree in both theory and practice. What has been lacking since devolution is a restatement of what it is to be a member of the UK, what *values* that membership expresses, and, from that, what the constants of state provision should be that all should enjoy no matter where they live. To get to that kind of restatement there has to be a better appreciation of how citizens negotiate multi-level government. How do Scottish citizens understand and give effect to their simultaneous relationships to Scottish and UK government? What do they want from two levels of government each claiming at the same time to act on their behalf? Do the Scottish want different things as compared to the dominant UK nation, the English? Does the devolution settlement give the Scots sufficient scope for expressing their distinctiveness in terms of identity and policy preferences *vis-à-vis* the English?

---

[1] For example, Robert Hazell's question 'Can the system take the strain?', in R. Hazell, 'Conclusion: the devolution scorecard as the devolved assemblies head for the polls', in R. Hazell (ed.), *The State of the Nations 2003: The Third Year of Devolution in the United Kingdom* (Thorverton, 2003), pp. 285–302, at pp. 300–1.

[2] As expressed in the very first recommendation in House of Lords Select Committee on the Constitution 2nd Report (HL Paper (2002–03) no. 28): *Devolution: Inter-Institutional Relations in the United Kingdom*, p. 5.

[3] Significantly, the Conservative shadow ministerial team was reshuffled after Michael Howard was elected leader to include a UK-wide devolution portfolio covering English regional and local government, Scotland, Wales, and Northern Ireland.

This chapter will argue that some quite good indicators are available of how the Scots view these relationships and express their expectations of multi-level government. What is lacking is a compass for understanding where they point. One of the ways to construct such a compass is through comparison with similar cases elsewhere, and that is what this chapter attempts. It commences by exploring the tensions which can exist between statewide commonality and territorial variation of policy standards, as exemplified in particular in the relationship of Quebec to Anglophone Canada. It then addresses how citizens as voters plot their ways through multi-level government by exploring how far and why voters behave differently at territorial as compared to statewide elections. The final two sections apply the findings to Scottish–English relationships in the UK, focusing first on territorial policy variation and 'multi-level voting', then on the importance of territorial financial arrangements in expressing ideas about the statewide solidarity of citizens in all territories.

Social Citizenship versus Territorial Culture

A useful starting point is to recall the suggestion made by Keith Banting and Stan Corbett that all decentralised states have to establish a balance between two sets of values:[4]

    a   commitments to what T. H. Marshall[5] coined as 'social citizenship', to be achieved by a common set of public services for all citizens across the entire country;

    b   respect for territorial communities and cultures, to be achieved through decentralised decision-making and significant scope for diversity in public services at the territorial level.

The 'compass' for understanding Scottish relationships with the UK and its dominant, English, component needs to point to how these two sets of values play out in practice. Are they in conflict with one another, so that the Scottish territorial community in the UK may find itself resisting pressure to accept uniform statewide public services? Or are the two sets of values complementary to one another, with the Scottish territorial community content with the balance of distinctive territorial public services alongside common statewide public services? An interesting benchmark for exploring the

[4] K. Banting and S. Corbett, 'Health policy and federalism: an introduction', in K. Banting and S. Corbett (eds), *Health Policy and Federalism* (Kingston/Montreal, 2002), pp. 1–38, at p. 18.
[5] T. H. Marshall, 'Citizenship and social class', in T. H. Marshall and T. Bottomore (eds), *Citizenship and Social Class* (London, [1950] 1992), pp. 3–51.

tensions and complementarities that occur when statewide social citizenship meets territorial culture is Canada, not least because of the parallels that get drawn between the relationships of Quebec to Anglophone rest-of-Canada and Scotland to the English-dominated rest-of-the-UK.

Often those parallels are not very well informed. They too easily get very one-sided, focusing on Quebecois separatism and inferring that Scotland faces the same issues. There are two points to make. First, Quebecois separatism reflects a dimension of territorial culture that Scotland lacks on a significant scale: fundamental linguistic difference. But second, and arguably a closer analogy to the Scottish–English relationship, separatist sentiment and other patterns of distinctiveness in Quebec are balanced by commonalities shared between the Quebecois and Anglophone Canadians. Pan-Canadian public attitudes surveys cast revealing light on this interplay of distinctiveness and commonality. There are, for example, notable differences on equality issues between Quebec and the rest of Canada, which would seem to reflect the history of the language issue. But in other areas there are rather more limited variations between Quebecois attitudes and the national average: on markers of Canadian national identity like the Charter of Canadian Rights and Freedoms; and on issues concerning the role of government, access to health care, and federal spending to support poorer regions.[6]

The latter point is especially interesting. In the 2001 'Portraits of Canada' survey, a battery of questions was asked on fiscal equalisation, including that in Table 8.1. Strikingly, *all* provinces, whether beneficiaries of equalisation or not, recorded at least 74 per cent strongly or moderately in favour, the Canada-wide average was 83 per cent, and Quebec scored spot-on the average of 83 per cent. Moreover, in all provinces with the exception of the wealthiest, oil-rich Alberta, more respondents felt that more money should be transferred than is currently the case from richer to poorer provinces than those who felt that less should be transferred.[7]

Indeed, in many cases Alberta has become as much as or more of an exception in Canada as Quebec. It has presented a strong, neo-liberal challenge to the broadly social democratic consensus established in Canada after the Second World War, mimicking some of the decentralist, anti-interventionist tendencies in the operation of US federalism since the 1980s, and routinely critical of the operation of a federal system designed to share

[6] See 'Portraits of Canada 2001', *The CRIC Papers*, no. 4 (Montreal: Centre for Research and Information on Canada), January 2002; 'The Charter: Dividing or Uniting Canadians', *The CRIC Papers*, no. 5 (Montreal: Centre for Research and Information on Canada), April 2002; 'Portraits of Canada 2002', *The CRIC Papers*, no. 8 (Montreal: Centre for Research and Information on Canada), December 2002.

[7] 'Portraits of Canada 2001', p. 16.

Table 8.1. Support for the equalisation programme in Canada

'As you may know, under the federal equalization program money is transferred from the richer provinces to the poorer ones, in order to ensure that Canadians living in every province have access to similar levels of public services. Do you strongly support, moderately support, moderately oppose, or strongly oppose the equalization program?'

	% strongly/moderately support equalisation
Manitoba	88
Ontario	87
Atlantic Provinces	87
Saskatchewan	85
British Columbia	84
Canada average	**83**
Quebec	**83**
Alberta	74

Source: 'Portraits of Canada 2001', *The CRIC Papers*, no. 4 (Montreal: Centre for Research and Information on Canada), January 2002, p. 16.

risks across provinces and citizens.[8] Quebec is not so much of an outlier on federalism matters. Quebec citizens are among the most positive (or least negative) about the clout their provincial government can wield in Canada. In 2001 only 31 per cent of the Quebecois felt that Quebec had 'less than its fair share' of influence 'on important national decisions in Canada'.[9] Only Ontarians felt more influential at national level. And on the questions whether Quebec is 'treated with the respect it deserves in Canada' and whether there is an appropriate balance between provincial and federal powers, Quebec is right in the heart of the provincial pack.[10]

This all adds up to a rather different image of Quebec's relationship to Canada than perhaps we are used to. It balances the received image of distinctiveness/self-assertion/separatism with a perhaps unexpected commitment to a social citizenship of Canada-wide values and Canada-wide solidarity. That balance is a fine one. The two referendums held on the renegotiation of Quebec's relationship with the rest of Canada were close-run, and support for the idea of Quebecois 'sovereignty-partnership' voted on in 1995 still runs at 40 per cent plus.[11] There may be a sense in striking this fine balance of being able to play the system to Quebec's advantage: the province is after all a recipient of the equalisation transfers of which it approves so much; and perhaps the spectre of separatism makes Quebec more influential in the Canadian federal system than it would otherwise be. But nonetheless

[8] 'Portraits of Canada 2002', pp. 15–16.
[9] 'Portraits of Canada 2001', p. 19.
[10] Ibid., pp. 19, 26.
[11] Ibid., p. 27.

there is a sense of a Canadian whole in play to which even Quebec and the Quebecois can subscribe.

That this is the case no doubt has something to do with the role the Canadian federal government has taken on itself in 'nation-building', in nurturing commonalities that help bind Canada together in its geographical and cultural diversity. The railroad was both a symbolic and a practical tool of nation-building in the nineteenth century; now it is probably a mix of the Charter, fiscal equalisation, and the Canadian Health and Social Transfer. The CHST uses federal subsidy to buy common social policy standards in areas for which the provinces are nominally responsible. Taken together with the impact of the fiscal equalisation programme, the CHST has also had the effect of promoting significant convergence in provincial per capita GDP and provincial per capita personal income onto the Canadian national average.[12]

This kind of 'nation-building' of course creates tensions between federal and provincial governments. The Quebec and Alberta provincial governments clearly resent it, albeit for different reasons. But there is evidently also sufficient, Canada-wide public approval of those standards for territorial distinctiveness in some policy fields to be overridden by expressions of Canadian citizenship.

There are plenty of other examples of decentralised states which express strong commitments to statewide values. In Australia there is an ideology of 'equal rights and equal treatment of citizens in all the states'.[13] This is reflected amongst other things in a commitment to inter-regional fiscal equalisation such that: 'Each State should be able to provide . . . services . . . of the same standard as other States without imposing higher rates of taxes or charges; differences in revenue-raising capacities and in the relative costs of providing comparable government services should be taken into account.'[14]

And in Germany the constitution insists that federal law outranks regional law in a long list of policy fields including civil law, education, energy, labour relations, agriculture, public health, foodstuffs regulation, transport, and the environment, 'if and to the extent that the creation of equivalent living conditions throughout the country or the maintenance of legal and economic unity makes federal legislation necessary in the national interest' (Article 72 of the German Basic Law). That constitutional provision

---

[12] F. Vaillancourt and S. Rault, 'The regional dimensions of federal intergovernmental and interpersonal transfers in Canada 1981–2001', *Regional and Federal Studies* 13:4 (2003), pp. 130–52.

[13] R. L. Watts, 'Equalization in Commonwealth federations', *Regional and Federal Studies* 13:4 (2003), pp. 111–29, at p. 116.

[14] Cited in M. Nicholas, 'Financial arrangements between the Australian government and Australian states', *Regional and Federal Studies* 13:4 (2003), pp. 153–82, at p. 162.

has supported a process of centralisation of legislative functions in Germany which leaves the German regions (*Länder*) with only a small set of residual primary legislative powers. The commitment to pursue statewide common standards has, over time, clearly outweighed ideas that federalism should be a guarantor of territorial difference.

Naturally enough some Australian States and German *Länder* governments dislike such expressions of statewide purpose, of 'equal treatment' or 'equivalent living conditions' across territories. That is especially the case for those with a stronger resource base, because commitments to equity allow central governments to limit the scope territorial governments would otherwise have for deploying their superior resource base to pursue more diverse territorial policy portfolios. They also allow central governments—directly or indirectly—to 'tax' richer territories in order to provide the resources for weaker territories to achieve common standards.

But though some *governments* may dislike all this, *citizens* tend to be more supportive of commitments to maintaining common, statewide standards. In Germany, that support for statewide standards even survived German unification despite the significant and direct cost to West Germans in terms of higher taxation to ensure that common standards were quickly reached in East Germany (unsurprisingly, East Germans were especially enthusiastic about the idea). Though the data available are less good for Germany than for Canada, it appears that high levels of public acceptance of statewide standards remain in policy fields like policing, education, transport, and environment, as does a commitment—as in Canada—to a high level of fiscal equalisation transfers from richer to poorer regions.[15]

Multi-Level Voting

A complementary route for assessing how citizens deal with the tension between state and territory, between statewide social citizenship and diversity of territorial cultures is to look at voting behaviour in territorial and statewide elections. The assumption common in the literature[16] is that territorial election results are little more than snapshot commentaries on the political situation in statewide politics, in UK terms the political situation

---

[15] N. Grube, 'Föderalismus in der öffentlichen Meinung der Bundesrepublik Deutschland', *Jahrbuch des Föderalismus 2001* (Baden-Baden, 2001), pp. 101–14, at pp. 105–10.
[16] Following the ideas of Karlheinz Reif and Hermann Schmitt on 'second order' elections. See K. Reif and H. Schmitt, 'Nine second order national elections: a conceptual framework for the analysis of European election results', *European Journal for Political Research* 8:1 (1980), pp. 3–44.

in Westminster. Comparative research[17] looking at Germany, Spain, and Canada shows, however, that to varying degrees territorial elections appear to be uncoupled in the minds of voters from statewide politics. In Canada voters seem to view the federal and provincial levels as more or less wholly unconnected when making their judgements at the ballot box. The parties standing for election are often different from province to province, and provincial election campaigns are strongly shaped by distinctive territorial political cultures—with Alberta and Quebec the extreme cases. In these circumstances provincial voting behaviour is shaped by sets of issues different to those that play into federal election campaigns.

In Germany there is much more uniformity in the parties standing for election at regional and federal levels and in the results they achieve at the two levels, reflecting a more homogeneous society and the commitment to common statewide standards noted earlier. But even in Germany there is some evidence that voters are beginning to take the opportunity in regional elections to express narrower territorial interests, and that the main statewide parties are finding it difficult to maintain the levels and patterns of support they enjoy in federal elections in regional ballots.[18]

But perhaps most interesting is Spain, which like the UK combines a dominant 'core' nation, Castilian Spain (broadly equivalent to England), with distinctive historic nationalities (equivalent to the Celtic nations in the UK). In the historic nationalities there are strong territorial parties (equivalent, say, to the SNP in Scotland) that compete in regional and Spanish elections alongside statewide parties (equivalent, say, to Labour and the Conservatives in the UK). The territorial parties in the historic nationalities score systematically better in regional than in statewide elections; the statewide parties score systematically better in Spanish than regional elections. This appears to reflect conscious decisions by voters a) to endorse the Spanish state in Spanish elections, b) to express territorial distinctiveness in regional elections, and c) in that way to shape the relation between the two arenas to ensure the region has maximum 'clout' in Spain.[19]

There are two points to draw out from this discussion. The first is that citizens, in their voting behaviour, seem well aware of a capacity to express the tension and shape the balance between statewide social citizenship and territorial cultures. The second, focused on the Spanish example, recalls the earlier point about Quebec: expressing territorial distinctiveness while *also*

---

[17] See C. Jeffery and D. Hough, 'Elections in multi-level systems: lessons for the UK from abroad', in Hazell (ed.), *State of the Nations 2003*, pp. 239–62.

[18] D. Hough and C. Jeffery, 'Landtagswahlen: Bundestestwahlen oder Regionalwahlen', *Zeitschrift für Parlamentsfragen* 33:1 (2003), pp. 49–66.

[19] Jeffery and Hough, 'Elections in multi-level systems', pp. 248–9, 260.

affirming a commitment to common, statewide values is a recipe for maximising influence and benefits from common statehood.

Reading Across into Scottish–English Relationships

The point of using comparisons in this contribution is to find pointers for understanding the relationships between Scotland and the UK and its dominant nation, England, that exist in the context of devolution. How do Scottish citizens negotiate these relationships? There are a number of points which can be 'read across' from these comparisons.

Elections

The first stays on the theme of elections. The two Scottish Parliament election results recorded so far, and all the opinion poll results published in between, reveal a pattern in which the SNP does systematically better when voters think of Holyrood. But at the same time the results in Scotland of the two Westminster elections of the devolution era, together with all the opinion poll results published in between, reveal that Labour (and to a lesser extent the Conservatives) do systematically better when voters think of Westminster. This pattern is confirmed in data from major public attitudes surveys done at the time of both devolved and Westminster elections in Scotland and Wales (Tables 8.2 and 8.3). Voters were asked in 2001 how they had voted in the Westminster election just past and at the same time how they would have voted had there been a devolved (constituency) contest on the same day (and in 2003 how they voted in the devolved elections and how they would have voted in a Westminster election on the same day).

Though some of the differences are small, the general pattern is clear. All the parties which operate Britain-wide—Labour, Conservatives, and Liberal Democrats—have a devolved election deficit, and the nationalist parties have a devolved election bonus. Voters appear quite clearly to want different things from different electoral processes. This split voting pattern, as Catherine Bromley and John Curtice have identified,[20] seems to be about the Scottish–UK relationship. It affirms Scottish membership of the union on the one hand, but wants as spikily Scottish a voice as possible representing Scottish interests in the union. And Labour in Scotland is not seen as entirely suited to that role, so its loses some support to more unambiguously Scottish

---

[20] C. Bromley and J. Curtice, 'Devolution: scorecard and prospects', in C. Bromley, J. Curtice, K. Hinds, and A. Park (eds), *Devolution: Scottish Answers to Scottish Questions?* (Edinburgh, 2003), pp. 7–29, at pp. 20–3.

Table 8.2. Differential voting preferences in Scotland 2001.

	Recalled 2001 Westminster vote	Hypothetical devolved constituency vote on the same day	Devolved minus Westminster
	%	%	%
Conservative	11	10	−1
Labour	53	49	−4
Liberal Democrats	17	15	−2
SNP	16	23	17
Other	4	4	=

Source: Scottish Social Attitudes Survey.

Table 8.3. Differential voting preferences in Scotland 2003.

	Recalled 2003 devolved constituency vote %	Hypothetical Westminster vote on the same day %	Devolved minus Westminster %
Conservative	19	22	−3
Labour	36	40	−4
Liberal Democrats	13	16	−3
SNP	25	18	+7
Other	7	3	+4

Source: Scottish Social Attitudes Survey.

voices in Scottish Parliament elections. Devolution in this sense is about Scottish voters expressing 'Scottish answers to Scottish questions' when they think of voting in the Scottish Parliament context, and 'UK answers to UK questions' when it comes to Westminster.[21]

Independence

Second, and reinforcing the point about the union, there has been no correlation between increased support for the Scottish National Party (and indeed the other pro-independence parties) in Scottish Parliament elections and increased support for Scottish independence. Support for independence has been flat-lining since devolution at 25–30 per cent, excepting a temporary surge at the time of the September 1997 devolution referendum (Table 8.4).

Multiple Identities

Third, and following on, the Scottish seem quite happy to combine Scottish and British identities. These are clearly not seen simply as exclusive and competitive identities, but also as complementary. The classic way of showing this

[21] Cf. L. Paterson et al., *New Scotland, New Politics?* (Edinburgh, 2001), p. 29.

Table 8.4. Constitutional preferences in Scotland, 1997–2003.

	May 1997 %	Sept. 1997 %	1999 %	2000 %	2001 %	2002 %	2003 %
Independence	26	37	28	30	27	30	26
Devolution with tax powers	42	32	50	47	54	44	48
Devolution without tax powers	9	9	9	8	6	8	7
No devolution	17	17	10	12	9	12	13

Source: John Curtice, 'Restoring confidence and legitimacy? Devolution and public opinion', in Alan Trench (ed.), *Has Devolution Made a Difference? The State of the Nations 2004* (Exeter, 2004), p. 230.

Table 8.5. Moreno national identity in Scotland and England, 2001.

	X, not British %	More X than British %	Equally X and British %	More British than X %	British, not X %
Scotland	36	30	24	3	3
England	17	13	42	9	11

Source: Michael Rosie and Ross Bond, 'Identity matters: the personal and political significance of feeling Scottish', in Catherine Bromley, John Curtice, Kerstin Hinds, and Alison Park (eds), *Devolution: Scottish Answers to Scottish Questions?* (Edinburgh, 2003), p. 119.

is to use the Moreno scale, which allows five identity options with 'Scottish, not British' at one end, 'British, not Scottish' at the other, and 'equally British and Scottish' in the middle. There have been no great changes in Moreno self-identification responses in surveys of public attitudes in Scotland since 1997 (Table 8.5).

'Scottish, not British' is the most frequent response, but with substantial self-identification also as 'more Scottish than British' and 'equally Scottish and British'. In total 60 per cent of the Scottish public had some level of British identity. English self-identification shows a different pattern, with fewer exclusively English and more—in total 75 per cent—claiming some level of British identity on the Moreno scale. The more significant point, however, is the level of overlap of the Scottish and the English publics in claiming an overarching British identity.

Policy Preferences

'British' may mean different things in Scotland and England (or in Wales or, most certainly, Northern Ireland). But the continued and seemingly stable affirmation of a British identity in Scotland does suggest a commitment to a common UK statehood, shared with the English (and the other nations), and to a set of common values associated with that statehood. Some of those values may be rooted in diffuse senses of shared history and are hard to tie down. Others are clearly visible in attitudes to the role of the state as a provider of public policies. As survey research over recent years has shown, there are perhaps fewer differences in these attitudes between Scotland and the biggest component of the UK, England, than might have been expected before devolution. In their 'devolution scorecard' Catherine Bromley and John Curtice compared surveys of Scottish and English opinion and found:[22]

a   that public opinion on the first big issue of policy divergence in Scotland—tuition fees—appears to be very similar in Scotland and England (and in both places, in contrast to Scottish policy, favours up-front student contributions to the costs of their higher education);

b   that public opinion on the next big issue of policy divergence—free personal care for the elderly—is also very similar in Scotland to that in England. In both there are overwhelming majorities (88 per cent in Scotland, 86 per cent in England) in favour of government making the main contribution to the costs of care. Scottish policy is therefore consistent with mainstream British opinion, and UK policy is not.

c   that 'on many key areas of public policy there appears to be little or no difference between attitudes in England and those in Scotland',[23] including levels of taxation and public spending, or the priority of extra spending on health care;

d   but that some differences do exist, with the Scottish more likely to favour comprehensive education than the English, and (a little) more likely to criticise the level of benefits for the unemployed as too low and the width of disparities between those with high incomes and those with low incomes as too wide.

This scorecard is a nuanced one. There are clearly some differences in priorities and underlying values, but also, it seems, more common values (and, it has to be said, a curious pattern of governmental response to those values, with Scottish policy more in line than UK/English policy with wider English and Scottish opinion on free personal care; and UK/English policy on tuition fees more in line with English and Scottish opinion than Scottish policy).

In Summary

These indicators on voting behaviour, constitutional choice, national identity, and policy preference suggest a variant on the relationship mentioned earlier

---

[22] Bromley and Curtice, 'Devolution: Scorecard and prospects', pp. 8–12.

[23] Ibid., pp. 11–12.

of Quebec to Canada (and no doubt also have equivalents in the relationships of, say, Victoria to Australia, Bavaria to Germany, and Catalonia to
Spain). They are

- *union-confirming*, affirming commonalities with the rest of the UK
  state and underlining elements of a UK-wide social citizenship;
- *territory-sensitive*, requiring recognition of a certain level of
  distinctiveness notwithstanding common statehood;
- *voice-giving*, demanding that Scotland's voice be taken seriously in
  the wider UK (in a way that it might not if Labour dominance were
  not challenged in Scotland by a strong nationalist party).

What is the UK for?

The previous section has identified more clearly what Scottishness and
Scottish preferences are in the post-devolution union. Scottish citizens have
been reasonably clear in articulating how they see the devolution settlement
as capable of expressing Scottish territorialism and commitment to the UK
union. And they are, as repeated surveys have shown, in principle content
with the institutional expression of devolution in Scotland (see Table 8.4), no
matter how disappointed they have been with particular issues (like the cost
overruns of the new Scottish Parliament building) or outcomes (the
perception that devolution has not yet made as much difference to health,
education, the economy and so on as they would have liked).[24]

But there is a wider point. As was made clear in the introduction to this
contribution, Scottish devolution is not just about Scotland, but also has
spillover effects for the wider UK union. What are the implications for the
union of this balance the Scots have struck between UK social citizenship
and Scottish territorial culture? What are the implications for the whole that
overarches the Scottish, the English and, indeed, the other parts of the UK
state? Robert Hazell and Brendon O'Leary have the prescription:

> [This] is a matter on which the [UK] Government needs to give a lead, in its
> actions and in its words, to bind the Union together in order to counterbalance
> the centrifugal political forces of devolution. The Government needs to under-
> stand and allow political space to those forces, and the regional and national
> loyalties that underpin them; but it also needs to understand and articulate

[24] C. Jeffery, 'Judgements on devolution? The 2003 elections in Scotland, Wales and Northern
Ireland', *Representation* 41 (2004).

clearly a sense of the wider loyalties which bind us together at the level of the nation state.[25]

But the government has not given a lead. It either does not recognise that devolution has changed its role as the voice of the union, or has pinned its hopes on muddling through. There have certainly been no systematic and convincing attempts to offer any new visions of what the union is for. The government's fullest statement of vision was in a speech by Tony Blair to the National Assembly for Wales in October 2001. They key passages were as follows:

> I believe devolution has left the UK stronger, not weaker ... It allows the energy and diversity of different parts of our country to breathe and develop ... [A]t the very time nations collaborate on a bigger stage, there is a greater desire to seize back control over local issues on smaller stages. Politics is [about] finding different levels appropriate to different types of issue ... There is merit in the simple argument that when it comes to the economy, defence, foreign policy, social security, bigger is stronger. We can then project that strength glob- ally. But within that unity, diversity can flourish. That is why devolution is important.[26]

Blair's words are at best a useful starting point, but they are hardly a full and considered statement of the new balance of whole and parts. If that is what the Scots are investing in when they say they continue to feel British as well as Scottish, then they may well have reason to feel disappointed. Something more active is required, something akin to the 'nation-building' efforts of the Canadian federal government, or of the expressions of statewide solidarity and common standards in Australia and Germany. It may be useful in this context to dwell on one of the most important mechanisms in those countries for balancing territorial identities and preferences with an overarching commitment to common statehood: territorial financial arrangements.

Territorial Financial Arrangements

In the earlier, comparative, discussion it was evident just how important ter- ritorial financial arrangements are as expressions and underpinnings of com- mon statehood and the common benefits of social citizenship that common statehood implies. In almost all decentralised systems, certainly in western

---

[25] R. Hazell and B. O'Leary, 'A rolling programme of devolution: slippery slope or safeguard of the Union', in R. Hazell (ed.), *Constitutional Futures: A History of the Next Ten Years* (Oxford, 1999), pp. 21–46, at pp. 45–6.

[26] T. Blair, 'Speech by the Prime Minister to the Welsh Assembly', 30 October 2001, download- able at http://www.number-10.gov.uk/output/Page1636.asp# .

democracies, it is felt to be important to have mechanisms which make it possible for all parts of the state to provide similar levels of public service,
despite territory-to-territory differences in income-raising capacity and costs.
Some parts of the state may of course not be very good at making good use
of that possibility in delivering services to citizens, and some parts may resent
the way they have directly or indirectly to subsidise other parts. But having
these mechanisms is a powerful statement of statewide solidarity and of a
commitment that all citizens should have access to some minimum level of
benefits from membership of the state.

Such mechanisms are lacking in the UK. The Barnett formula and the
historical baselines to which increments to the Scottish, Welsh, and Northern
Irish blocks are added are clearly not mechanisms designed, over the long
run, to allow each part of the UK to provide similar levels of public service,
whatever their differences in income-raising capacity and costs. There are,
though, some signs, albeit still rather subterranean, which point in the direction of expressing UK-wide solidarity in some more explicit way. One is in
the rudimentary commitment of the UK government to reduce regional economic disparities in England. There are a number of problems with how that
commitment has been expressed.[27] However, raising the issue, even in a rudimentary way, and even just for England alone, suggests a notion of the role
of the centre in ensuring a certain level of cross-territorial equity. Put another
way, the 'north–south divide' and the differences in opportunity it creates for
citizens on the wrong side of the divide have been acknowledged as a problem that needs rectifying in the pursuit of what some have called 'territorial
justice'.[28]

At the same time there has been a renewal of a discourse of territorial
'need' in debates about the allocation of resources to the UK's nations and
regions. The terminology of need has been much used in arguments for
devolution in northern England,[29] but also in pleas for recognition of the

---

[27] The commitment is expressed in a way that may actually allow a widening of absolute disparities, even if regional growth rates converge. Moreover, as a number of pieces of recent
research have shown, government lacks obvious and potent policy levers to achieve its aim. See
J. Adams, P. Robinson, and A. Vigor, *A New Regional Policy for the UK*, Institute for Public
Policy Research (London, 2003); HC Select Committee on the Office of the Deputy Prime Minister 9th Report (HC Paper (2002–03) no. 492–i): *Reducing Regional Disparities in Prosperity*.
[28] Adams, Robinson, and Vigor, *A New Regional Policy for the UK*, p. 7.
[29] Cf. J. Tomaney, 'The Regional governance of England', in R. Hazell (ed.), *The State and the
Nations: The First Year of Devolution in the United Kingdom* (Thorverton, 2000), pp. 117–48, at
pp. 141–2. See also the regional calculations of public expenditure relevant to 'need' measured
by social security payments in D. Bell and A. Christie, 'Finance—the Barnett Formula: nobody's
child?', in A. Trench (ed.), *The State of the Nations 2001: The Second Year of Devolution in the
United Kingdom* (Thorverton, 2001), pp. 135–52, at pp. 141–2.

problems of ensuring balanced economic development and social cohesion in an ostensibly 'rich' region like London.[30]

That this debate has arisen largely reflects a misguided notion that some kind of recognition of special needs underpins the current territorial financial arrangements for Scotland (and Wales and Northern Ireland). The needs assessment conducted by HM Treasury in 1978 did not in fact determine the size of the baseline blocks onto which the Barnett formula has added increments since. Nonetheless, the terminology—and, implicitly, the inter-regional comparability—of 'need' drives English regional debates about the reform of territorial finance. And claims to special needs in England are eas-ily perceived as a threat to the particular structure of territorial finance in Scotland (and Wales and Northern Ireland), and easily evoke renewed expressions of special 'need' there too. This chorus of special needs might appear to be an implicit endorsement of some kind of process of territorial financial compensation, or equalisation, by need. There is, though, an impor-tant element missing. Those making claims about their special needs do not recognise or articulate the corollary: special needs in one place that require compensation also require tacit or explicit consent from those places that do not have such special needs that compensation will be given.

To put it more bluntly, *why should taxpayers in the southern half of England pay for everyone else's needs?* The answer, presumably, has to do with a sense of mutual commitment which has to do with the shared values inher-ent in common statehood. On the basis of that mutual commitment it follows easily enough—as in Australia, in Germany, even in Quebec–Canadian rela-tionships—that measures should be taken to ensure that places disadvan-taged by their specific economic structure, or topography, or public health problems remain in a position to provide much the same quality of public services for citizens as other, less disadvantaged places.

There is a veiled assumption here about the desirability of UK-wide soli-darity and about the importance of all citizens having access to minimum lev-els of public service wherever they happen to live. But because it is so veiled there has never been an open and sensible debate about who should get what and why. That kind of debate would be a necessary building block in (re-) defining the content of UK social citizenship for the post-devolution era, in working out just what it is that the Scots and the English should still enjoy in common from the state. And protagonists in the debate should remember that those who help compensate for others' needs now might in future have needs that require compensation. That implicit bargain, that essential social

---

[30] Cf. J. Tomaney, 'Reshaping the English regions', in A. Trench (ed.), *The State of the Nations 2001*, pp. 107–34, at p. 129; C. Jeffery, *Fiscal Federalism: A Comparative Investigation*, Report for the Brussels Regional Government (2003).

solidarity is what membership of a union ultimately means. Citizens in Scotland, in their balance of claims to distinctiveness alongside shared values with the English and their shared commitment to Britishness seem quite capable of articulating that bargain. It is a shame that UK's governments—in Westminster, Edinburgh and elsewhere—seem to lack that same capability.

Note. The ideas in this contribution reflect work undertaken in the Economic and Social Research Council's research programme on Devolution and Constitutional Change, which the author directs, as well as the project on 'Multi-Level Electoral Competition in Decentralised States' he carried out with Dan Hough as part of the Leverhulme Trust's research programme 'Nations and Regions: The Dynamics of Devolution' at the Constitution Unit, University College London.

IDENTITIES

9

Varieties of Nationalism in Scotland and England

ANTHONY HEATH AND SHAWNA SMITH

THE AIM OF THIS PAPER IS TO EXPLORE THE NATURE OF UNIONISM AND NATIONALISM in Scotland and England and the prospects for the union. It has been customary to distinguish between British nationalism, an inclusionary and civic form of nationalism emphasising the union between England and Scotland, and a minority nationalism which seeks to secure statehood for the Scottish nation.

British nationalism has usually been seen as a relatively recent construct, forged through the Napoleonic and more recent wars and the shared project of the British empire.[1] In the most recent past it has been particularly associated with the Conservative party under Margaret Thatcher and has usually been assumed to be propagated by the dominant ethnic and economic groups.[2] However, British nationalism is likely to be in decline as younger generations grow up who do not remember the Empire or Second World War but are part of the European project.[3] Under Labour, official British nationalism has taken a weaker form, with official blessing for devolution, albeit intended to preserve the union.

Minority nationalism is the nationalism of politically subordinate groups that seek statehood. It is usually seen to have an ethnic base, and historically the driving force has been exclusion from political (and perhaps economic) power.[4] It has, of course, been most powerful in Ireland, where Catholics

---

[1] L. Colley, *Britons: Forging the Nation 1707–1837* (New Haven, 1992).

[2] M. Hechter, *Internal Colonialism: The Celtic fringe in British National Development 1536–1966* (London, 1976).

[3] J. Kellas, *The Politics of Nationalism and Ethnicity* (London, 1991); A. F. Heath and J. Kellas, 'Nationalisms and constitutional questions', in *Understanding Constitutional Change*, special issue of *Scottish Affairs* (1998), pp. 110–29.

[4] E. Gellner, *Nations and Nationalism* (Oxford, 1983); Hechter, *Internal Colonialism*.

Proceedings of the British Academy **128**, 133–152. © The British Academy 2005.

were indeed excluded from power in the Protestant-dominated British state. More contemporary arguments look to postmaterialism and postmodernism as possible sources of nationalism—individuals are increasingly free to choose their identities, and with the waning of traditional bonds, younger generations are free (but not compelled) to choose a nationalist identity.[5]

In general we might expect England, as historically the dominant partner (or at least believing itself to be the dominant partner), to embrace unionism and British nationalism, and for the English therefore to be less supportive of devolution or separatism for Scotland. Indeed, the English generally seem to find it difficult to distinguish Britain from England and to have a fuzzy conception of their national identity.[6] However, there is another possibility, namely that devolution has itself undermined support for unionism and that the English have now become more aware of their separate interests and identity from Scots. A sense of national identity may, as Hobsbawm has suggested, be promoted by conflict with opposing national groups,[7] and a sense of conflicting interests between Scots and English may be one consequence of devolution. This could lead to the erosion of British nationalism and its replacement by a new form of English nationalism.

The form that English nationalism might take is of particular interest. Scottish nationalism has had none of the characteristics of the far-right nationalism that has blighted many European societies, but would English nationalism be quite so benign? It might take on an ethnic and exclusionary character and be marked by the xenophobia of European far-right movements, hostile not only to migrants and asylum seekers but also to Scots and the other nations that have historically been part of Great Britain.

Another possibility is that the decline of official unionism may lead not to English nationalism but to a more general distaste for, or indifference towards, nationalism in all its forms. As Mattei Dogan has argued, we may be entering an era of post-nationalistic politics.[8] Rather than active hostility towards Scots, there may simply be indifference; lack of commitment to the union may mean that the English do not care particularly either way about devolution or independence for Scotland.

---

[5] R. Inglehart, *Modernisation and Postmodernisation: Cultural, Economic and Political Change in 43 Societies* (Princeton, 1997).

[6] L. Hazelden and R. J. Jenkins, 'The national identity question: methodological investigations', *Social Survey Methodology Bulletin* 51 (2003), pp. 18–26.

[7] E. J. Hobsbawm, *Nations and Nationalism since 1780* (Cambridge, 1990).

[8] M. Dogan, 'The decline of nationalisms within Western Europe', *Comparative Politics* 26 (1994), pp. 281–305.

Aspects of Nationalism

To explore these issues we begin by looking at three different aspects of nationalism, namely emotional attachments to Britain, perceptions of conflicts of interest between England and Scotland, and constitutional preferences. We would expect those who embrace official nationalism to have an emotional attachment to Britain, to perceive shared interests rather than conflicting interests between the two countries, and to prefer the maintenance of the union. At the other extreme we would expect minority nationalists in Scotland to lack emotional attachment to Britain, to perceive a conflict of interest between the two countries and to prefer independence for Scotland.

In addition to these two archetypal groups whose attachments, perceptions of conflict, and constitutional preferences make up coherent, internally consistent packages, there could be a range of other more mixed groups which may reveal rather more of the potential strains within the union. On the one hand, there may be potential nationalists in Scotland who lack attachment to Britain or who perceive a conflict of interest but have yet to embrace a thoroughgoing nationalist ideology advocating independence. In contrast, in England there may again be people who perceive a conflict of interest but have yet to embrace an exclusionary ideology or to have rejected unionism.

Our data come from the 2003 round of surveys conducted as part of the Economic and Social Research Council's Devolution and Constitutional Change programme. Co-ordinated modules of questions were asked in the 2003 British Social Attitudes and the 2003 Scottish Social Attitudes surveys.

We have two key questions that enable us to measures attitudes towards the union and constitutional arrangements, one about Scotland and one about England, but both asked in both countries.

> About Scotland:
> Which of these statements comes closer to your views: Scotland should
> —become independent, separate from the UK and the European Union;
> —become independent, separate from the UK but part of the European Union;
> —remain part of the UK, with its own elected parliament which has some taxation powers;
> —remain part of the UK, with its own elected parliament which has no taxation powers;
> —remain part of the UK without an elected parliament.

About England:
With all the changes going on in the way the different parts of Great Britain are run, which of the following do you think would be best for England?
—for England to be governed as it is now, with laws made by the UK parliament;
—for each region of England to have its own assembly that runs services like health;
—or, for England as a whole to have its own new parliament with law-making powers.

The Scottish question reflects the kinds of constitutional options that were being discussed at the time of the referendum in 1999 by the political parties, ranging from independence to the maintenance of the status quo. A particular debate had focused on the question of tax-raising powers. In the event, the Scottish people had voted for the third option, namely for Scotland to remain part of the UK with its own elected parliament and limited taxation powers. For simplicity, we group responses to this question, simply distinguishing independence, devolution, and maintenance of the status quo ante. In England, debates on constitutional questions were not so advanced. The major constitutional initiative had been the proposal for regional assemblies, a proposal particularly associated with John Prescott, the Deputy Prime Minister.

Table 9.1 shows the distribution of preferences on these constitutional questions in England and Scotland respectively. Broadly speaking, the table shows big differences in constitutional preferences for England and Scotland, but remarkable similarity in the views of residents in the two territories. Residents both of England and Scotland overwhelmingly support devolution for Scotland, while residents of both territories incline towards no change in the constitutional position for England. On neither issue, then, is there any real difference of opinion between the residents of the two territories. To be sure, people in England appear to be less interested in questions of Scotland's constitutional position than are people in Scotland: in England 12 per cent did not have a view on Scotland's position. Correspondingly, residents in Scotland were less interested in England's constitutional position, with nearly 14 per cent having no view.

There is just one, rather modest, divergence between England and Scotland: slightly more people in Scotland favour independence for Scotland (26 per cent versus 17 per cent in England). This hardly suggests a major conflict, however. The dominant impression is that England and Scotland are alike in their constitutional preferences. It is simply not the case, for example, that Scots want independence whereas the English want to maintain the union.

However, while support for Scottish independence is slightly greater in Scotland than in England, the reverse is not the case. Indeed, English and

Table 9.1. Attitudes towards England's and Scotland's constitutional positions.

Scotland's constitutional position	Residents in England (N = 1,917)	Residents in Scotland (N = 1,508)
Agree that . . .	%	%
Scotland should remain part of UK without a parliament	13	13
Scotland should remain part of UK with a parliament	58	55
Scotland should be independent	17	26
None of these / don't know	12	6
Total	100	100

England's constitutional position	Residents in England (N = 975)	Residents in Scotland (N = 1,508)
Agree that . . .	%	%
Laws should be made by UK parliament	54	53
Each region should have its own assembly	23	16
England should have its own new parliament	17	18
None of these / don't know	5	14
Total	100	100

Scottish residents are quite similar in their support for a separate parliament for England, with Scots slightly more likely to support independence (18 per cent versus 17 per cent). There is a simple explanation for this asymmetry. Scottish separatists also tend to prefer separatism for England, since the latter is the natural corollary of the former. More generally, we find that people's preferences for constitutional arrangements in the other territory tend to reflect their preferences for arrangements in their own territory.

But while there seem to be few differences between England and Scotland in their constitutional preferences, there are much bigger differences in their sense of attachment to the union. We have measured these affective attachments with questions about feelings of national pride. We asked respondents:

> How proud are you of being British, or do you not see yourself as British at all?
>
> And how proud are you of being English/Scottish, or do you not see yourself as English/Scottish at all?

In contrast to the previous question on constitutional preferences, this question taps affective attachments rather than policy preferences.

Table 9.2. Pride in being British, English, or Scottish.

Pride in being British	English residents' pride in being British (N = 1,917)	Scottish residents' pride in being British (N = 1,508)
Feeling . . .	%	%
Very proud	43	24
Somewhat proud	37	41
Not very proud	10	13
Not at all proud	2	5
Not British	7	16
Don't know	1	1
Total	100	100

Pride in being English/Scottish	English residents' pride in being English (N = 1,917)	Scottish residents' pride in being Scottish (N = 1,508)
Feeling . . .	%	%
Very proud	45	71
Somewhat proud	33	17
Not very proud	8	3
Not at all proud	2	0
Not English/Scottish	12	9
Don't know	1	1
Total	100	100

The numbers for Scotland and England differ quite dramatically with regard to these measures. In terms of pride in being British, nearly 80 per cent of English residents claim to be proud or very proud, compared to only 64 per cent of Scottish residents. In addition, 16 per cent of Scottish residents claim to not identify as British at all, compared to only 7 per cent of English residents. Turning to the lower panel of the table we see that, in England, pride in being English is at a very similar level to pride in being British with 78 per cent proclaiming themselves proud. However more than 88 per cent of those in Scotland declare themselves to be proud of being Scottish, with an extraordinary 71 per cent claiming to be very proud. Similarly, whilst 12 per cent of English residents stated they were 'not English', only 9 per cent of Scottish residents did the same. These findings show that while levels of English and British pride remain similar in England, in Scotland levels of Scottish pride trump levels of British pride to a significant degree.

This puts a rather different complexion on the national differences in attitudes towards the union. Table 9.2 demonstrates that Scots feel much greater attachment to Scotland than they do to Britain, a phenomenon that has no parallel in England. The differences between England and Scotland in policy

Table 9.3. Perceptions of conflict of interest between England and Scotland.

Agree that . . .	Residents in England (N = 1,917) %	Residents in Scotland (N = 1,508) %
England's economy benefits more	6	31
Scotland's economy benefits more	38	23
Equal benefits	40	39
Neither/both lose	3	1
Don't know	13	5
Total	100	100

preferences are rather small, but the emotional differences are much larger. The 'glue' holding Scots together seems to be much stronger than that holding the English together.

There are also big differences when we look at people's perceptions of the benefits of the union. We asked our respondents:

> On the whole, do you think that England's economy benefits more from having Scotland in the UK, or that Scotland's economy benefits more from being part of the UK, or is it about equal?

We can think of this question as indicating the extent of a perceived conflict of interest between the two nations. (See Table 9.3.)

Again we see a marked difference between the two territories. Whilst 'equal benefits' is the most frequent response in both territories, in England nearly as many respondents felt that Scotland benefited more (38 per cent) and only 6 per cent felt England benefited more. In Scotland the reverse was true. Thus, while there are many respondents in both territories who feel that the benefits are equal, sizeable minorities in both countries do perceive a conflict of interest. Interestingly, the net balance (the percentage who think the other country benefits more, less the percentage who think their own country benefits more) is actually greater in England, at 32 percentage points, than it is in Scotland, where it is only 8 points.

We thus get very different impressions of relations between England and Scotland depending on whether we consider constitutional preferences, affective attachments, or perceptions of national interest. To obtain an overall picture of the pattern of sentiments, we can carry out a cluster analysis, based on these normative, cognitive, and affective measures, to distinguish the main groupings in the two countries. Table 9.4 gives the resulting typology for Scotland while Table 9.5 shows the typology for England.

We distinguish four groups in each country. In Scotland our first group is a classic example of minority nationalism, making up around a fifth of the

Table 9.4. A typology of Scottish residents.

	Scottish nationalists (N = 333) %	Potential Scottish nationalists (N = 191) %	Unionists (N = 714) %	Disengaged (N = 268) %
Prefer Scottish independence	80	0	13	11
Prefer separate parliament for England	31	13	13	17
Believe Scotland benefits most	0	0	36	35
Believe England benefits most	82	100	0	3
Proud to be British	21	100	100	0
Proud to be Scottish	97	96	89	69

Table 9.5. A typology of English residents.

	Separatists (N = 196) %	Potential separatists (N = 483) %	Unionists (N = 874) %	Disengaged (N = 362) %
Prefer Scottish independence	77	0	16	12
Prefer separate parliament for England	25	14	17	15
Believe Scotland benefits most	91	100	0	20
Believe England benefits most	0	0	8	14
Proud to be British	52	100	94	35
Proud to be English	86	90	100	0

sample. These Scottish nationalists have very high levels of affective attachment to Scotland and conversely low attachment to Britain. They overwhelmingly believe that England benefits most from the union, and they tend to favour independence for Scotland. They also want to see constitutional change in England, with a third supporting a separate English parliament. In cognitive, normative, and affective terms they have rejected the union.

Our second group, a smaller group, can be regarded as potential Scottish nationalists or perhaps as ambivalent unionists. Like the archetypal Scottish nationalists, they are proud of Scotland and they perceive a conflict of interest with England. However they do not (as yet?) favour independence for Scotland and they remain proud of Britain.

We then have a large group of unionists. This is the largest of our four groups and makes up just under half of the sample. They are proud of Britain, although this coincides with a high level of attachment to Scotland too. They do not perceive a conflict of interest with England, and have little desire for independence. So this is a distinctly Scottish form of unionism — this group is both Scottish and unionist.

The remaining Scottish residents can be classified as 'disengaged'. They are akin to the unionists in their lack of support for independence for either England or Scotland, nor do they perceive a conflict of interest between the two countries; indeed, they feel in much the same way that the unionists do that Scotland benefits from the union. However, they lack the pride in Britain of the unionist group, and even their levels of pride in Scotland are relatively low, at least when compared with our other three groups in Scotland. This begins to look rather like a 'post-nationalist' group, for whom issues of national identity and independence are not especially salient.

In England we find a broadly similar typology, although some of the details vary. While we do not have an exact equivalent to the Scottish nationalists, the first group does have quite a lot in common with them. Like the Scottish nationalists, this group perceives a conflict of interest between England and Scotland, and like the Scottish nationalists, favours independence for Scotland. They are also proud to be English and, like their Scottish equivalents, have relatively low levels of pride in Britain. However, while they are the group in England that is most likely to support a separate English parliament, their support for this constitutional change is still pretty low. In other words, they do not seem to have a distinct English nationalist political agenda in the way that the Scots do. For this reason we prefer to term them separatists (reflecting their desire for Scotland to be independent) rather than thoroughgoing English nationalists. This group is also much smaller than its Scottish equivalent, covering only 10 per cent of our respondents in England.

Next, we have a larger group, which bears strong similarities to the potential Scottish nationalists. This group perceives a conflict of interest with Scotland but is proud of Britain (as well as of England) and do not favour independence for Scotland (nor a separate parliament for England). We can term these potential separatists, and they outnumber the actual separatists, making up a quarter of the sample in England.

Our third group's members are archetypal unionists; they are proud of Britain, perceive no conflict of interest between the nations, and have no liking for Scottish independence. As with their Scottish equivalents, pride in Britain coexists with national pride in England. The only way in which they differ from the Scottish unionists is in their perception of the benefits of the union; the English unionists think both countries benefit, whereas many Scottish unionists actually thought that Scotland benefited more. In other words, the English unionists do not appear to see distinctive benefits for England from the union. Like their Scottish equivalents they make up just under half the sample.

Finally, as in Scotland, we have a group who can best be characterised as disengaged. Like their Scottish equivalents, they have no liking for Scottish independence and perceive no conflict of interest between the two countries.

And they have low levels of affective attachment to Britain, and none at all to England.

The cluster analysis, then, has produced roughly comparable groups in the two territories, and they make up roughly comparable proportions of the two samples. There are some subtle differences between them, perhaps the biggest difference being the character of the nationalist/separatist groups. Scottish nationalists are a larger group (one-fifth rather than one-tenth of the sample) and they appear to be more politicised (not surprisingly, given the success of the SNP in Scotland). English separatists are a smaller group and seem to lack a distinctive political agenda for England.

Looked at from the perspective of this typology, the prospects for the union are not particularly encouraging. To be sure, there is only a small group of Scottish nationalists in Scotland and an even smaller group of English separatists. However, in both countries the unionists fall somewhat short of an overall majority and there are large groups that are either disengaged post-nationalists or ambivalent unionists.

Our key research question is, then, to understand more of these patterns of nationalism and unionism, disengagement and ambivalence. What sorts of people are they? Do they fit the usual stories about the sources of British nationalism and minority nationalism? Are the potential separatists in England the same sorts of people as the potential nationalists in Scotland, or do they exhibit more of the traits of far-right nationalism? And are they composed of older generations that are likely to be a waning political force? Or are they a younger, rising generation?

What Sorts of People?

We first check that our cluster analysis tallies with the other questions that we have on national identities and that our interpretation of the groups as nationalists, unionists, and so on makes sense. (In essence we can think of this as a validation of our typology.)

The two surveys contained a number of questions relevant to national identity. First, there is the widely used 'Moreno' question asking respondents to choose between British and national identities.[9] Respondents were asked:

[9] L. Moreno, 'Scotland and Catalonia: the path to Home Rule', in D. McCrone and A. Brown (eds), *The Scottish Government Yearbook* (Edinburgh: Unit for the Study of Government in Scotland, 1988).

Some people think of themselves first as British. Others may think of themselves first as English/Scottish. Which, if any, of the following best describes how you see yourself?
—English/Scottish not British
—More English/Scottish than British
—Equally English/Scottish and British
—More British than English/Scottish
—British not English/Scottish
—Other description

In addition to the Moreno question, respondents were also given a multiple choice question on national identity, and were asked which of the multiple choices represented the best self-description.

We also asked respondents which nationality they would like to appear on their passport. We asked:

Say you were allowed to choose the nationality that appears on your passport. Which one of the descriptions on this card would you choose? British, English, European, Irish, Northern Irish, Scottish, Ulster, Welsh, Other answer.

In Table 9.6 we give selected responses to these three questions on national identity.

Table 9.6 shows the expected pattern, with unionists in both countries tending towards a British identity rather than a national one and the nationalists tending towards a Scottish or English identity. However, the table also reinforces our earlier remarks about the somewhat different character of

Table 9.6. National identities of the four clusters.

	England			
Agree that . . .	Separatists %	Potential separatists %	Unionists %	Disengaged %
Identify as English and not British	35	17	17	6
Want British passport	37	61	59	53
British best national identity	31	50	51	44

	Scotland			
Agree that . . .	Nationalists %	Potential nationalists %	Unionists %	Disengaged %
Identify as Scottish and not British	65	26	15	42
Want British passport	4	19	42	14
British best national identity	2	17	33	9

nationalism and unionism in the two countries. Thus, the Scottish nationalists are much more likely than the English separatists to have an exclusively
national, non-British identity. And the Scottish unionists are less likely than
the English unionists to adopt a British identity. While there are strong parallels, then, between the two typologies, it is also important to recognise the
different character of the four groups in the differing contexts provided by
England and Scotland. In Scotland the general context makes all four groups
more Scottish and less British than their counterparts in England, whereas in
England there is a stronger sense of Britishness in all four groups.

In Table 9.7 we move on to present some of the key demographic characteristics of our different groups of unionists and nationalists in the two countries. Previous research has shown that unionists in Scotland tend to be rather
older (reflecting, we suspect, generational differences), are more likely to
come from advantaged social classes, and are more likely to be members of
the established church. Scottish nationalists tend to be the obverse.[10] Do we
find the same patterns among the four groups in England?

Table 9.7 shows the expected pattern for unionists and nationalists in
Scotland. Scottish unionists tend to be older, with nearly a third being over
sixty-five, relatively highly educated, with many having professional or man-
agerial jobs in the salariat, and the majority religious, most likely as members
of one of the established churches in Scotland. We may—informally—think
of the unionists as being more closely allied with the privileged establishment. Nationalists, on the other hand, tend to be younger, less religious, less
well educated, and less advantaged economically. Potential nationalists contain a combination of these characteristics, but in general are quite similar to
the unionists. The disengaged post-nationalists are perhaps the most interesting group: they tend to be young and non-religious, like the nationalists,
but differ in being much more highly educated. Thus the data suggest that,
whereas amongst older respondents higher education was associated with
unionism, amongst the young it has been accompanied by disengagement.
This suggests a potentially worrying prospect for the union—in Scotland
unionism is under threat both from the younger generation of nationalists
and also, although in a different way, from the younger generation of highly
educated post-nationalists.

Is this same pattern replicated in England? The results for England show
some intriguing parallels and differences. First, we find that the English separatists have a lot in common with the Scottish nationalists: they tend to be

---

[10] Heath and Kellas, 'Nationalisms and constitutional questions'; A. Brown, D. McCrone, L.
Paterson, and P. Surridge, *The Scottish Electorate: The 1997 Election and Beyond* (Basingstoke,
1999).

Table 9.7. Demographic profile of the four clusters.

	England			
	Separatists %	Potential separatists %	Unionists %	Disengaged %
Aged 65 or older	19	26	27	13
With university degree	11	19	10	25
Working class	33	23	32	26
In the salariat	32	35	25	39
No religion	49	40	39	45

	Scotland			
	Nationalists %	Potential nationalists %	Unionists %	Disengaged %
Aged 65 or older	12	34	29	13
With university degree	7	7	16	23
Working class	39	25	27	23
In the salariat	20	24	27	29
No religion	51	30	39	53

younger, less educated, less privileged occupationally, and less likely to be religious. The disengaged post-nationalists also show many similarities with their Scottish equivalents: they are young but better educated and somewhat more privileged economically.

However, we find that there is a major difference between the unionists in England and in Scotland. In England we find that the unionists, like their Scottish equivalents, are rather older and somewhat more likely to be members of the established church. But they are not especially privileged either educationally or occupationally. Instead, it is the potential separatists and the disengaged that are the most privileged.

Thus, a comparison of these groups in England and Scotland seems to indicate that whilst the demographic roots of separatism and disengagement are rather similar in the two countries, the roots of unionism are rather different. In Scotland, the conventional theory about the sources of official nationalism hold, with the unionists being a relatively privileged stratum. In England, however, what we might term the 'establishment' is rather lukewarm about the union. The English unionists cannot be characterised as a privileged group—they are ordinary men and women in relatively humble circumstances.

Civic and Ethnic Nationalism

Having identified our four groups, our next step is to explore the character and behaviour of each group and the implications for relations between the two countries. A key distinction in the literature on national identities is between civic and ethnic nationalism.[11] Civic nationalism has a more inclusive character and promotes the acceptance of citizens irrespective of their ethnicity. Ethnic nationalism is more exclusionary and in the extreme case has been xenophobic. As Breton has suggested, in the case of ethnic nationalism 'a central preoccupation is with the cultural character of the community and its preservation'. In the case of civic nationalism, by contrast, Breton suggests that 'the basis of inclusion or exclusion . . . is by birth or on the basis of legally established criteria and procedures. Theoretically anyone who meets the criteria can become a member.'[12] Broadly speaking, therefore, ethnic nationalism has an ascriptive character and is therefore exclusionary, whereas civic nationalism can be acquired and is potentially inclusive.

According to the standard accounts, we might expect official British nationalism to have a more civic character and to be more inclusive, while minority nationalisms which fight for independence have usually been expected to have a more ethnic character. However, it is not entirely clear that this simple division between ethnic and civic nationalism will fit the Scottish case. On the surface Breton's account of ethnic nationalism might seem to be more applicable to Welsh nationalism, with its emphasis on the preservation of the Welsh language and culture, than to Scottish nationalism.

Table 9.8 provides us with some measures of civic and ethnic nationalism in the two countries. Unfortunately, we have somewhat different items in the two questionnaires and so we cannot make strict comparisons. However, the results are at the very least suggestive.

First of all, in England we asked questions that tap what we might term an exclusionary conception of nationhood:

> I'd like you to think of someone who was born in Scotland but now lives permanently in England and said they were English. Do you think you would consider them to be English?

> And now think of a non-white person living in England who spoke with an English accent and said they were English. Do you think you would consider them to be English?

---

[11] R. Brubaker, *Citizenship and Nationhood in France and Germany* (Cambridge MA, 1992).
[12] H. Breton, 'From ethnic to civic nationalism', *Ethnic and Racial Studies* 2 (1988).

Should the number of immigrants to Britain increase a lot, increase a little, remain the same, decrease a little or decrease a lot?

Do you agree that those born abroad have a right to be British if their mother or father was British?

In England we find that the separatists are clearly the most exclusionary of our four groups; they are the most likely to want the number of immigrants reduced, the least willing to accept Scots or non-whites as English and, perhaps surprisingly, are even unwilling to accept as British people born overseas of British parents. The pattern of responses suggests that this group are not simply hostile to non-whites but are generally hostile to those they see as 'other', as coming from outside England.

At the other extreme we find the disengaged, who appear to be the least prejudiced and the most accepting of people born overseas. They have more of the characteristics of a civic and inclusive form of nationalism than do the main unionist group and are by far the most tolerant of immigration. This reinforces our interpretation of this group as a post-nationalist one.

The unionists come in between these two extremes. As Tilley and his colleagues have shown in further analyses of these data, the dominant pattern in England is for respondents to have combined civic and ethnic conceptions of Britishness, rather than for civic and ethnic conceptions to have an either/or character.[13] This seems to be the pattern exemplified by our unionist group.

In Scotland we have a parallel question on whether someone born in England but now living in Scotland could be considered Scottish, together with some additional questions that also tap the civic/ethnic distinction:

> People have different views about what it takes to be truly Scottish. Some say that as well as living in Scotland, to be truly Scottish you have to have been born in Scotland. How much do you agree or disagree with this?

> And some say that as well as living in Scotland, to be truly Scottish you have to be white—rather than Black or Asian. How much do you agree or disagree with this?

> Suppose that Scotland became independent. Who do you think should be entitled to a Scottish passport and full Scottish citizenship? Do you think it should be only people who in your view are truly Scottish, or anyone permanently living in Scotland?

---

[13] J. Tilley, S. Exley, and A. Heath, 'What does it take to be truly British?', in Alison Park et al. (eds), *British Social Attitudes: The 21st Report* (London, 2004).

Table 9.8. Civic and ethnic nationalism in the four clusters.

	England			
Agree that . . .	English separatists %	Ambivalent unionists %	Unionists %	Disengaged %
Scottish residing in England are English	25	32	41	32
Non-whites residing in England are English	60	72	67	63
Number of immigrants should be reduced	88	78	75	52
Individuals born abroad are British if parents were British	51	73	63	80

	Scotland			
Agree that . . .	Nationalists %	Potential nationalists %	Unionists %	Disengaged %
English residing in Scotland are Scottish	38	45	45	39
Non-whites residing in Scotland are Scottish	68	59	70	69
Must be born in Scotland to be Scottish	58	51	54	52
All permanent residents entitled to Scottish passport	30	21	35	23
Only truly Scottish entitled to Scottish passports	61	67	53	62

In Scotland, the nationalists do not stand out in quite the same way as the English separatists did in the exclusionary character of their nationalism. Indeed, a striking feature of Table 9.8 is how similar the four Scottish groups are to each other. To be sure, this may be because we have a rather different set of questions available in Scotland, but it is striking that Scottish nationalists are as liberal as the unionists or the disengaged post-nationalists in their attitudes towards non-whites residing in Scotland, and there are only modest differences on attitudes towards the English. On the passport question, they are little different in their inclusivity from the other groups.

We should not exaggerate the civic qualities of Scottish nationalism, however. Fewer than a third were willing to see permanent residents securing a Scottish passport and fewer than half were willing to accept Scottish residents born in England as being Scottish. However, the parallel question in England shows that, among all four groups alike, the English were even less accepting of Scots than the Scots were of the English. For example, 38 per cent of Scottish nationalists were accepting of English migrants to Scotland, but only 25 per cent of English separatists were accepting of Scottish migrants. There were similar differences between most of the other groups in the two territories, suggesting that Scots as a whole are somewhat more inclusive than the English.

Finally, we have some additional questions on political efficacy that enable us to check further whether English separatism has the same character as Scottish nationalism. One theory of far-right nationalism (such as that of the British National Party or of the French Front National) is that it is a protest by the politically excluded, voicing anti-system sentiments.[14] If our hypothesis about the differing characters of Scottish nationalism and English separatism is correct, we would expect to find that these anti-system sentiments were more distinctive in the English case.

We have a number of questions that tap a sense of political exclusion. Respondents were asked whether they agreed with the following statements:

> (In both England and Scotland) Parties are only interested in people's votes, not in their opinions.

> (In England only) People like me have no say in what the government does.

> (In England only) It doesn't really matter which party is in power, in the end things go on much the same.

> (Scotland only) Some people say that it makes no difference which party wins in elections, things go on much the same ... How much of a difference do you think it makes who wins in general elections to the UK House of Commons? A great deal, Quite a lot, Some, Not very much, None at all.

We have somewhat different questions in the two countries, but a similar pattern can be detected (see Table 9.9). In both countries we find that the nationalist/separatist group are more likely to express disillusionment and cynicism about the political system, while the other groups are broadly similar to each other. However, in the case of Scotland the difference between the nationalists and the other three groups is relatively small, while in England the separatists stand out much more clearly as a disillusioned group. The theory of nationalism as a response to a sense of political exclusion holds better for the English separatists than it does for the Scottish nationalists.

[14] N. Mayer, *Ces Français qui votent FN* (Paris, 1999).

Table 9.9. Perceptions of political efficacy in England and Scotland.

	England			
	English separatists	Ambivalent unionists	Unionists	Disengaged
Agree that . . .	%	%	%	%
Parties only interested in votes	89	75	76	74
People like me have no say in government	81	62	67	64
Doesn't matter which party is in power	76	60	71	71

	Scotland			
	Nationalists	Potential nationalists	Unionists	Disengaged
Agree that . . .	%	%	%	%
Parties only interested in votes	83	75	70	73
Makes no difference who wins general election	12	9	6	10

Conclusions

We have used our questions on constitutional preferences, perceived conflicts of interest, and affective attachments to distinguish four broadly parallel groups in England and Scotland—unionists, nationalists, potential nationalists, and disengaged post-nationalists. In both countries unionists are the largest single group, but in both countries they fall short of a majority. Moreover, unionists tend to be rather older than other respondents, and on the basis of the theory of generational change we would expect them to be a declining force.

There are clearly tensions, too, with quite large numbers on both sides of the border who perceive a conflict of interest, although not as yet wishing to see separation between England and Scotland. And among younger generations we see a growth in one direction of Scottish or English nationalism, and in the other of disengagement. With continuing generational change, we expect that the forces maintaining a shared commitment to Britain will continue to weaken.[15]

These processes seem to be more or less common between the two countries. However, there are also important differences. In Scotland it appears

[15] For a detailed analysis of generational change in British identity see J. Tilley, A. Heath, and S. Exley, 'The decline of national pride in Britain', paper presented at the 15th Annual Elections, Public Opinion and Parties Conference, Oxford University 10–12 September 2004.

that nationalism has a more benign, inclusive character. English separatism in contrast has worrying features, and has parallels with the far right and, for example, the French Front National. And while this is a relatively small group, it is much larger than current political support for the far right in England would suggest. Moreover, the xenophobia of the English separatists does not appear to be specific to non-whites but also seems to extend, albeit weakly, to the Scots. Here then is a potential for overt conflict. However, this potential has not as yet been harnessed to any specific political agenda in the way that Scottish nationalism has been politicised by the SNP. While the threat from the BNP in England should never be ignored, the current direction of politicisation in England is anti-European rather than anti-Scotland. We suspect that parties like the Referendum Party in 2001 and currently the UK Independence Party are the most likely to harness the potential English nationalism and to direct it against Europe rather than against Scotland.

However, the most likely development in England is towards a post-nationalism with a young, highly educated generation of the disengaged who may well become the future English opinion leaders. Unlike the English separatists, this group does not perceive any conflict of interest with Scotland but nor does it have any strong sense of attachment to the union. If Scotland were to vote for greater independence, it is unlikely that this group would stand in its way.

Note. We are very grateful to the Economic and Social Research Council, which funded this research (Grant no. L219252018) as part of its programme on Devolution and Constitutional Change. We are particularly grateful to Professor Charlie Jeffery, the director of the programme, for his encouragement and support and to our colleagues in the Centre for Research into Elections and Social Trends for their comments and advice.

Appendix

The first half of Table 9.10 shows a strong relationship among residents of Scotland between their attitudes towards the constitutional positions of the two countries. Respondents who favour the maintenance of the status quo ante for Scotland also show strong support for maintaining the status quo for England (58 per cent) and are very disinclined to see a separate English parliament (14 per cent). In contrast, respondents who favour independence for Scotland are much less likely to favour the status quo for England (only 32 per cent), while they are much more likely than other groups to favour a separate English parliament (36 per cent). And, not surprisingly, people who are not interested in Scottish constitutional arrangements tend to have no views

Table 9.10. Relationship between attitudes towards English and Scottish constitutional positions.

	Residents in Scotland (row percentages)				
	Laws should be made by UK parliament	Each region should have its own assembly	England should have its own new parliament	None of these/ Don't know	N
Scotland should remain part of UK without parliament	83	7	5	4	193
Scotland should remain part of UK with a parliament	58	19	14	9	833
Scotland should be independent	32	19	36	13	387
None of these/don't know	22	4	4	70	95

	Residents in England (row percentages)				
	Scotland should remain part of UK without parliament	Scotland should remain part of UK with a parliament	Scotland should be independent	None of these/ Don't know	N
Laws should be made by UK parliament	16	64	13	6	523
Each region should have its own assembly	8	57	23	12	225
England should have its own new parliament	10	58	26	6	164
None of these/ don't know	8	29	11	52	63

about English arrangements either. Residents in Scotland, then, tend to show a rather high level of consistency in their attitudes towards arrangements in the two territories.

The second half of Table 9.10 shows that in England the degree of consistency is much weaker, although there is still some tendency for the attitudes towards the two issues to go together.

This may well be because constitutional arrangements, whether for Scotland or for England, simply have not been of great salience to the English public and their ideas are much less structured.

10

Brought Together or Driven Apart?

JOHN CURTICE

CRITICS OF DEVOLUTION ARGUED THAT THE CREATION OF A SCOTTISH PARLIAMENT would have an adverse impact on the relationship between England and Scotland. By providing Scots with a powerful symbol of their separate nationhood, support for the union would be undermined and the country would be set on the slippery slope towards independence.[1] Moreover, England could not be expected simply to acquiesce.[2] After all, Scottish MPs would be able to vote on English legislation while English MPs would no longer have any say in Scottish domestic legislation. Meanwhile, Scotland would still retain its favourable public spending settlement. In short, the impact of devolution on both sides of the border would drive the two countries apart.

Of course, the advocates of devolution had a riposte. For some of those of a unionist persuasion at least, devolution was regarded as a means of strengthening the union.[3] By creating a Scottish Parliament with the autonomy to pursue a different public policy from that being implemented in England, the union would demonstrate that it had the ability to accommodate Scotland's distinctive circumstances and policy preferences, thereby helping to put the nationalist genie back in the bottle. Equally, many hoped that the creation of the Scottish Parliament, the Welsh Assembly, and the Northern Irish Assembly would be the beginning of a process of implementing devolution all round, thereby assuaging any English discontent at the favourable treatment afforded to the smaller territories of the union.

---

[1] T. Dalyell, *The End of Britain* (London, 1977); M. Forsyth, 'The governance of Scotland', in L. Paterson (ed.), *A Diverse Assembly: The Debate on the Scottish Parliament* (Edinburgh, 1998), pp. 245–52.

[2] J. Paxman, *The English: a Portrait of a People* (Harmondsworth, 1998).

[3] A. Aughey, *Nationalism, Devolution and the Challenge to the UK* (London, 2001); V. Bogdanor, *Devolution in the UK* (Oxford, 1999).

Proceedings of the British Academy **128**, 153–170. © The British Academy 2005.

This chapter examines which of these perspectives appears to be correct, at least so far as developments in public opinion are concerned. It does so by looking at how the attitudes of those living on both sides of the border have developed in the immediate wake of the creation of the Scottish Parliament. In particular it focuses on three sets of attitudes that might be thought to be central to the relationship between two countries that share the same state: constitutional preferences, policy preferences, and identities.

The legitimacy of a multinational state and its constitutional arrangements clearly depends on its ability to command public support. If people in England and Scotland disagree about how they should be governed, their co-existence within the same state can at best only be an uneasy one. So first of all we examine the extent to which people in the two countries have similar or different constitutional preferences. But even if their constitutional preferences are similar, their relationship could still suffer if they have very different expectations of what public policy should be. Two societies with very different social outlooks are likely to struggle to reach an accommodation about those laws that are still intended to apply across the state as a whole. Meanwhile, if they do opt to pursue very different policies in line with the policy preferences of their respective publics, the spill-over effects of the divergent policies may frustrate their fulfilment. So, secondly, we look at how far people in England and Scotland do or do not share similar policy preferences. Lastly, we need to bear in mind that nations and societies are held together and even defined by their affective attachments and symbols.[4] A multinational state is strengthened by the existence of identities and symbols that are held in affection by all those living in its component countries. It is potentially weakened if those in different countries owe adherence to different identities, and especially if these identities are regarded as antipathetic to each other. So in the final section of this chapter we look at how far people in England and Scotland do or do not share a set of identities and symbols in common.

Our evidence comes from two parallel surveys, the British and Scottish Social Attitudes Surveys. These are high-quality surveys conducted by the National Centre for Social Research that are designed to facilitate both the academic study of public opinion and the evaluation of public policy. Conducted annually, the British survey interviews around 3,500 people throughout Great Britain (south of the Caledonian Canal) while its Scottish counterpart contacts around 1,500 people throughout Scotland. Both surveys have in recent years been tracking our three sets of attitudes on the two

---

[4] E. Gellner, *Nations and Nationalism* (Oxford, 1983).

sides of the border, thanks to funding from the Leverhulme Trust, the Economic and Social Research Council, and the Office of the Deputy Prime Minister. Because the two surveys have included the same or functionally equivalent questions they are ideal for establishing just how similar or different attitudes in the two countries are. And because the two surveys have asked many of these questions on a regular basis over the last four years or so, they also enable us to establish whether in the wake of devolution attitudes have come together or been driven apart.

Constitutional Preferences

Our first task, then, is to examine attitudes on both sides of the border towards how Scotland and England should be governed. We begin with Scotland. In Table 10.1 we show how people on both sides of the border have responded since the 1997 General Election when asked to choose between independence for Scotland (either inside or outside the European Union), some form of devolved parliament, or no legislative devolution at all. There is in truth little sign of tension here. The level of support for Scottish devolution in Scotland is more or less matched by the proportion in England who favour it. In both countries some form of devolved parliament has regularly commanded the support of between 50 and 60 per cent of the population over the last six years. Meanwhile, such opposition as there was in both countries to there being some kind of parliament in Edinburgh at all appears to have receded once the body was up and running in 1999, and on the most recent readings amounts to little more than one in eight.

Not that similarity of response to this question is sufficient evidence there is a close relationship between the two countries. After all, those on both sides of the border who advocate independence clearly want to loosen the ties between them. And the proportion who take this view appears to have been rather higher in England since the Scottish Parliament has been in operation, a development that might be regarded as some evidence of an English backlash. At the same time there is no consistent evidence that support in Scotland for Scottish independence has increased, though equally the hopes of some that it might fall have not been fulfilled either. Independence appears to continue to command the support of between 25 and 30 per cent of the Scottish public. Still, for the moment at least it seems that the existence of a devolved Scottish Parliament is in tune with majority public opinion on both sides of the border.

But what about the governance of England? Are people there unhappy about the fact that Scotland has devolution while they do not? And might people in Scotland be reluctant to grant England the advantages that they

Table 10.1. Attitudes in England and Scotland towards how Scotland should be governed.

	England						
	May 1997	Sept. 1997	1999	2000	2001	2002	2003
Scotland should . . .	%	%	%	%	%	%	%
be independent, separate from UK and EU, or separate from UK but part of EU	14	na	24	20	19	na	17
remain part of UK with its own elected parliament which has some taxation powers	38	na	44	44	53	na	51
remain part of the UK with its own elected parliament which has no taxation powers	17	na	10	8	7	na	9
remain part of the UK without an elected parliament	23	na	13	17	11	na	13
	Scotland						
Scotland should . . .	%	%	%	%	%	%	%
be independent, separate from UK and EU, or separate from UK but part of EU	28	37	28	30	27	30	26
remain part of UK with its own elected parliament which has some taxation powers	44	32	50	47	54	44	48
remain part of the UK with its own elected parliament which has no taxation powers	10	9	8	8	6	8	7
remain part of the UK without an elected parliament	18	17	10	12	9	12	13

na: not asked
Source: British and Scottish Election Studies 1997; Scottish Referendum Study 1997; British and Scottish Social Attitudes Surveys.

themselves now enjoy? Table 10.2 suggests that the answer to the first question is 'No', thereby rendering the answer to the second largely redundant. The table shows the answers that people on both sides of the border gave when asked to choose between an English parliament with powers similar to that of the current Scottish body, regional assemblies with responsibilities similar to those of the National Assembly for Wales, and no devolution at all. Although, as we have seen, people in England are supportive of a devolved parliament for Scotland, they do not appear to feel the need for something similar for themselves. The status quo of rule from Westminster continues to

Table 10.2. Attitudes in England and Scotland towards how England should be governed.

	England				
	1999 %	2000 %	2001 %	2002 %	2003 %
England should be governed as it is now, with laws made by the UK parliament	62	54	59	56	55
Each region of England to have its own assembly that runs services like health	15	18	21	20	24
England as whole to have its own new parliament with law-making powers	18	19	13	17	16
	Scotland				
England should be governed as it is now, with laws made by the UK parliament	na	45	49	na	53
Each region of England to have its own assembly that runs services like health	na	15	17	na	17
England as whole to have its own new parliament with law-making powers	na	28	23	na	18

na: not asked
Source: British and Scottish Social Attitudes Surveys.

enjoy the support of over half of those living in England. Meanwhile, this proves to be the most common view in Scotland too.

But even if the broad contours of the current devolution settlement seem to be in tune with public opinion on both sides of the border, it could still give rise to important sources of tension. Even if people in England are happy to be ruled by Westminster, we cannot assume that this means they believe that Scottish MPs should continue to have a vote in the Commons on legislation that only applies to England. We cannot assume either that people in England or indeed Scotland are content with the financial details of the current devolution settlement whereby public spending per head is higher in Scotland than in England while at the same time the Scottish Parliament itself has little or no influence over just how much it actually has to spend. Meanwhile, behind any such tensions might well lie disagreements about how the economic benefits of the union are distributed.

Table 10.3 indicates that there is indeed considerable opposition in England to allowing Scottish MPs to vote on English legislation. No fewer than 60 per cent agreed and only 11 per cent disagreed when this question was last asked in 2003. But in this they are largely at one with opinion north of the border. Around half of people in Scotland also agree that their representatives at Westminster should not be meddling in England's affairs, a view which those in favour of independence are particularly likely to hold, while

Table 10.3. Attitudes towards the constitutional relationship between England and Scotland.

	Attitudes in England			Attitudes in Scotland		
	2000 %	2001 %	2003 %	2000 %	2001 %	2003 %
Scottish MPs should no longer be allowed to vote on English legislation						
Strongly agree	18	19	22	14	15	15
Agree	46	38	38	39	36	36
Neither agree nor disagree	19	18	18	17	21	21
Disagree	8	12	10	19	16	16
Strongly disagree	1	2	1	4	8	8
Now that Scotland has its own parliament, it should pay for its services out of taxes collected in Scotland						
Strongly agree	na	20	22	na	7	5
Agree	na	53	52	na	45	46
Neither agree nor disagree	na	12	12	na	18	16
Disagree	na	11	10	na	25	25
Strongly disagree	na	1	*	na	3	4
Compared with other parts of the UK, Scotland's share of government spending is . . .						
Much more than fair	8	9	9	2	2	3
Little more than fair	12	15	13	8	8	8
Pretty much fair	42	44	45	27	36	35
Little less than fair	10	8	8	35	32	35
Much less than fair	2	1	1	23	15	13
Whose economy benefits more from Scotland being part of the UK?						
England's	8	7	7	43	38	30
Scotland's	38	42	39	16	18	24
About equal	39	38	40	36	39	30

* less than 0.5%
na: not asked
Source: British and Scottish Social Attitudes Surveys.

only just under a quarter disagree. And attitudes towards this subject appear to be quite stable on both sides of the border. So while the so-called 'West Lothian question' may be a potential source of tension amongst political elites on both sides of the border, there is little evidence that resolving it by ending the right of Scots MPs to vote on English legislation would give rise to much tension between the two publics.

The higher levels of public expenditure per head enjoyed by Scotland have also exercised elites in recent years.[5] However, despite this concern, most people in England still do not believe that Scotland gets more than its fair share of public spending. Only 22 per cent take that view, little different from the position three years earlier. A plurality reckon that the current position is more or less fair. Indeed the apparent failure of this subject to generate much public interest south of the border, let alone actual concern, is underlined by the fact that a quarter say they simply do not know whether Scotland gets more than its fair share or not. Meanwhile, although Scots themselves are still inclined to believe that they do not get a fair share, this perception seems at least to be a little less common now than it was three years previously.

There does, though, exist a rather different source of potential tension between the two publics so far as the economic consequences of the current settlement are concerned. In both countries people are inclined to think that the other partner to the union benefits more from membership of the United Kingdom than their own country. But even so in both countries only a minority actually believe that their country is losing out. Moreover, there is no sign at present that this perception is growing; indeed if anything in Scotland at least the opposite is true. In short while there is some potential for resentment about the financial and economic relationship between the two countries, it appears at the moment at least to be relatively muted.

Even so, this does not stop people in England from contemplating a change in the way that public expenditure in Scotland is funded. Nearly three in four reckon that now Scotland has its own parliament, it should pay for its own services against taxes raised in Scotland. Nevertheless, on the surface at least this is not a source of tension between the two publics because around half of people in Scotland take the same view. However, there are two possible motives for supporting 'fiscal autonomy'. On the one hand it might be seen as a way of curbing public expenditure in Scotland and keeping the ambitions of the Scottish Parliament in check; on the other it could be regarded as a way of enhancing the parliament's power and status. Perhaps the former motive is predominant in England, the latter in Scotland. Of this there is some evidence. In England those who believe that Scotland gets more than its fair share of public spending are nine points more likely to support fiscal autonomy than those who think it gets less than its fair share. At the

[5] D. Bell and A. Christie, 'Finance—the Barnett Formula: nobody's child?', in A. Trench (ed.), *The State of the Nations 2001: The Second Year of Devolution in the United Kingdom* (Thorverton, 2001), pp. 135–51; I. McLean and A. McMillan, 'The distribution of public expenditure across the UK regions', *Fiscal Studies* 24 (2003), pp. 45–71.

same time, those who think that Scotland gets most economic benefit out of the union are fourteen points more likely to favour fiscal autonomy than those who think England gets most benefit. Between them these figures suggest that some of the support in England for greater fiscal powers for the Scottish Parliament reflects resentment at the current position. In Scotland, by contrast, it is those who think that England gets most benefit out of the union who are six points more likely to favour fiscal autonomy, while perceptions of the balance of public expenditure between the two countries do not make much difference to attitudes at all. So it would appear that north of the border fiscal autonomy is more likely to be regarded as a means of enhancing the parliament's power.[6]

The current asymmetric devolution settlement gives rise to a number of logical anomalies. But it appears that it largely matches an asymmetry of opinion on the two sides of the border. Both England and Scotland support Scottish devolution. Neither England nor Scotland sees much need for English devolution. Further, even where there are doubts about the current settlement, as appears to be the case with the West Lothian question and the fiscal powers of the Scottish Parliament, the two publics at least appear to be in agreement on the changes that should be made, albeit perhaps from somewhat different motives. In short, while the current constitutional settlement could be changed in a manner that might bring it more in line with public opinion, there is little evidence that it has driven the two countries apart.

Values and Attitudes

But even if they are largely in agreement about how they are governed, are the two countries in agreement too about the values that they wish to see upheld and the public policies that they support? After all, it is commonly argued that people in Scotland are more 'left-wing' than their counterparts south of the border and that it was a peculiarly Scottish resistance to the policies introduced by Mrs Thatcher's Conservative government that helped fuel the renewed demands for devolution in the 1980s and 1990s.[7] It is also often suggested that as a small country that is less enamoured of the appeal to British nationalism, Scotland adopts a less antagonistic attitude towards Europe. Meanwhile the furore that greeted the attempt in 2000 to remove the

[6] Further support for this conclusion comes from the fact that in Scotland support for fiscal autonomy is higher amongst those who say they would like the parliament to have more powers. As many as 63 per cent of those who believe that the Scottish Parliament should have more powers support fiscal autonomy compared with just 35 per cent of those who disagree.

[7] D. McCrone, 'Thatcherism in a Cold Climate', in Paterson (ed.), *A Diverse Assembly*, pp. 205–10.

legislation (known as Section 28 or Clause 2A) that barred local authorities (and thus the schools that they ran) from promoting homosexuality persuaded many people that Scotland is a distinctly socially conservative society. And even if there was little difference between Scottish and English attitudes before the advent of devolution, by creating a policy process in Scotland that is separate from that in England, devolution itself may have started to drive public opinion in the two countries apart.

On the other hand, we should remember that the social structures of the two countries are similar to each other. Thus 48 per cent of people in Scotland have at least one Higher or its equivalent, just as 44 per cent of people in England have acquired at least one A level pass. Scotland is only slightly less middle-class than England with 32 per cent employed as professionals or managers compared with 36 per cent in England. Meanwhile, on the most recent reading, exactly the same proportion, 12 per cent, claim to attend a religious service once a week while in both countries the largest religious community is Protestant (albeit different branches thereof). In so far as values are the product of social structure there is little reason at all to believe that these two societies should be very far apart.

Table 10.4 looks at some indicators of left–right values that have been carried regularly in recent years on both the British and the Scottish Social Attitudes Surveys. In each case the table compares the proportion giving a left-wing response in Scotland with the equivalent proportion in England. The first two items in the table are taken from scales that are designed to measure where people stand along a socialism versus *laissez-faire* dimension.[8] The third is an item about attitudes towards unemployment benefit which previous research has indicated discriminates particularly well between Conservative and Labour supporters.[9] Meanwhile, the final two items tap attitudes towards the welfare state including what is thought to be the appropriate balance between taxation and spending.

Together this set of items provides some support for the claim that Scotland is a more left-wing or social democratic society than England.[10] Since 1999 people in Scotland have been a little more likely to say that there

[8] G. Evans, A. Heath, and M. Lalljee, 'Measuring left–right and libertarian–authoritarian values in the British electorate', *British Journal of Sociology* 47 (1996), pp. 93–112; A. Heath, G. Evans, and J. Martin, 'The measurement of core beliefs and values: the development of balanced socialist/laissez faire and libertarian/authoritarian scales', *British Journal of Political Science* 24 (1994), pp. 115–31.

[9] J. Curtice and S. Fisher, 'The power to persuade: a tale of two Prime Ministers', in A. Park, J. Curtice, K. Thomson, L. Jarvis, and C. Bromley (eds), *British Social Attitudes: The 20th Report. Continuity and Change over Two Decades* (London, 2003), pp. 233–53.

[10] For a similar analysis of the evidence prior to 1999 see, A. Brown, D. McCrone, L. Paterson, and P. Surridge, *The Scottish Electorate: The 1997 Election and Beyond* (Basingstoke, 1999).

Table 10.4. Indicators of left–right values in England and Scotland.

Agree that . . .		1999 %	2000 %	2001 %	2002 %	2003 %
There is one law for the rich and one for the poor						
	Scotland	66	67	68	61	57
	England	61	64	56	61	57
Ordinary working people do not get their fair share of the nation's wealth						
	Scotland	58*	71	61*	64	54*
	England	60	61	58	61	60
Benefits for unemployed people are too low and cause hardship						
	Scotland	36	43	41	41	45
	England	32	40	34	28	36
Increase taxes and spend more on health, education and social benefits						
	Scotland	55	54	63	60	58
	England	58	51	60	61	51
Disagree that . . .						
Large numbers of people these days falsely claim benefits						
	Scotland	79	83	79	na	85
	England	80	79	79	na	79

* shows proportion disagreeing with statement that 'Ordinary working people do get their fair share of the nation's wealth.'
na: not asked
Source: British and Scottish Social Attitudes Surveys.

is one law for the rich and one for the poor, to agree that unemployment benefits are too low, and to favour more spending on health, education, and social benefits. In the one instance where Scotland appears to be notably less left-wing than England—in 2003 on the question of whether ordinary people get their fair share of the nation's wealth—the gap could well be accounted for by a difference in the way that the question was administered in the two countries. (Respondents in Scotland were asked whether they agreed or disagreed that ordinary people do get their fair share of the nation's wealth, whereas those in England were asked whether they agreed or disagreed that they did not do so.)

But, equally, the differences in the pattern of responses in the two countries are no more than 'little'. If Scotland is to be characterised as a predominantly social democratic country, then England qualifies for that description as well. Meanwhile there is no consistent evidence that such difference of perspective as exists in the two countries has become any wider. True, there are signs that the gap in attitudes towards unemployment benefit has widened somewhat, but at the same time such difference as there ever was in response to the question about one law for the rich and one for the poor appears to have disappeared. Meanwhile, on the remaining items there is no more than trendless fluctuation. In short, there is little evidence here that Scotland and England are being driven apart.

Our second suggestion about possible differences between England and Scotland was that the latter has a more pro-European attitude. This does indeed prove to be the case. In 2003 27 per cent of people in Scotland said that they believed that Britain's long-term policy should be to increase the EU's powers or even to work for the formation of a single European government, whereas only 17 per cent of people in England took that view. But even so the difference is no more than a relative one. The predominant mood in Scotland is still one of scepticism towards the EU, much as it is in England. Equally there has been no significant increase in the gap between Scotland and England, as there was already an eight point difference in 1999.

Of the final claim—that Scotland is a more socially conservative society—there is, however, no evidence at all. In Table 10.5 we show the responses given on both sides of the border to a set of items designed to measure where people stand on a libertarian–authoritarian dimension, that is whether people are inclined to take a liberal stance on social issues, inclining to the view that morality is an individual choice, or whether they prefer to adopt a more authoritarian perspective that emphasises the need for society as a whole to uphold moral values.[11] In each case the table shows the proportion backing the authoritarian view. There are few differences between the answers given by people in Scotland and those in England.[12] So while the fact that most of the items secure majority support suggests that Scotland is indeed a socially conservative society, its claim to that title is no greater than England's. Moreover, people in the two countries have given largely the same answers to these questions on each and every occasion that they have been asked since 2000.

This apparent lack of difference in attitudes can even be found on subjects where the Scottish Executive and Parliament have made a high-profile decision to adopt a different policy from that being pursued by the UK government in England. As Table 10.6 shows, even when the Scottish Executive was abolishing 'up-front' tuition fees north of the border in

[11] Evans, Heath, and Lalljee, 'Measuring left–right and libertarian–authoritarian values'; Heath, Evans, and Martin, 'The measurement of core beliefs and values'.
[12] See also Brown et al., *The Scottish Electorate*, pp. 78–85.

Table 10.5. Indicators of Liberal–Authoritarian Values in England and Scotland.

Agree that . . .	Scotland %	England %	Gap %
Young people today don't have enough respect for traditional British values	60	68	−8
People who break the law should be given stiffer sentences	79	79	0
For some crimes, the death penalty is the most appropriate sentence	53	58	−5
Schools should teach children to obey authority	80	83	−3
The law should always be obeyed, even if a particular law is wrong	44	40	+4
Censorship of films and magazines is necessary to uphold moral standards	64	65	−1

Source: British and Scottish Social Attitudes Surveys 2003.

Table 10.6. Policy attitudes in England and Scotland.

Agree that . . .	1999 %	2000 %	2001 %	2002 %	2003 %
No students or their families should pay towards their tuition costs while they are studying					
Scotland	na	38	31	na	29
England	na	30	33	na	28
Government should mainly be responsible for paying for the care needs of elderly people living in residential and nursing homes					
Scotland	86	na	88	na	88
England	80	na	86	na	84
All children should go to the same kind of secondary school, no matter how well or badly they do at primary school					
Scotland	63	na	63	na	65
England	49	na	51	na	48

na: not asked
Source: British and Scottish Social Attitudes Surveys.

2000, only 38 per cent of people in Scotland said that no students should have to pay fees while they were studying, a figure that was just eight points higher than in England. Meanwhile, even that gap now seems to have disappeared. In contrast the Scottish Executive's decision to pay for the personal care costs of older people does appear to have been in tune with public opinion, at least as evidenced by near universal support for the argument that the government should be mainly responsible for paying for the care needs of people in nursing and residential homes. However, support for that proposition is almost as strong in England.

There is, though, one clear exception to this picture of a similarity of attitudes in the two countries. Nearly two-thirds of people in Scotland support the principle of comprehensive secondary education, whereas in England no more than half do so. It would appear that in being reluctant to embrace such UK policy initiatives as 'specialist schools' and 'city academies' the Scottish Executive has reflected a distinctive public mood in Scotland. But even here there is no evidence that the difference of view has become any greater since the advent of devolution.

Scotland and England appear then for the most part to share the same values and similar policy preferences. Scotland is at most a little more left-wing or social democratic, while it is just somewhat more pro-European. At the same time there is no sign that it is a more socially conservative society or that such differences of view as do exist between Scotland and England have widened consistently since 1999, including on subjects where the Scottish Executive has adopted a distinctively different policy from that being pursued in England. So far as values and attitudes are concerned, there is then no sign at all that the two countries are being driven apart.

Identities and Symbols

So far we have demonstrated that people in Scotland and England have largely similar views about the structure of the United Kingdom and the values and attitudes that they believe should be upheld by government and society. But it does not necessarily follow that they also share the same emotions. They may still exhibit an affective attachment to different identities and symbols. And they could even regard those different symbols and identities as being in conflict with each other. On the other hand, perhaps people in the two countries adhere to a common set of identities and symbols, identities and symbols that are associated with the British state and which provide an emotional glue that helps keep the two countries together.

One such symbol that might help bring them together is the Union Jack. This flag incorporates the symbols of the constituent nations of the union and in so doing implicitly suggests that people may identify with the British state while also maintaining an adherence to the English or Scottish nation. In Table 10.7 we show what people in England and Scotland said in 2001 and 2003 when they were asked how they felt when they saw the Union Jack. At the same time it also shows how they said they felt when they saw their own national flag, that is the St George's Cross and the Saltire respectively.

Table 10.7. Feelings towards flags in Scotland and England.

	Scotland			
	Union Jack		Saltire / St George's Cross	
	2001 %	2003 %	2001 %	2003 %
Very proud	11	14	40	48
A bit proud	20	22	31	28
Not much either way	60	55	28	22
A bit hostile	5	4	1	*
Very hostile	2	3	*	*
	England			
Very proud	33	34	21	28
A bit proud	26	27	19	19
Not much either way	37	36	56	49
A bit hostile	2	2	2	2
Very hostile	1	1	1	1

* less than 0.5%

Source: British and Scottish Social Attitudes Surveys.

People living in England are markedly more likely to say they feel proud when they see the Union Jack than are those in Scotland. In 2003 as many as 61 per cent of people in England said that they felt proud, compared with just 36 per cent who did so in Scotland. In contrast, people in Scotland are markedly more likely to feel proud of the Saltire than people in England do of the St George's Cross. As a result, those living in Scotland are more likely to feel proud when they see the Saltire than they are when they see the Union Jack, whereas in England the Union Jack is more likely to be an object of pride. Meanwhile there are signs too in both countries that pride in the national flag has increased.

So the glue that binds the union does not appear to be very strong here. In particular, people living in Scotland exhibit a relatively weak affective attachment to the Union Jack. But at the same time we should note that few people in Scotland say that they feel hostile towards this flag. This symbol of the British state is not so much a source of hostility as indifference. Well over half say they do not feel much either way about the Union Jack.

The emotional glue of the union looks even weaker when people are asked to say which of a range of possible national identities best describes them (see Table 10.8). If forced to choose, only one in five people in Scotland now say they are British, only just over half the proportion who did so in 1979. Meanwhile even in England only half, if that, now say they are British, whereas as recently as ten years ago nearly two-thirds chose that option. It

Table 10.8. Trends in forced choice national identity.

	1974 %	1979 %	1992 %	1997 %	1999 %	2000 %	2001 %	2002 %	2003 %
In England									
English	na	na	31	34	44	41	43	37	38
British	na	na	63	59	44	47	44	51	48
In Scotland									
Scottish	65	56	72	72	77	80	77	75	72
British	31	38	25	20	17	13	16	18	20

na: not asked

Source: Scottish Election Studies 1974–97; British Election Studies 1992–7; Scottish Social Attitudes Surveys 1999–2002; British Social Attitudes Surveys 1999–2002.

seems as though feeling British is no longer a majority choice on either side of the border.

Yet two words of caution are in order. First, the decline in Britishness that apparently occurred in England in the immediate wake of Scottish and Welsh devolution has, it seems, come to a halt. Equally, what had appeared to be an inexorable decline in adherence to Britishness in Scotland appears not only to have stopped but even to have been reversed to some degree. Second, and perhaps more importantly, for many people identities are not exclusive. In both countries consistently around two in five people say they are British and English/Scottish. As a result, as Table 10.9 shows, around seven in ten people in England and at least half in Scotland acknowledge some adherence to Britishness. While Britishness may not be many people's primary bond, particularly in Scotland, it still coexists alongside feeling English or Scottish, and

Table 10.9. Trends in free choice national identity.

	1997 %	1999 %	2000 %	2001 %	2002 %	2003 %
In England						
British	77	71	67	67	73	70
English	55	65	59	63	57	59
In Scotland						
British	52	47	52	50	52	58
Scottish	82	84	87	86	87	84

Source: British and Scottish Election Studies 1997; British and Scottish Social Attitudes Surveys 1999–2002.

as a result is an identity that many people on both sides of the border share in common.

Much the same point is evident if we look at an alternative way of asking about national identity that explicitly acknowledges the possible existence of a dual national identity. Here respondents are asked to say whether they feel exclusively English/Scottish or British, or whether they feel some mixture of both. As Table 10.10 shows, around three-quarters of people in England acknowledge that they are British to some degree, while even in Scotland as many as three in five do so. It is true that this measure also shows that the proportion who feel exclusively Scottish or exclusively English has risen since the advent of devolution, while in Scotland more than half of those who say they are to some degree British also say they are more Scottish than they are British. So here too the pattern of responses suggests that the bonds of Britishness are neither predominant nor as strong as they once were, but at the same time they have evidently still far from disappeared.

People in Scotland do then have a rather different set of identities from their counterparts in England. In particular, both feeling British and adherence to symbols of British identity are weaker north of the border. And it is a difference that devolution has done little to narrow; indeed, initially at least devolution may have made people in England more aware of their Englishness. But Britishness is far from dead. Even in Scotland it is a form of identity that many are prepared to acknowledge and one that only a minority reject with hostility. The identities and symbols of the British state may no

Table 10.10. Trends in Moreno national identity.

	England					
	1992 %	1997 %	1999 %	2000 %	2001 %	2003 %
English not British	na	7	17	19	17	17
More English than British	na	17	15	14	13	19
Equally English and British	na	45	37	34	42	31
More British than English	na	14	11	14	9	13
British not English	na	9	14	12	11	10
	Scotland					
Scottish not British	19	23	32	37	36	31
More Scottish than British	40	38	35	31	30	34
Equally Scottish and British	33	27	22	21	24	22
More British than Scottish	3	4	3	3	3	4
British not Scottish	3	4	4	4	3	4

na: not asked

Source: Scottish Election Study 1992; British and Scottish Election Studies 1997; British and Scottish Social Attitudes Surveys.

longer always be capable of bringing the two countries together, but they certainly do not seem to be pushing them apart.

Conclusion

Devolution has so far not helped to drive England and Scotland apart from each other. They share a common commitment to the asymmetric devolution settlement. They appear to expect government to uphold similar values and attitudes. All they lack is a strong common commitment to a shared set of identities and symbols, but even here they appear to have enough in common for them to be capable of sharing the same multinational state. Little wonder then that whatever the potential strains and fissures created by the current devolution settlement, there is, as Table 10.11 shows, relatively little sense on either side of the border that there is much conflict between those living in the two nations. Even in Scotland fewer than two in five say that there is serious conflict between the Scots and the English—a figure that falls to just one in four when respondents are asked to set sporting rivalries aside!—while in England only one in five take that view.

Further, even if some of the potential tensions thrown up by the devolution settlement were to come to the fore, they appear capable of amicable resolution at least so far as the two publics are concerned. Denying Scots MPs the right to vote on English legislation or requiring the Scottish Parliament to raise more of what it spends might well be applauded on both sides of the border. Meanwhile there seems to be little prospect that the publics of Scotland and England would wish to try and insist on diametrically different public policies.

Yet we should bear in mind those differences of identity and symbolism. At present the fact that they are differences rather than points of antagonism renders them benign so far as Anglo-Scottish relations are concerned. Indeed without some such differences of identity and symbolism it could hardly be

Table 10.11. Perceptions of conflict between the Scots and the English.

Conflict between the Scots and the English is . . .	England 2000 %	Scotland 2000 %	Scotland 2003* %
Very serious	4	10	5
Fairly serious	16	28	20
Not very serious	54	53	66
There is no conflict	21	9	8

* In 2003 respondents were invited to 'leave aside what might happen in sports like football'.
Source: British and Scottish Social Attitudes Surveys.

said that England and Scotland were two different nations at all. Still they are rallying calls that political elites could potentially attempt to use in, say, some future serious dispute between governments of very different political colour in London and Edinburgh, a dispute that might perhaps be exacerbated by a tougher financial and economic climate than devolution has enjoyed so far. Even so at present there seems no reason to believe that such calls would necessarily be heeded to the extent that the two countries would want to part. After all, most marriages have to endure at least the occasional row.

11

National Identities and Twentieth-Century Scottish Migrants in England

ANGELA McCARTHY

Introduction

ALTHOUGH DEVOLUTION WITHIN THE UK HAS REAWAKENED ACADEMIC CURIOSITY in national and regional identities, scholars of Scotland have been mainly concerned with exploring Scottishness and its coexistence with Britishness *within* Scotland.[1] Analyses of Scottish national identities among migrants, meanwhile, have focused largely on the experience of Highlanders and those other Scots who settled in Canada.[2]

Such explorations have also predominantly been confined to the pre-twentieth-century period.[3] This is somewhat surprising given that throughout the twentieth century approximately two million people left Scotland, a figure paralleling estimates of Scottish migration in the preceding century.

---

[1] See, for instance, D. Broun, R. J. Finlay, and M. Lynch (eds), *Image and Identity: The Making and Re-making of Scotland Through the Ages* (Edinburgh, 1998); T. Devine and P. Logue (eds), *Being Scottish: Personal Reflections on Scottish Identity Today* (Edinburgh, 2002).

[2] M. Harper, *Adventurers and Exiles: The Great Scottish Exodus* (London, 2003).

[3] The major exception is M. Harper, *Emigration from Scotland Between the Wars: Opportunity or Exile?* (Manchester, 1998). See also I. Lindsay, 'Migration and motivation: a twentieth-century perspective', in T. M. Devine (ed.), *Scottish Emigration and Scottish Society* (Edinburgh, 1992), pp. 154–74 and A. McCarthy, 'Personal accounts of leaving Scotland, 1921–1954', *The Scottish Historical Review* 83 (Oct. 2004), pp. 196–215. Broad overviews of Scottish society have also consistently failed to address the significance of twentieth-century emigration from Scotland. An edited collection of articles on Scotland in the twentieth century, for instance, excludes migration as a central defining topic for investigation, while analysis of mobility in T. M. Devine's sweeping synthesis of Scottish history since 1700 is largely confined to the nineteenth-century outflow of Scots. See T. M. Devine and R. J. Finlay (eds), *Scotland in the Twentieth Century* (Edinburgh, 1996); T. M. Devine, *The Scottish Nation, 1700–2000* (London, 1999). In addition, the most recent survey of Scotland in the twentieth century only briefly touches on migration in Scottish society. See R. J. Finlay, *Modern Scotland, 1914–2000* (London, 2004).

Proceedings of the British Academy **128**, 171–182. © The British Academy 2005.

Table 11.1. Scottish-born population in England and Wales, 1921–71.

	Numbers	% of total England and Wales population
1921	333,517	0.9
1931	366,486	0.9
1951	580,806	1.3
1961	653,626	1.4
1971	775,495	1.6

Source: Calculated from the Census of Population, England and Wales, 1921–1971. I am grateful to Enda Delaney for these figures.

Although statistics for Scottish mobility are notoriously unreliable, an estimated 800,000 departed in the period prior to 1920 with almost half a million leaving during the inter-war years.[4] At least another half a million Scots left in the 1950s and 1960s.[5]

Generally, these Scots were as likely to settle overseas as in other parts of the UK. But increasing numbers of Scots moved to other parts of the UK from the 1920s onwards, until by the 1950s and 1960s a balance was struck between those settling elsewhere in the UK and overseas, a pattern which was a feature of their mobility in certain periods of the nineteenth century.[6] Between 1841 and 1931, for instance, it is estimated that 748,577 Scots moved elsewhere in the UK.[7]

Despite this movement, there has been little study of the historical migration of Scots to England. Such negligence of Scottish migration in the twentieth century is surprising for, as Table 11.1 shows, there were considerable numbers of Scottish migrants in England, even though they formed only a small percentage of the total population.

What factors, then, account for the scholarly disregard of Scottish settlement in England? In part, Scottish migrants in England were less associated with issues such as crime and politics which have attracted the interest of historians of other migrant groups. Additionally, unlike the Irish and several other ethnicities entering England, the Scots were predominantly Protestant and not viewed as 'alien'. Their dual Scottish and British identities meant too that they were rarely conceived of as an exotic 'other'. That Scottish movement to England is conceptualised as internal migration, together with a

---

[4] M. Flinn, *Scottish Population History from the Seventeenth Century to the 1930s* (Cambridge, 1977), Table 6.1.1, p. 441.

[5] M. Anderson, 'Population and family life', in T. Dickson and J. H. Treble (eds), *People and Society in Scotland*, III: *1914–1990* (Edinburgh, 1992), pp. 12–47, at p. 14.

[6] Flinn, *Scottish Population History*, p. 442; Anderson, 'Population and Family life', 14; T. M. Devine, 'The paradox of Scottish emigration', in Devine (ed.), *Scottish Emigration and Scottish Society*, pp. 1–15, at pp. 11–12.

[7] Flinn, *Scottish Population History*, Table 6.1.2, p. 442.

greater propensity for return migration compared with overseas flows, has perhaps also led to its being viewed as less exciting and vigorous compared with the relocation of Scots abroad.

In light of this manifest neglect, this chapter attempts to provide a preliminary examination of the twentieth-century Scottish migrant experience within England, by investigating notions of national identity as articulated by individual migrants. The utilisation of oral testimony enables the experience of migration to be viewed from the perspective of the participants, thereby providing a more nuanced interpretation of Scottish national identities, rather than conveying a homogeneous portrait of collective group identity. Oral sources also allow penetrating analysis of themes that are best explored through individual stories. Furthermore, the longitudinal nature of oral testimony gives it 'a crucial competitive edge', as Eric Richards has argued, over the contemporary document.[8] By the mapping of individual accounts over time the consequences of past events can be examined. For instance, a Scot moving to England in the 1920s would live through a rapidly changing relationship between the two countries. Crucially, oral testimony enables exploration of aspects of the migration experience that would otherwise be lost to scholars. Few historians, however, have drawn upon such rich and abundant material in the Scottish migrant context.[9]

The six interviews used here for the exploration of Scottish identity were sourced from the National Sound Archive at the British Library. All the interviews were part of the Millennium Memory Bank, a project that collected the testimonies of some 6,000 people reflecting on themselves and their communities during the twentieth century. The interviews were structured under sixteen main themes, with the theme relating to 'who we are' providing the impetus for discussion of identity.[10] That the majority of the interviews utilised were conducted more than thirty years after the interviewees' migration suggests that reflections of twentieth-century Scottish migrants on their national identities occasionally indicate current rather than historical manifestations of their identity. Two aspects of their testimonies, however, can be used to provide historical insight into their Scottishness: personal ethnic networks and the perceived differences between origin and destination. While the former enabled the maintenance of aspects of their identity, the latter

---

[8] E. Richards, 'Hearing voices: an introduction', in A. J. Hammerton and E. Richards (eds), *Speaking to Immigrants: Oral Testimony and the History of Australian Migration* (Canberra, 2002), pp. 1–19, at p. 8.

[9] One exception is E. Buettner, 'Haggis in the Raj: private and public celebrations of Scottishness in late imperial India', *The Scottish Historical Review* 81 (Oct. 2002), pp. 212–39.

[10] These themes were: where we live; house and home; living together; who we are; belonging; crime and the law; growing up; getting older; technology; eating and drinking; money; playtime; going places; life and death; beliefs and fears; what's next.

reveals a number of customs that Scottish newcomers perceived as distinguishing them from their English neighbours.

How, though, should Scottishness be defined? Clearly the term has multiple meanings, evoking various facets for different people. As a concept, identity is not only a sense of what is intrinsically felt, but is shaped by the wider environment. A broader definition of Scottish identity, however, would embrace those of Scottish descent and consider how Scottishness transferred itself across generations.

For the purposes of this discussion, however, expressions of identity are confined to Scottish-born migrants. In exploring what Scottish identities meant to these migrants, it is mainly concerned with personal manifestations of Scottishness. This emphasis is adopted because the interviews show that migrant Scots in twentieth-century England primarily exhibited a social and mental version of Scottishness rather than the institutional Scottish identity, influenced by church and school, that scholars stress operated in the nineteenth century. This fashioning of an intimate, *internal* sense of Scottishness is discernible in their language, their interaction with other Scots, and their possession of allegedly distinct characteristics. By contrast, their fellow expatriates who settled abroad were more inclined to exhibit an *external* form of Scottishness, particularly in relation to their involvement in Scottish societies. What emblems of expatriate ethnic identities, then, did Scottish migrants exhibit in England?

Expressions of Identities

In 1950, following the accidental death of her brother, killed by a lorry, the infant Ann Dean moved with her parents to Corby from Lanark. Reflecting on the move almost fifty years later, Ann explained the decision as follows:

> I think my mum had a nervous breakdown and my father felt that the only way to move on was to move out of the area and I guess really at that time the only thing that was offering a house with employment was Corby in the steelworks where my father was furnaceman so he came down first. We had relatives down here and we took residence up in 52 Rowlett Road and they never moved.

While the immediate impetus, according to Ann, was her brother's tragic death, other factors were essential in the move from Lanark and the selection of Corby: the opportunity for her father to obtain employment and lodging; and the presence in the town of family connections. Presumably Corby's robust Scots community and ongoing links with family and friends in Scotland played a vital role in the nurturing of Ann's identity as Scottish, which she emphasised almost fifty years later. 'I'm Scottish. I'm definitely

Scottish', Ann exclaimed. She further elucidated on the components of this sustained connection: 'Being Scottish . . . a lot of my ties are up there. My grandma. My brother's obviously buried up there. All my grandparents are buried up there. We go back every year . . . just to keep ties with cousins.'[11] Corby was also a major place of settlement for Irish Protestants in the 1940s and 1950s. The presence in Corby, then, of substantial numbers of other ethnic groups may have further fostered this sense of being Scottish for Ann Dean.

Other migrants also drew upon networks of friends in moving south of the border, such connections often proving vital in securing access to employment. As Joyce Savage, from Kilwinning, described her move to England: 'I had a friend working for a similar company who were based in Harpenden in Hertfordshire and she recommended it to me and so I thought well I mean I have no ties, nothing, so I just moved and that was it.'[12]

Not all Scots in England, though, had such initial personal networks to facilitate their settlement. Jean Taylor Balls from Balfron, Stirlingshire, for instance, moved to Suffolk where she had no family or friends settled. Nevertheless, it did not take long before Jean was interacting with other Scots:

> I came against a lot of Scots obviously when I first came south. A lot of them came and spoke to me. Again family histories or someone knows someone else and word soon gets round that there's someone new in the locality who's come from Scotland, who's got a relative, who's connected to so and so back in Scotland so you've obviously got a meeting point to begin with and I was welcomed in many Scottish families.[13]

These accounts represent a social Scottishness and show that personal testimony can provide a different perspective on how identities are constructed. Another migrant interviewed more than fifty years after her initial migration from Sutherland was Catherine Marshall. Aged in her mid-twenties, Catherine relocated to Shropshire in 1945. Unlike Ann Dean, however, Catherine emphasised her regional rather than national identity: 'I'm a Gael, Highlander. I don't know that probably the average English person sees any difference between that. I don't suppose there is much. But, but I'm aware

[11] Interview with Ann Dean by BBC Radio Northampton, recorded 15 December 1999, Millennium Memory Bank, British Library Sound Archive (BLSA), C900/12094 C1, copyright BBC.

[12] Interview with Joyce Savage by Eva Simmons, recorded 14 January 1999, Millennium Memory Bank, BLSA, C900/01074, copyright BBC.

[13] Interview with Jean Taylor Balls by Ivan Howlett, recorded 25 February 1999, Millennium Memory Bank, BLSA, C900/17074, copyright BBC.

of the Gaelic culture which makes you a Gael I suppose.'[14] For Catherine Marshall, then, her regional rather than national identity took priority.

While Ann Dean and Catherine Marshall did not reflect on what their national or regional identities exemplified, Joe Hendry, a migrant from Glasgow to Cumbria, eloquently described his emotional awareness of what constituted being Scottish: 'It's a sense of your time and your place and your identity, a sense of belonging and it's not just, it's what and who you belong to. It's not just what you feel within yourself you are although that's part of it.' He continued vibrantly, extending his sense of identity from being Scottish to encompassing stereotypical features romantically attributed to the Celtic races: 'It's a sense of being a Celt . . . a temperamental thing . . . quite fiery sometimes . . . sense of fun, sense of laughter, sense of gaiety, singing, good company, what they call the craic . . . the social side of things, being with people.' In conclusion Joe stated, 'Most Scottish people like most Celtic people are very, very sociable, outward going, slightly extrovert, maybe sometimes more than slightly extrovert.'[15] Joe's reflections, made in 1999, are reminiscent of the 1940s emphasis on the Celtic character of Scottish culture, though Joe demonstrates a social and internal rather than physical and exterior representation of Scottishness.[16]

Despite the stereotype of the typical Celt evident in Joe Hendry's reflection, other Scots in England likewise identified some characteristics as more endemic to Scotland than England, thus reaffirming a sense of Scottishness. Vibrant community ties and good humour were two vital and distinctive components specified by Joyce Savage of Kilwinning as embodying a Scottish identity:

> I think the sense of humour in Scotland is second to none. There's a huge difference which, of course, I wouldn't be able to think of an example of, of the sense of humour. And I think there's more of a sense of community in Scotland. People are friendlier, more willing to help you whereas down here they're quite insular and maybe people have come from different areas to here for work and so they keep themselves to themselves more here.[17]

Despite this comment, Joyce Savage maintained that she had an amicable relationship with her English neighbours. She felt, however, that an English migrant in Scotland would encounter more difficulties attempting to integrate due to culturally inherited antipathies towards England:

---

[14] Interview with Catherine Marshall by Chris Eldon Lee, recorded 15 January 1999, Millennium Memory Bank, BLSA, C900/15065 C1, copyright BBC.

[15] Interview with Joe Hendry by John Watson, recorded 3 February 1999, Millennium Memory Bank, BLSA, C900/02594 C1, copyright BBC.

[16] R. Weight, *Patriots: National Identity in Britain 1940–2000* (London, 2002), p. 128.

[17] Interview with Joyce Savage.

If the reverse were true and someone had come up to Scotland they would be, they would feel left out, definitely, but I haven't felt that at all. People have been nothing but nice to me and, you know, taken me on my own merits. They either like you or don't like you as a person and nothing to do with the fact that you're Scottish. It's definitely a one way thing the Scottish hating the English 'coz the English couldn't really give two hoots about the Scottish. You know they don't like them or hate them or worry about them at all. They're just other people. In Scotland it's quite inbred that you don't like the English. You're sort of brought up not through anything anyone says but that's just part of the whole culture.[18]

By contrast, Doug Black, a native of Glamis Castle who went to England in 1964, indicated that the English were concerned about the relationship with Scotland:

One of the things that gets me about being a Scotsman living in England, the English are absolutely determined that we can't abide the English. Now they actually claim that when England are playing another team at football that we in Scotland will support the other team against England and it doesn't matter how much I tell them that that is complete nonsense they still insist that that is the fact.[19]

Clearly Joyce's and Doug's reflections are not representative of the relations between English and Scots. Their accounts do, however, show the conflicting assumptions surrounding such contact. Possibly Joyce's comment is a result of a more social interaction with English friends while Doug's is a verdict arising from male sparring during international sporting fixtures, though such rivalry existed throughout the twentieth century. Such comments also seemingly reflect contemporary cultural attitudes rather than being an expression of experiences encountered after their initial arrival in England. In order to ascertain to what extent a sense of Scottish identity existed at the time of migration, other factors need to be examined. In this respect, the differences between Scotland and England, as noted by Scots, are perhaps the most useful insight.

For Jean Taylor Balls the most striking change she recollected, among many differences between Stirling and Suffolk, were the cuts of meat. As she described this seemingly mundane contrast:

Well obviously there are different cuts of the Scottish beef, the different cuts of Scottish lamb. Lamb was the main problem. There was different parts that I had been used to cooking in Scotland at home with my mother and I remember once going to a local butcher and asking for a shank of lamb and he looked at me in total amazement: 'I don't know what you're talking about.' And I had

---

[18] Ibid.

[19] Interview with Doug Black by Lucy Ashwell, recorded 7 April 1999, Millennium Memory Bank, BLSA, C900/07169 C1, copyright BBC.

to learn then that the actual lamb was cut differently and you either had a whole leg or a half leg and that was it.[20]

Intriguingly, Scots migrants primarily recalled ordinary, day-to-day contrasts in customs between Scotland and England. Joyce Savage, for instance, remembered having to purchase alcohol from a local off-licence in Glasgow through a metal grill and hatch. The climate also proved a considerable contrast. Joyce recollected that during winters in Glasgow 'we used to have to defrost all the pipes with a hairdryer in the morning to be able to run the water to get the kettle boiled. And you know it was freezing. It was minus 18 and ice on the inside of the windows.' These memories prompted Joyce in bemusement to contrast this experience with the weather she encountered in England where her neighbours 'used to moan about the summer and things. Used to say "Oh God we've had an awful summer this year", and I used to think, "That was an awful summer? My god, I've never had such a good summer in my life." Or they'd complain that they'd had two cold days in a row and you'd think god you don't know you're living, you just don't know.' Apart from such mundane contrasts, Joyce also reflected on the grim character of Glasgow:

> Life in Glasgow where, you know, if you went into an off-sales to buy you know a bottle of wine to take out for the evening like down here the, the shelves are all open to you and you can walk along and select your bottle of wine from the shelf but in, well, in the particular area of Glasgow where I was then there was a grill, there was a counter and a grill, a metal grill, and a hatch and you told the man through the hatch what bottle of wine you wanted and he brought it to the grill and showed you and if you wanted it you handed him the money and then he handed you the bottle of wine . . . All the shops had metal shutters and graffiti and litter. I mean, not all of Glasgow's like that, just the bit that I was living in at the time but it's definitely, you know, rough.

Her new locality, by contrast, was 'a much more gentle atmosphere'.[21]

By contrast, other migrants expressed nostalgia for the Scottish landscape. After relocating to Shifnal in 1945, Catherine Marshall reflected, 'Looking back on it, it took me a long time to live in what is a relatively flat landscape. I did miss the mountains and I missed the waters, the sea lochs.'[22] Encountering such contrasts, positive and negative, in England served to remind Scots of their differing identity. Intriguingly, though, such contrasts were not so overtly disparaging as the criticism of London and British life

[20] Interview with Jean Taylor Balls.
[21] Interview with Joyce Savage.
[22] Interview with Catherine Marshall.

levelled by Australian women which served to reinforce their sense of national identity.[23]

One of the ways in which Scottish identities could be reinforced and re-invented arose from visits home. This return flow also documents the ongoing sense of being Scottish for migrants in England. Doug Black, who was born near Glamis Castle in the north of Scotland in 1941, went to England in 1964. His testimony, however, reveals that despite the short-distance nature of his mobility, returning home was not always a ready option: 'I used to claim that it was being easier for me to emigrate to Australia than find a train fare to go home because you could emigrate to Australia for a tenner in 'em days.' According to Doug, 'to be able to go home for a few days meant to me leading the life of a monk for a month or more.'[24]

Return visits, while reinforcing their personal sense of Scottishness, also demonstrated to migrants that family and friends did not always view them as Scots. This is particularly evident in relation to language and accent, one of the major means by which migrants from Scotland identified themselves as Scottish, and were identified by others as Scottish. One migrant who reflected at length on the issue of the Scottish accent was Jean Taylor Balls. Jean moved from Stirlingshire to Suffolk and recalled:

> At first, obviously, I was different and of course I felt strange to begin with. I remember being struck very forcibly. I went back to a family wedding in Scotland only six months after I was married and a very dear friend said to me, 'Oh you're English', and I said, 'Pardon', and he said, 'You've lost your Scottish accent.' And, to be honest, I was horrified because down in Suffolk everyone said, 'Oh you're Scottish, where do you come from?' . . . I was appalled to think that this person thought I had changed my accent. Having said that I remember meeting a friend who lived in a local village who'd come down to work in London. She came back with a Cockney accent after six months and of course I've got memories of that and it upset me to think that he thought I sounded English. But of course over the years, yes, I've been told my accent has changed. It doesn't take many minutes back in with my family in Scotland to find it's as broad as ever. My husband's often remarked on that.[25]

For Jean Taylor Balls her accent was not a means of exclusion. Rather, she saw it as providing her with the opportunity to make very amicable friendships. Her extract, however, reveals the ways in which Scottish identities could be reinforced and confirmed by others. Doug Black from Glamis Castle who went to England in 1964 in his early twenties and settled in Yorkshire likewise emphasised the importance of language in being accepted

[23] A. Woollacott, *To Try Her Fortune in London: Australian Women, Colonialism, and Modernity* (Oxford, 2001), p. 163.
[24] Interview with Doug Black.
[25] Interview with Jean Taylor Balls.

in England: 'Collective view in Yorkshire is that they see themselves far more closely associated with other communities further north than they do with communities further south so in some ways they probably accept me more than they would if I was—say had a Cockney accent.'[26]

Accents also serve to show the way in which regional identities distinguished Scots from each other. Joe Hendry, for instance, professed, 'I'm very comfortable with the accent I have. Part of the problem with the Glasgow accent it's a very fast tongue. Therefore as you move further south you've got to remember to modulate your vowels a little and speak more slowly.' He further elucidated upon the linguistic variance of the Glaswegian tongue: 'I find that the Scots language and so much that goes with that which when I was a child at school was referred to as slang and which I discovered later wasn't slang it was the Scottish Glasgow dialect, wonderful words like dreich.'[27] Of course, not all migrants shared Joe's view of the Glaswegian tongue. According to Catherine Marshall of Sutherland, 'They're very correct speakers the Invernesians, the people north of Inverness. They're very correct. They're not like the broad Glasgow with the glutteral [glottal] stop. They're not like that. They're very correct.'[28] Joe and Catherine's testimonies highlight the divisions between regions of Scotland, once again reaffirming a sense of regional rather than solely national identity.

Although their accents marked them as outwardly different from their English neighbours, for Scottish migrants in England their accent was not suppressed or modified in public. Instead it was nourished and powerfully asserted. Although for some migrants their accent altered, their recollections do not view this as a means of conformity. This, together with their predominantly favourable accounts of life in England, suggests that Scots did not receive a hostile reception.

Intriguingly, these migrants failed to reflect on their use or non-use of Gaelic or the Scots language. This contrasts significantly with their compatriots who settled elsewhere who frequently alluded to the Scottish language.[29] Unlike their fellow expatriates, however, Scots in England were more inclined to include consideration of a British identity. This may in part be related to devolution and debates taking place before devolution. Such reflections, therefore, indicate that current events are significant in influencing memory. Catherine Marshall, for instance, not only felt a regional attach-

---

[26] Interview with Doug Black.
[27] Interview with Joe Hendry.
[28] Interview with Catherine Marshall.
[29] A. McCarthy, 'Scottish national identities among inter-war migrants in North America and Australasia', *Journal of Imperial and Commonwealth History* (forthcoming, 2005).

ment to Scotland but also proclaimed, 'I'm British too you see.'[30] Joe Hendry also explained, 'I think too in recent years that sense of Scottishness has actually grown . . . that sense of being Scottish first and being British second and for some people just being Scottish and not being anything else.' Despite acknowledging the identities of others, Joe felt particularly British:

> I feel very British. I know that not everybody in Scotland now seems to feel British but I feel part of Britain and Scotland's a part of Britain and whether we like it or whether we don't it's all one big island and you can draw lines across it anywhere you like but history tells us that lines tend to move a bit.

Later in the interview, however, Joe qualified this by stating, 'I don't feel British in an emotional sense.'[31] Such reflections reveal that even if by the close of the twentieth century a sense of Britishness declined among Scots in their homeland, as Richard Weight has argued,[32] some Scottish migrants in England still felt a shared British and Scottish identity. Indeed, such awareness of a British identity may also explain why there has been little study of the Scots in England.

Conclusion

The internal character of Scottishness briefly outlined in this paper, largely invisible to observers, can misleadingly suggest that Scots were integrated into the societies they settled in. Yet internal components of their identities were merely configured in different ways to other ethnic groups, such as the Irish, whose identities were more institutionalised and visible.

Although the Scottish migrant testimonies utilised in this paper did not dwell at length on national identities, the fact that such reflections arose in an interview concerned with identity as part of a larger project suggests the importance of Scottishness for Scots in England. While specific recollections are ambiguous as to whether a Scottish identity is a current development, other aspects of oral testimony, such as contact with other Scots, differences between origin and destination, and accent and language show a sense of identity *at the time of migration*. In this way Scots in England, as with their expatriate counterparts abroad, articulated a range of manifestations of their identities.

Few Scots who settled in England in the twentieth century, however, proclaimed the public nature of their identities. Nor did they reflect much on

[30] Interview with Catherine Marshall.
[31] Interview with Joe Hendry.
[32] Weight, *Patriots*, p. 11.

cultural representations of their identities such as literature, paintings, and music. For Scots in England their national identity was less 'institutional' and 'cultural' and more a 'social-mental' conceptualisation. In this sense they were similar to their compatriots interviewed in New Zealand.[33]

Scots in the United States, Australia, and Canada, by contrast, sharply proclaimed an exterior identity through vigorous participation in ethnic societies. Two reasons may account for this divergence. First, much of the testimony from the United States, Canada, and Australia emerges from migrants who departed in the 1920s, while the sources derived for the migrant experience in England and New Zealand emanated from a later time period. Second, in both England and New Zealand the oral histories utilised were not specifically concerned with the migration experience. The interviews drawn upon for the United States, by contrast, were conducted by the Ellis Island Museum and were predominantly focused upon the migrant experience.[34]

Furthermore, the testimonies in this chapter suggest that interpretations of Scottish identity have for too long been reliant on domestic conditions in Scotland. Where constructions of migrant identity exist they too have been influenced by developments about identity within Scotland, specifically a focus on Highlandism, and by a disproportionate concentration on Canada. By incorporating the migrant component of identity as portrayed by Lowlanders and Highlanders in England a more nuanced interpretation of identity has been revealed, particularly the blending of Scottishness and Britishness and the representation of regional affiliations. Being Scottish in England was therefore powerful and dynamic and shows a Scottish world coexisting within a British one.

Note. The author would like to thank Dr Enda Delaney and Dr Andrew Mackillop for their comments on an earlier draft of this chapter.

---

[33] McCarthy, 'Scottish national identities'.
[34] Ibid.

12

The Auld Enemy in the New Scotland

ASIFA HUSSAIN AND WILLIAM L. MILLER

Antipathy towards the Auld Enemy is the one form of racism which still seems to be acceptable today in an otherwise politically correct Scotland.[1]

MUCH OF THE RESEARCH AND DEBATE ABOUT MULTICULTURALISM HAS FOCUSED ON ENGLAND.[2] And within England it has traditionally focused on the 'visible' minorities. But the numbers of 'visible' minorities within Scotland are much smaller than in England and more attention has focused on 'invisible' minorities—notably the Irish minority. Sectarian divisions have been labelled 'Scotland's Shame'.[3]

In the 2001 Scottish Census, however, only 1 per cent say they were born in Ireland and fewer than 1 per cent call themselves Irish. By contrast, over 8 per cent (408,948) say they were born in England. By far the largest minority in Scotland is English and if Kidd is correct then Scottish attitudes towards the English could well bid for the title 'Scotland's Other Shame'.

Traditional Scottish self-consciousness, the long debate over devolution, and the eventual creation of a Scottish Parliament have all posed a challenge to this English minority. Both devolutionists and more independence-minded nationalists consistently proclaimed a non-ethnic, inclusive, 'civic' concept of nationalism.[4] That included their attitude towards the English. SNP leader Alex Salmond, for example, regularly claimed to be an 'anglophile':

---

[1] C. Kidd, 'Unenlightened days when racism was thought to be trendy', *The Scotsman*, 13 January 2003, p. 13; see also C. Kidd, 'Race and the Scottish nation, 1750–1900', Royal Society of Edinburgh Lecture, 13 January 2003.

[2] T. Modood et al., *Ethnic Minorities in Britain: Diversity and Disadvantage. 4th PSI survey* (London, 1997), esp. ch. 9, 'Culture and identity'.

[3] T. M. Devine (ed.), *Scotland's Shame? Bigotry and Sectarianism in Modern Scotland* (Edinburgh, 2000).

[4] A. Henderson, 'Political constructions of national identity in Scotland and Quebec', *Scottish Affairs* 29 (1999), pp. 121–38, at p. 138.

Proceedings of the British Academy **128**, 183–199. © The British Academy 2005.

I have often pronounced myself one of the most anglophile of all Scottish Members. I am prepared to defend that. I have certainly forgotten more about English history than many Conservative Members have ever learnt. We present our case for Scotland in a positive way. We do not spend our time being antagonistic about other nations. That contrasts heavily with the attitude of the Conservative Party.[5]

Ethnic nationalism is 'in essence exclusive', stressing the ethnic group and common descent but civic nationalism claims to be 'inclusive in the sense that anyone can adopt the culture and join the nation'.[6]

Yet there are problems with this simple 'civic versus ethnic' distinction. First, civic nationalism can easily degenerate into ethnic nationalism. Pulzer argues that 'nationalism degenerates ... Though often inspired in its first stage by the urge to emancipate, it finds its logical conclusion in a paroxysm of destructiveness.'[7] The early leaders of nationalist movements may be personally cosmopolitan, highly educated, inclusive-minded, aware and respectful of diversity, as keen to cherish other cultures as their own, defensive rather than aggressive. Their enemy may be global homogeneity rather than internal diversity. But that complex perspective can get simplified and degraded as it filters down and is put into practice.

Second, although nationalists may sincerely believe that they are advocating a civic conception, minorities may view it as ethnic nationalism.

Third, minorities may not be able—and/or may not be willing—to 'adopt the culture and join the nation'.

Fourth, liberal notions of tolerance and equality may be welcome but grossly insufficient for a small insecure minority: 'One might enjoy all the rights of citizenship and be a formally equal member of the community, *and yet feel an outsider* who does not belong' (our emphasis).[8] The problem is compounded by the significance of 'political symbols, images, ceremonies, collective self-understanding and views of national identity'.[9]

The increasing emphasis on Scottish history, the enthusiasm publicly expressed by senior politicians for the film *Braveheart*,[10] even the romantic

---

[5] Hansard, HC (series 5) vol. 299, col. 396 (30 July 1997).

[6] J. Kellas, *The Politics of Nationalism and Ethnicity* (Basingstoke, 2nd edn 1998), p. 65.

[7] P. Pulzer, *The Rise of Political Anti-Semitism in Germany and Austria* (London, revised edn 1988), p. 287, quoted in B. Porter, *When Nationalism Began to Hate: Imagining Modern Politics in Nineteenth-Century Poland* (New York, 2000), p. 4.

[8] B. Parekh, *Rethinking Multiculturalism: Cultural Diversity and Political Theory* (Basingstoke, 2000), p. 237.

[9] Ibid., p. 203; see also T. Modood and P. Werbner (eds), *The Politics of Multiculturalism in the New Europe: Racism, Identity and Community* (London, 1997), p. 263.

[10] T. Edensor, 'Reading Braveheart: representing and contesting Scottish identity', *Scottish Affairs* 21 (1997), pp. 135–58, at p. 147.

and nostalgic if inaccurate claim (to the applause of MSPs, however) that 'the Scottish Parliament, adjourned on 25 March 1707, is hereby reconvened',[11] or SNP leader John Swinney's more recent call to use Scotland's 'Patron Saint' to promote the new Scotland,[12] could be exclusionist to those—including the English—whose ethnic identity makes it difficult for them to identify with historic (as distinct from contemporary) Scotland. Figures from the Commission for Racial Equality showed a sharp increase in racial incidents in Scotland after the Devolution Referendum,[13] and the press printed a rash of stories about harassment of the English minority.[14] While there may have been an element of media hype in this, such coverage can by itself increase the insecurity of the minority.

Devolution and nationalism challenge the identities of the English in a unique way. Their invisibility gives them some protection from the casual harassment that afflicts other minorities—though focus-group participants told us they had to keep their mouths shut in threatening situations. But England is '*the* significant other', with a key role in defining Scottish identity.[15] Though Scotland and England were united in a voluntary union, it sometimes had an imperial flavour. And the position of the English in the new Scotland could have a classic post-imperial-minority flavour—like that of the English in the Irish Free State after 1922, or of Russians in Uzbekistan in more recent times.

The threat to Scottish minorities under devolution is not intentional oppression by new institutions, but unintentional stimulation of nationalist passions and minority fears. Despite the inclusive rhetoric at the top, minorities might still fear harassment by a more consciously nationalistic public, and still resent being overlooked on symbolic occasions by the authorities.

But on the other hand they might not. Multicultural nationalism may be in principle an oxymoron, but against all simple (or simplistic) logic perhaps it can work in practice. It is an empirical question and one that is best answered from the perspective of minorities themselves.

We used 6 focus-group discussions followed by 751 telephone interviews to discover the experiences and perspectives of the English minority in post-devolution Scotland. To gauge majority attitudes towards them, we also

---

[11] Scottish Parliament, Debate I: col. 5, 9 June 1999.

[12] J. Swinney, 'Patron saint should promote Scotland', *The Scotsman*, 19 November 2002, p. 8.

[13] Commission for Racial Equality, *Racial Attacks and Harassment* (London, 1999) accessible at www.cre.gov.uk .

[14] J. Rafferty, 'Scotch wrath', *Sunday Times Magazine* 4 October 1998, pp. 16–22; Commission for Racial Equality, *CRE-Scotland 1999/2000 Report* (Edinburgh, 2000), p. 8.

[15] K. Wright (convener), 'Part 1: Identities', *People and Parliament: Reshaping Scotland* (People and Parliament Trust, 1999), accessible at www.alastairmcintosh.com/articles/1999_p&p/summary.htm .

placed a module of questions in the 2003 Scottish Social Attitudes Survey (SSAS).

For focus groups we sought participants who said they had been 'born in England'. For the English minority survey, however, we widened the scope to include anyone who lived in an English 'household'—defined as one containing someone who had been 'born in England'—or who had such people amongst their 'very close relatives: parents, children, brothers, sisters'. But all the findings presented in this chapter are based on the 579 core respondents who were *themselves* born in England—those who therefore were literally 'English immigrants' living in Scotland.

Spatially, our sampling procedures reflected the spatial distribution of the English, who are concentrated in Edinburgh and southern Scotland.[16] Survey respondents were selected by random digit dialling using filter questions to select the English-born. Finally, 2001 Census figures were used to weight the sample and bring it into line with the age-by-gender pattern for all English-born adults within Scotland.

Sympathy versus Belonging

English immigrants show far more respect than other minorities (such as Pakistanis, whom we also surveyed) for Scottish history, culture, and national symbols. But English identities are simple, rigid, and primarily territorial. In consequence, their own criteria for national identity prevent them from identifying with Scotland. They are indeed willing 'to adopt the culture' but (psychologically) unable to 'join the nation'.

History, Culture, and Symbols

Permanent outsiders they may be, but relatively sympathetic and engaged outsiders—though, in the focus groups they did take care to emphasise the difference between their concept of factually accurate history and 'Hollywood' romances such as *Braveheart*. We asked whether it was 'good for people to pay more attention to Scottish history, or should people focus more on Scotland's future and less on Scotland's past?' Although a majority feel people should focus on the future, a large minority of the English immigrants (27 per cent) think it is good to 'pay more attention to Scottish history'. And a mere 4 per cent feel there should be 'special history lessons' for 'English children'.

---

[16] Although the English-born constitute only 8 per cent of the population of Scotland, they constitute around 12 per cent in the area covered by the Edinburgh telephone directory and over 16 per cent in the area covered by directories for the Borders and South-West Scotland.

They also hold relatively positive views about assimilation, that is about whether 'those who come from outside Scotland, often bringing their own customs, religion, and traditions with them' should 'try to adapt and blend into the locality' or 'stay different and add to the variety of customs and traditions in the locality'. In focus groups some recalled that their Scottish neighbours had found them particularly useful when a bagpipe player was required, and none of their Scottish neighbours could play! Others were regular Burns Night speakers. And overall, almost half the English (47 per cent) explicitly favour 'adapting and blending' rather than 'adding variety'—in sharp contrast to other Scottish minorities that we interviewed.

A third of the English immigrants criticise the Scottish Parliament for being an exercise in nostalgia. But they rather enjoy nostalgia and see the Scottish Parliament as part of a continuous history. That is reflected in their attachment to historical symbols—notably the future of the Saltire, and the parliament's location in a Church of Scotland building.

'Should Scotland have a new flag to help the new parliament identify with all the people of today's Scotland? Or should it keep the *historic* white X-shape on the blue background—often called the Saltire or the *St Andrew's Cross*?' English immigrants could hardly be expected to enthuse over a symbol associated with the annual nationalist festivities on the historic battlefield of Bannockburn—or indeed with the more contemporary battlefield of Wembley. But, surprisingly, they do: only a negligible 4 per cent would replace the Saltire. Our survey finding is confirmed and explained by the focus-group discussions. Given the excessive expenditure on the parliament building, there is some distaste for wasting money on new symbols of any kind:

> I think now we are almost getting into a backlash against too much spinning and too many logos—and a new flag? I think a lot of people would feel that was a waste of resources—they should put up with the existing Saltire [E2-D].[17]

But participants in several different focus groups spontaneously outlined a different and more positive reason for their attachment to the Saltire: it is an integral part of the Union Jack and therefore as much a 'British' symbol as a Scottish symbol.

> The Saltire makes up the Union Jack along with all the rest, doesn't it, you know the St George's Cross and the Saltire and the Welsh one [E2-F]; it is part of the Union flag and actually to my mind it's their bit of the Union flag, isn't

---

[17] [E2-D] indicates a comment by participant D in Focus Group 2 of the six focus groups with English immigrants.

it and possibly reflects that Scotland is also part of the UK [E3-C]; I think it's fine, the Saltire [E4-C] . . . I mean the St Andrew's Cross is part of the Union Jack—but in the same way that the St Andrew's Cross has kind of been hijacked by the independence lobby, so has the Union Jack been hijacked by the fascists and the bother boys and the national party [E4-G] . . . that's true in England [E4-E].

So, what to those at the annual Bannockburn rally is a Scottish nationalist or even anti-English symbol turns out to be, for English immigrants, a treasured British symbol.

From 1999 to 2004, the new parliament was sited in a Church of Scotland building. Most of the English immigrants are not presbyterian (or United Reformed), let alone Church of Scotland. And the Church of Scotland's Westminster Confession of faith recalls the unsuccessful attempt of the Scottish Church to impose its belief and practices on the English, largely by force of arms. Relatively few of today's English immigrants (25 per cent) are offended by the use of a Church of Scotland building, however, though there is some evidence of religious sensitivities: it is criticised by only 12 per cent of those who were brought up as presbyterians; but by 21 per cent of those brought up as 'other' Protestants, by 23 per cent of episcopalians, by 32 per cent of Catholics, and by 32 per cent of those who were brought up in no religion.

However, the greatest difference between English immigrants and other minorities over symbols concerns representation in the Scottish Parliament. The English-born, at 8 per cent of the population (and rather more than that of the adult population) could expect at least ten MSPs on a strictly proportionate basis—though there are considerably more.[18] But they neither knew nor cared: 'I do not think it matters' [E5-A, B, C]; 'I don't feel the need to have somebody who is English represent me in the Scottish Parliament' [E3-E]. Only 41 per cent say there should be some English-born MSPs, 53 per cent do not care, and 6 per cent even go so far as to say there should *not* be any English-born MSPs in a Scottish Parliament—conceding an ethnically 'Scottish Parliament for a Scottish people'! By contrast, MSPs from 'visible' minorities were highly conspicuous by their absence and these minorities did care.

Identities

Most people in Britain have 'hyphenated' or 'nested' national identities,[19] though some have even more complex ethno-territorial identities. Coming from Scotland's 'significant other', the English immigrants are reluctant to

---

[18] M. Spicer (ed.), *The Scotsman Guide to Scottish Politics* (Edinburgh, 2002).
[19] D. Miller, *Citizenship and National Identity* (Oxford, 2000), ch. 8.

Table 12.1.   Identities: Scottish versus British.

	Amongst English-born %	Amongst majority Scots* %
Exclusively British	43	1
More British than Scottish	20	2
Equally British and Scottish	24	21
More Scottish than British	8	38
Exclusively Scottish	1	36
None of these	5	1

* Based on a tight definition of majority Scots: excluding those born outside Scotland or living with partners who were born outside Scotland.
Source: Minorities Survey by Hussain and Miller. Don't Knows etc. excluded from calculation of percentages.

accept the label 'Scottish' even in hyphenated form. But in marked contrast to the major ethnic minorities within England, the English in Scotland are inclined to use the term 'British' as a *synonym* for 'English' rather than an *antonym*.

We asked English immigrants to place themselves on the standard 5-point Moreno scale that runs from exclusively Scottish to exclusively British. Few object, but they crowd the 'British' end of the scale.

The criteria people use to determine whether someone else is a 'true Brit' or a 'true Scot' vary from person to person, but amongst those most frequently cited are birthplace, parentage, and race.[20] Almost half of the English immigrants (43 per cent) feel that to be 'truly Scottish' it is essential to be born in Scotland—implying that they themselves can never be 'truly Scottish' *in their own eyes*. Well over a third (36 per cent) feel it is essential to have Scottish parents, though relatively few (14 per cent) feel it is essential to be white. Only 42 per cent feel someone can be 'truly' Scottish without at least one of these characteristics. Even when faced with the more persuasive proposition that residents who 'were not born in Scotland and do not have Scottish parents' but 'have lived in Scotland for a long time' should be regarded as truly Scottish, only 65 per cent of English immigrants agree.

Amongst Scottish minorities, this emphasis on birthplace is peculiarly English. Two-thirds of the English immigrants feel 'more British than Scottish' or even 'exclusively British'. By contrast only 15 per cent of ethnic Pakistani *immigrants* (i.e. those born outside Scotland) in Scotland feel 'more

[20]   D. McCrone et al., 'Who are we? Problematising national identity', *The Sociological Review* 46 (1998), pp. 629–52; L. Paterson et al., *New Scotland, New Politics?* (Edinburgh, 2001), pp. 117–19.

Table 12.2.   True Brits, True Scots?

	Amongst English-born %
To be truly British it is necessary . . .	
to be born in Britain	39
to have British parents	32
to be white	8
To be truly Scottish it is necessary . . .	
to be born in Scotland	43
to have Scottish parents	36
to be white	14
none of these required	42
Someone should be regarded as truly Scottish . . .	
if they have lived in Scotland for a long time but were	
not born in Scotland and do not have Scottish parents	65

Source: Minorities Survey by Hussain and Miller. Don't Knows etc. excluded from calculation of percentages.

British than Scottish'. It is peculiarly difficult for the English to 'join the nation'.

Perhaps, if given a wider choice, the English-born would describe themselves as 'English'? After all, they were only interviewed because they agreed they were 'English-born' when we were filtering out whom to interview. But surprisingly perhaps, when faced with the wider choice of 'English, British, Scottish, Catholic, Protestant, Episcopalian', or some combination of religious and territorial identity, less than a quarter opt for 'English' as their primary identity.

An absolute majority (56 per cent) opt for 'British', followed a long way behind by 'English' (24 per cent). Overall, only 3 per cent opt for a religious identity as either a primary or joint identity, though the figure is somewhat higher amongst regular church attenders and especially Catholics (14 per cent). So for English immigrants, their identity is primarily territorial rather than cultural, though 'British' rather than 'English'. More surprisingly, perhaps, given the historic sectarian divide in Scotland, our SSAS data also indicate that very few majority Scots now regard religion as their primary identity[21] (as once they did, according to Richard Finlay in Chapter 2),

---

[21] R. Bond and M. Rosie, 'Becoming Scottish—what does it take?', paper to Scottish Social Attitudes Conference, *The New Scotland Four Years On*, Edinburgh, 6 February 2004; see also R. Bond and M. Rosie, 'National identities in post-devolution Scotland', *Scottish Affairs* 40 (2002), pp. 34–53, table 5.

Table 12.3.   Identities: ethno-religious identification?

	Amongst English-born %
English	24
British	56
Scottish	11
Catholic + Protestant + Episcopalian	2
English and British*	3
English and Scottish*	3
English and some religious identity*	1

* Respondents were not invited to choose these combined 'territorial and religious' options, but interviewers were instructed to note them if they were spontaneously given. (The questionnaires included 'silent codes' for them, as a reminder to the interviewers.)
Source: Minorities Survey by Hussain and Miller. Don't Knows etc. excluded from calculation of percentages.

though religion is the primary identity for two-thirds of Scotland's largest visible minority (Pakistani Muslims). Consistent with their overwhelmingly territorial and largely 'British' identities, English immigrants have come to terms with devolution but remain overwhelmingly opposed to Scottish independence.

Age and generation have only a relatively small impact on identities, though the *direction* of the impact is significant: the young are significantly more inclined to stress their English identity at the expense of both Scottish and religious identities—though over half of both young and old feel primarily British rather than anything else.

Table 12.4.   Identities: ethno-religious identification—by age.

	Amongst English-born %	
	Younger	Older
English	29	20
British	54	57
Scottish	9	13
Catholic + Protestant + Episcopalian	1	3
English and British	3	3
English and Scottish	3	4
English and Catholic, Protestant, or Episcopalian	0	1

Younger = aged up to 39 yrs; older = 40 plus.
Source: Minorities Survey by Hussain and Miller. Don't Knows etc. excluded from calculation of percentages.

'As others see us'

Very few of the English immigrants sense much social exclusion. Few suspect that Scots would be 'unhappy' to have an English work-place colleague (8 per cent) or family member (5 per cent). And only about a quarter (27 per cent) imagine that 'most Scots' think they 'take jobs, housing, and health-care from Scots'. But almost half (48 per cent) imagine that 'most Scots' think they 'will never be committed to Scotland', and a huge 78 per cent imagine that 'most Scots' think they 'will always be more loyal to England than to Scotland'. So they feel surrounded by nationalist distrust rather than economic resentment.

In that they are correct. Our module of questions in the 2003 SSAS shows that the majority of Scots do recognise the positive economic contribution of English immigrants, but most Scots (81 per cent of those with a view) do indeed think English immigrants will always be 'more loyal to England'. Does this indicate an immediate crisis? Probably not. We could soften these findings—put them 'out of focus' would be a better description—by factoring in those with 'no opinion' or 'neutral' views. But that would only cover up a potential problem. The real reason why Scottish perceptions of English disloyalty do not indicate an immediate crisis is the absence of a sufficiently acute conflict—a point that we address directly below.

Table 12.5.   To see ourselves as others see us: perceptions of perceptions.

	Amongst English-born (*perceptions* of Scots' feelings about English) %	Amongst majority Scots* (*actual* Scots' feelings about English) %
Think Scots feel English people living in Scotland . . .		
take jobs, housing, and healthcare from Scots	27	18
will never be committed to Scotland	48	44
will always be more loyal to England	78	81
Think Scots would be unhappy to have an English person now living in Scotland as . . .		
a work-mate	8	na
a relative by marriage	5	5

* Based on a tight definition of majority Scots: excluding those born outside Scotland or living with partners who were born outside Scotland. Note: this column shows the percentages of Scots who really do feel this way.
na: not asked
Source: Minorities Survey by Hussain and Miller. Don't Knows etc. excluded from calculation of percentages.

Discrimination and Harassment

Most English immigrants (87 per cent) feel Scots treat those they do not regard as 'truly Scottish' worse than they treat other people. And 40 per cent feel that happens 'more than rarely'.

What kind of Scots do they think would be 'most prejudiced against those they regard as not being truly Scottish?': not so much politicians and officials (8 per cent) as 'ordinary people' (75 per cent). And on balance English immigrants feel Scotland has 'become more welcoming to people who are not completely Scottish' since devolution (28 per cent 'more welcoming' against 17 per cent 'less welcoming'). Once again they attribute that to the changing behaviour of ordinary Scots rather than politicians, however: devolution has calmed the prejudices of the Scots.

Ideological minorities are reputedly subject to a 'spiral of silence'.[22] They become increasingly unwilling to articulate their views. Ethnic minorities may not react in quite the same dynamic way. But ethnic minorities may, like ideological minorities, find it necessary or desirable to suppress their grievances. One possibility is that they may voice their grievances within their own community while moderating their criticism when speaking to those outside it. And since English immigrants are exposed by their speech rather than their skin colour, they may be particularly sensitive to the danger of voicing criticisms to relative strangers. To investigate this possibility we asked:

> When you are speaking to Scots people *that you do not know very well*, do you feel you can say what you think about Scotland and Scottish things? Or do you feel you have to be careful what you say? Is it OK to praise Scottish things but not to criticise them, for example?

Just under half (48 per cent) say they 'have to be careful'. But on balance they say it has become easier since devolution to criticise Scotland and things Scottish. Three-fifths say devolution has made no difference, but the remainder split more than two to one (27 per cent versus 11 per cent) in favour of saying it has become *easier to criticise* things Scottish. Indeed, focus-group participants indicated that criticising the parliament (usually for 'waste')—if not other things Scottish, or Scotland itself—has become something of a bonding experience:

> I think it's become easier politically because I think so many real Scots are criticising their own parliament, so one can join in the criticism [E4-C].

Although they suffer much less harassment than some other minorities in Scotland, almost a third of the English immigrants (29 per cent) report that

---

[22] E. Noelle-Neumann, *Schweigespirale: The Spiral of Silence* (Chicago, [1984] 1993).

Table 12.6. Treatment of those who are 'not truly Scottish'.

	Amongst English-born %
Scots would treat someone worse if they regarded them as 'not truly Scottish' . . .	
usually	2
at least sometimes	40
at least rarely	87
Most prejudiced against those they regard as not being truly Scottish are . . .	
politicians and officials	8
ordinary people	75
mixed / depends	16
Since the Scottish Parliament was set up, feel that Scotland has become . . .	
more welcoming to people who are not completely Scottish	28
less welcoming to people who are not completely Scottish	17
no difference / neither / mixed	55
More/less welcoming mainly because of . . .	
politicians	13
ordinary Scots	46
mixed / depends	41

Source: Minorities Survey by Hussain and Miller. Don't Knows etc. excluded from calculation of percentages.

they or someone in their household has been harassed or discriminated against for being English. Nearly all say that was 'mainly' by 'ordinary people', not the police, officials, or employers. Indeed, 57 per cent feel the new parliament is 'really committed' to fighting such discrimination.

Mostly, English immigrants feel they can live with low-intensity harassment or are merely irritated or annoyed rather than frightened by it. Typical comments are:

> My daughters were certainly teased when they first came up, for their English accent [E5-C]; My boss used to wind me up something terrible about my English accent [E4-H]; this fellow would not shut up all the time about my accent, on and on, and on and on . . . we just got up and walked out [from a bar in Stirling] in the end [E6-G].

Occasionally it gets much worse, and really frightens: one woman, a Scot herself, returned with her family to a very pleasant rural part of Scotland. Her young daughter had been born in England, however, and:

> because she spoke with an English accent . . . was physically, verbally and emotionally abused by a group of six boys . . . [they] held her physically while they all rubbed their Scottish flags in her face and then taunted her . . . [R]eporting

it to the school brought little support . . . I felt ashamed for the first time in my life of being Scottish . . . such racism in a rural school, I dread to think what happens in inner-city schools. (Letter to the authors.)

In an industrial area focus-group participants complained of:

the inability of Scottish people to recognise their racism towards the English [E6-E]

and the inability of school authorities to recognise its seriousness:

our boys came home from school one day and they had been spat at all down the backs of their coats, not long after we had been here . . . I went to see the head master . . . and he just said 'what do you expect, you are English' [E6-B].

And the old were guilty too:

when our oldest child was only 10, he went next door to ask this elderly lady if her grandson could come out to play with him and—I've got to say what she said—'F off back to England, you effing English bastard'—and slammed the door in his face [E6-E].

But the problem is not limited to school-children:

I felt vulnerable when I stood at the bus stop—and have heard people slagging off the English and I thought to myself if I open my mouth I could be in trouble here, I'm on my own [E6-A].

Fully 83 per cent report being subjected to ethnic 'comments which were intended as humorous but which irritated' them; and 45 per cent have had such experiences 'more than rarely', though only 10 per cent say it has really 'hurt and annoyed' them. The rest say it 'never happens' or they 'can live with it'.

In addition, 42 per cent report being 'deliberately insulted or abused'; and 16 per cent have had that experience more than rarely. When it does occur it seldom 'frightens' English victims, however (only 1 per cent). Mostly they are

Table 12.7. Irritating ethnic humour.

	Amongst English-born %
Subjected to irritating humour . . .	
very often	13
at least sometimes	45
at least rarely	83
Response . . .	
can live with it	78
hurts and annoys	10
never happens	12

Source: Minorities Survey by Hussain and Miller. Don't Knows etc. excluded from calculation of percentages.

Table 12.8. Intentional insults and abuse.

	Amongst English-born %
Subjected to intentional insults . . .	
very often	4
at least sometimes	16
at least rarely	42
Response . . .	
frightens	2
just annoys	39
never happens	53
Such insults . . .	
are not by typical Scots	45
say openly what ordinary Scots feel	15
never happen	40
Scots are generally anti-English	39

Source: Minorities Survey by Hussain and Miller. Don't Knows etc. excluded from calculation of percentages.

simply 'annoyed'. Mostly they have not had such experiences or they imagine the perpetrators are 'not typical Scots', but 15 per cent imagine this abuse merely expresses openly what other Scots are quietly thinking. Indeed, 39 per cent of English immigrants think 'Scots are generally anti-English'.

But, in their view, the move towards devolution has not increased the level of abuse, though the efforts of the Scottish Parliament have not reduced it either. Roughly as many detect an increase as a decrease, and far more detect no change.

Table 12.9. At ease in Scotland?

	Amongst English-born %
Feel 'at ease living in Scotland'	97
Since the Scottish Parliament was established . . .	
feel more at ease	12
feel less at ease	6
neither / mixed	82
See their long-term future in . . .	
Scotland	89
England	6
other	5

Source: Minorities Survey by Hussain and Miller. Don't Knows etc. excluded from calculation of percentages.

Despite all this, almost all the English feel 'at ease living in Scotland'. Most of the English (82 per cent) feel the Scottish Parliament has made no difference in this respect, though—by a margin of two to one—the few who do detect a difference feel its impact has been positive. Almost all the English immigrants (96 per cent) have 'close' friends who are '*not* English' and most (89 per cent) see their future in Scotland.

Perceptions of Conflict

There is a self-conscious perception amongst English immigrants that while they might have some conflict with majority Scots, other conflicts were worse.

The classic, much-researched sectarian conflict between Catholics and Protestants in Scotland provides a 'benchmark'. But it is essential to specify the context. In focus-group discussions, participants would not comment on conflicts between Catholics and Protestants—nor between Scots and English—without spontaneously specifying whether the context was sport or something other than sport. We could hardly avoid doing the same in our surveys. So we asked:

> Thinking now about Protestants and Catholics in Scotland—*apart from football and sport*, how serious would you say conflict between them is?

In a similar format, we asked:

> . . . about the Scots and the English—*apart from football and sport*, how serious would you say conflict between them is?

And finally we asked about perceptions of conflict 'between Muslims and non-Muslims in Scotland'. Here there is no need to specify sport or non-sport as the context.

Outside the narrow confines of sport only 16 per cent of English immigrants feel there is at least 'fairly serious conflict' between themselves and the majority of Scots; and only 2 per cent that there is 'very serious conflict'. By comparison, over twice as many English immigrants feel there is at least 'fairly serious conflict' between Protestants and Catholics or between Muslims and non-Muslims in Scotland; and around 7 per cent that these conflicts are 'very serious'.

Our SSAS data show that majority Scots detect only a little more conflict with English immigrants than the English themselves realise: 25 per cent of Scots feel it is at least 'fairly serious conflict', and 5 per cent 'very serious'. And Scots also rate conflict between themselves and the English as much less serious than between Protestants and Catholics or between Muslims and non-Muslims in Scotland.

Table 12.10. Perceptions of conflict.

	Amongst English-born %	Amongst majority Scots* %
Excluding sport: conflict between Scots and English is . . .		
very serious	2	5
at least fairly serious	16	25
Comparisons		
Excluding sport: conflict between Protestants and Catholics in Scotland is . . .		
very serious	8	10
at least fairly serious	37	41
Conflict between Muslims and non-Muslims in Scotland is . . .		
very serious	6	4
at least fairly serious	36	42

* Based on a tight definition of majority Scots: excluding those born outside Scotland or living with partners who were born outside Scotland.
Source: Minorities Survey by Hussain and Miller. Don't Knows etc. excluded from calculation of percentages.

It is in this context that our earlier finding concerning the 'suspect loyalty' of English immigrants in Scotland must be placed. The overwhelming view of majority Scots that English immigrants are more loyal to England than to Scotland is only potentially—but not actually—significant as long as so few on either side see the conflict as 'very serious'.

Conclusions

The long debate over devolution has intensified Scottish self-consciousness and challenged the identity of English immigrants by making them more explicitly aware that they are strangers in a foreign land. But devolution itself has not—by their own report—added to their problems. It has been part of the solution rather than part of the problem. So far at least, Scottish politicians have succeeded in their expressed aim to create a devolved Scotland that is no more exclusive than in the past and to some extent more inclusive. That is particularly true for the 'visible' minorities in Scotland, especially the Pakistani Muslims.

The English immigrants are a very special minority, however. Not so much because they are 'invisible' nor because they are so numerous, but because they are identified with the 'significant other' that plays such an

important role in defining Scottish identity itself. Pakistanis in Scotland overwhelmingly identify themselves as Scots and are largely accepted as 'Asian
Scots', despite their cultural distinctiveness. But the 'Auld Enemy' cannot
bring itself to identify itself as Scottish, however much it sympathises with
(historic) Scotland and however culturally assimilated it may be. Nonetheless,
the English also feel more relaxed, more 'at ease' in post-devolution Scotland,
if only a little more.

English immigrants cope with the problem of identity by describing
themselves as 'British' rather than 'English'. They interpret the Saltire as a
union symbol rather than a nationalist symbol. A majority of English immigrants now support devolution, though they overwhelmingly oppose independence (unlike the Pakistanis, who support Scottish independence). Like
other people in Scotland, English immigrants are divided about the performance of the new parliament, but no worse than divided. They do not feel
harassment has increased and, even if only by a very narrow margin, they feel
Scotland has become more welcoming rather than less since devolution. By a
larger margin they feel it has got easier to criticise Scotland in public than
before devolution.

Harassment of the English, though less extensive and less serious than the
harassment suffered by other minorities, is still enough to make some Scots,
such as the Scotswoman (quoted above) whose children had been born in
England, 'ashamed to be Scottish'. And devolution has not had a great positive impact on this problem. But its impact should not be judged against a
zero-change baseline. The impact of devolution has at least been positive
when the history of nationalism elsewhere suggests it could have been negative. It is a considerable political achievement to become even the slightest bit
more inclusive while moving in a nationalist direction.

Scottish politicians have proved notoriously bad at containing the
financial cost of the new parliament building. But so far they have proved
very good at containing the social and political costs of nationalism. And the
problems for English immigrants within Scotland are attributed by them to
ordinary prejudiced Scottish people, not to political leaders, nor to
constitutional change.

Note. This research was supported by the Economic and Social Research Council
(Grant no. L219252118) and the Nuffield Foundation (Grant no. OPD/00213/G).
We are particularly grateful to Professor Charlie Jeffery, the director of the ESRC
programme on Devolution and Constitutional Change, for his encouragement and
support.

UNFINISHED BUSINESS

13

W(h)ither the Union? Anglo-Scottish Relations in the Twenty-first Century

DAVID McCRONE

'When I use a word,' Humpty Dumpty said, in a rather scornful tone, 'it means just what I choose it to mean—neither more or less.'
(Lewis Carroll, *Alice Through the Looking Glass*, ch. 6)

Problematising the Union

WHAT ASSESSMENT CAN WE MAKE OF THE UNION AFTER ALMOST 300 YEARS? What impact has devolution had on Anglo-Scottish relations in particular? In the constitutional ferment of the 1990s, it was argued by some nationalists and unionists alike that creating a Scottish Parliament would be something of a slippery slope leading to independence and the break-up of the United Kingdom. Nationalists, of course, welcomed the possibility, and unionists abhorred it, but metaphors such as 'the slippery slope', and 'the thin end of the wedge' were certainly prominent in the constitutional debates of the last decade. Perhaps, like Chou En-Lai, who, when asked what he thought was the significance of the French Revolution, is reputed to have replied 'It is too soon to tell', we should put our judgement on hold. Nevertheless, this is an opportune moment to ask about the union, given that it is 400 years since the Union of Crowns, and almost 300 years since the Union of Parliaments.

Undoubtedly, much writing on the union in the last decade or so has been elegiac rather than celebratory. Books with titles like *The Break-Up of Britain, After Britain, The Divided Kingdom, The Day Britain Died*, and so on represent current conventional wisdom. As a sociologist who has been look-ing at such matters for over thirty years, I want to counsel caution, and to argue that things are more complicated than they seem without in any way

Proceedings of the British Academy **128**, 203–215. © The British Academy 2005.

suggesting that there is not something of a crisis for the British state in general, and Anglo-Scottish relations in particular.

Evolving Union

The first and obvious thing to be said is that much depends on what we mean by 'the union', for patently it is not the same phenomenon as it was at the outset of the eighteenth century, nor the nineteenth, nor even the twentieth century. We cannot debate the future of the union simply by assuming that it is the same creature it was almost 300 years ago. The union may mean what we want it to mean, as Humpty Dumpty observed. My own take on the original Union of 1707 was that it was something of a 'marriage of convenience' for both parties, Scotland and England, a *mariage de raison*.[1] At this point I am usually taken to task for ignoring the considerable corruption and public protest involved, and the fact that one prominent figure discovered he had an urgent appointment at the dentist that day and could not vote the bill through. Be that as it may, and it indubitably was, the eighteenth century union was a negotiated deal between two sets of patricians at a time when proper democracy had not yet been invented. Put simply, the Scots got access to English markets at home and abroad, and the soudrons got rid of the troublesome alliance their northern neighbours had with France. So far, so historical. What the union did mean, of course, was that Scottish civil society was not only left to its own devices but also was allowed to prosper in the union as long as it did not rock the constitutional boat. However, an anomalous incubus lay at the heart of this union: it governed a unitary state, while allowing considerable latitude in its civil institutions.[2] Notwithstanding the 'incorporating' theory espoused by its English architects, the eighteenth-century union, as far as the Scots were concerned, was a way of having your cake and eating it: being internally self-governing, while benefiting from the power and scope of Empire.

By the nineteenth century, this arrangement was in full flow, in essence because the union was an imperial rather than a state arrangement. Britain was, in Eric Hobsbawm's apt phrase,[3] a 'semi-automatic switchboard' for controlling a global economy, and one in which internal state power was

[1] D. McCrone, *Understanding Scotland: The Sociology of a Nation* (London, 2nd edn 2001), p. 216.
[2] N. MacCormick, 'The English constitution, the British state and the Scottish anomaly', in *Understanding Constitutional Change*, special issue of *Scottish Affairs* (1999), pp. 129–45.
[3] E. Hobsbawm, *Industry and Empire* (Harmondsworth, 1988).

fairly underdeveloped. Naval power was the most significant because it guaranteed the trade routes of the day. It has always struck me as significant that the British state had no properly developed 'ministry of the interior' along the lines of the French or German states, and for good reason. Power in Britain was turned outwards rather than inwards unless rebellions, like the Forty-five, erupted within. Put another way, the British state is something of a 'convenience'—a *gesellschaftlich* arrangement—rather than an 'entity'—The State—run along continental lines.[4]

This was the context in which one could be Scottish and British in roughly equal measure, in Graeme Morton's happy phrase, a unionist-nationalist.[5] One of the main reasons was that being British was much more of an imperial than a national reality. I am struck by the similarities between Britain and Rome in this respect: *civis britannicus sum*. In other words, being a subject of the Crown (too often confused with the monarchy, in my view, rather than the personification of the state) on whose realm the sun never set presented few inherent contradictions to speak of. One could be Australian, Canadian, even Scottish, as well as British, because these were not mutually exclusive categories until the second half of the twentieth century when independent dominions wanted greater control of their immigration policy, and hence, citizenship. It is significant, it seems, that even as late as mid-twentieth century, Scottish nationalists wanted Home Rule in an imperial context, and saw no real contradiction in that.[6]

It took a long time during the twentieth century for this to begin to unravel. What both made and unmade the British state were the twin processes of warfare and welfare. British identity had been forged and sustained in the course of war against 'others', first French, then German. It was necessary to define ourselves in terms of who we were not—French, German, and so on. This was so much easier to imagine because Britishness was in essence an imperial identity, though a fuzzy one, defined more by an allegiance to the Crown than residence in these islands.[7] The historian John Stevenson has commented that 'as the great imperial power, patriotism and national pride were almost part of the Edwardian psyche'.[8] Note the juxtaposition of 'imperial' with 'national'. Britain, in other words, existed as an imperial state—with colonies and dominions which came to embody its

---

[4] G. Poggi, *The Development of the Modern State* (London, 1978), p. 100.

[5] G. Morton, *Unionist-Nationalism: Governing Urban Scotland 1830–1860* (East Linton, 1999).

[6] R. Finlay, *Independent and Free: Scottish Politics and the Origins of the Scottish National Party, 1918–1945* (Edinburgh, 1994).

[7] R. Cohen, *Frontiers of Identity: The British and Others* (London, 1994); H. Goulbourne, *Ethnicity and Nationalism in Post-Imperial Britain* (Cambridge, 1991).

[8] J. Stevenson, *British Society 1914–45* (Harmondsworth, 1984), p. 49.

identity. It took a New Zealander, P. A. Pocock,[9] to define 'British' history as something quite different from English, Scottish, Welsh, and Irish history, and also something which belonged to those living beyond these shores: hence the significance of *civis britannicus sum*.

The irony is that the imperial connection has in large part reinforced the contradictions of British national identity. After 1945 the Dominions wished to redefine citizenship in line with their growing status as independent states, and began promulgating their own nationality laws for immigration purposes. The 1948 British Nationality Act—whereby people were defined as 'citizens of the UK and colonies'—was grafted on to an older conception of Britishness as being a subject of the Crown rather than citizen of a territory, embedded in the 1914 British Nationality and Aliens Act, which did not refer to Britain as a physical territory as such. The 1931 Westminster Statute had given the Dominions the power to enact their own laws of citizenship so as to restrict immigration into *de facto* national territories.

The preferred stance of British governments was that people were British subjects first and citizens of states second, but they were increasingly unable to hold the line against growing independence. The fuzziness of British identity was the result of a complex legacy of imperial rule focused on allegiance to the monarchy rather than the state. Goulbourne has argued that both Labour and Conservative parties in the post-1945 period found themselves caught up in this confused game of identity politics.[10] On the one hand, Labour sought to develop a non-ethnic, multi-racial strategy for its erstwhile colonies, based on a sense of place rather than a sense of tribe, at home and abroad. (It found itself in difficulties coping with Scottish and Welsh nationalism in the 1970s, which it saw as a betrayal of its 'non-ethnic' definition of Britain.) On the other hand, the Conservative party found itself moving to a more 'ethnic' definition of nationality, especially under pressure from the Powellite wing of the party, and embedded the concept of 'patriality', first introduced in the 1971 Immigration Act, in Mrs Thatcher's Nationality Act of 1981. This meant that being able to prove you had a grandparent born in the UK gave you right of entry to these shores, something much closer to a law of blood (*ius sanguinis*) than a law of territory (*ius soli*).

[9] P. Pocock, 'British history: a plea for a new subject', *Journal of Modern History* 4 (1975), pp. 601–21.

[10] Goulbourne, *Ethnicity and Nationalism*.

Detaching Scotland

Before exploring issues of identity, let me return to the core of my argument. Warfare and welfare in the twentieth century reshaped the union by making the UK a more centralist and unitary state. After all, you could not practise modern warfare without involving everyone, and the post-war welfare state required homogeneous rights and obligations covering the whole territory. The United Kingdom developed along two contradictory lines. On the one hand, it was a unitary state, a 'nation-state', with a single parliament at its core making laws for the whole kingdom. On the other hand, it remained multinational with Scottish institutions which had actually been strengthened (under Tom Johnston) rather than weakened by the practice of a war economy. Thus an inherent contradiction lay at the heart of the British state, namely, that it was not only unitary but multinational, and, for Scotland at least, institutionally diverse. Although these contradictions were not to become politically manifest until the final quarter of the twentieth century, they were becoming so as early as mid-century. After 1955, Scotland and England began to diverge in electoral behaviour. This was not simply a function of the growing strength of the SNP; indeed, the rise of the SNP is, to my mind, a symptom rather than a cause of fundamental changes in the union. What really did for the mid-century union was electoral divergence in the two parts of the kingdom, underpinned by alternative frames of political reference.

With the benefit of hindsight, we can see that electoral divergence between Scotland and England really came into its own from the 1970s. All too often, this was taken simply as a reflection of the rise of the Scottish National Party, but there is far more to it than that. Divergence reached its height in 1992, but the elections of Labour in 1997 and 2001 did not produce the status quo ante. Indeed, as we can see from Figure 13.1, it is not Labour's strength in Scotland that matters so much as Conservative weakness which accounts for most of the differential. Labour's advantage in Scotland over its vote in England peaks at 12.9 per cent in 1987, but Conservative shortfall in Scotland compared with England is well above that figure for all of the last twenty-five years.

A unitary system of government in the UK, especially majoritarian democracy, always had the potential for disrupting the delicate balance of the union between small and large neighbours, and the remarkable thing was that it took so long to express itself in electoral terms. What Scotland needed, and usually got, was clever and sensitive governance, a Scottish Office alert to the nuances of being both British and Scottish, of bridging one to the other, and for much of the next twenty-five years after the Second World War it worked tolerably well.

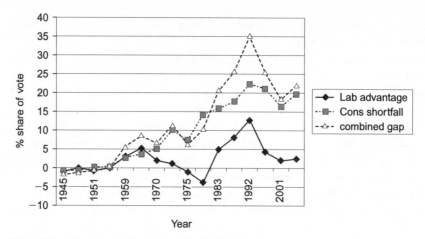

Figure 13.1. Elections in Scotland and England, 1945–2001.
Note. This graph shows the differentials in popular vote between Scotland and England with regard to Labour advantage and Conservative shortfall in Scotland, together with a summary of the combined gap.

This seemed surprising to some, because there has long been an argument that there is something antediluvian about the British state. Only up to a point, one might say. Writers like David Marquand have observed that the UK is 'un-modern', not in the sense that it is socially and economically unreconstructed—Britain was, after all, the home of the industrial revolution and almost single-handedly invented market capitalism, but that in constitutional-political terms it did not try to resolve its inherent contradictions.[11] Thus, it has, at its jurisprudential heart, no written constitution, no proper set of citizenship rights, an unelected second chamber, a doctrine of democratic dictatorship—Crown sovereignty—all underpinned by a powerful social and economic elite—the 'Establishment'. The unwillingness or inability of the UK to modernise its political institutions reflected in part the fact that its success had been built upon its role as a nightwatchman state, with underdeveloped state structures except where, as in the case of the armed forces, they were needed to defend and extend the empire. It left civil society to its own devices, such that the British state sat lightly upon it. Marquand has called the UK an 'unprincipled' society because its state structures were modernised and integrated by default rather than by design. In truth, it is hard to sustain the argument that Britain was never modern, for as Linda Colley observes, up to the beginning of the nineteenth century, it was one of the most modern and democratised in Europe.[12]

---

[11] D. Marquand, *The Unprincipled Society* (London, 1988).
[12] L. Colley, *Britons: Forging the Nation 1707–1837* (New Haven, 1992).

Scotland's rise and fall as part of this world power are closely related. There is little to sustain the argument that Scotland was some kind of oppressed colony of England. On the one hand, the lowlands of Scotland were in a position to take advantage of the exceptionally favourable European and British conjuncture of the end of the eighteenth century, and prospered as a result. On the other hand, Scotland was so well adapted to imperial opportunities in the nineteenth century that the collapse of the economy after the First World War was catastrophic. The roots of Scotland's economic decline lie much more in a surfeit of, an over-adaptation to, British imperialism than any failure to embrace it wholeheartedly. When the international order collapsed, Scotland was so locked into it that it suffered along with the UK as a whole,[13] without the benefit of economic restructuring as happened in the south of England.

This, of course, is history, but it explains how the British 'marriage' became less and less convenient as far as the Scots were concerned. They had entered the relationship with England in a fairly cold-eyed, practical manner, without any serious loss of national identity. Being Scottish and British made economic and political sense. It did not mean that everyone became 'English'. Indeed, it is the relationship between 'state' and 'national' interests which is the key to understanding nationalism and national identity in the British islands. What did not happen here was an aggressive programme of 'nation-building' on the British model. One might even say that the UK is less misconceived than under-conceived, an absent-minded state, a state-nation, rather than a nation-state. In other words, the state came after nations, and in the Scottish case, sat lightly on top of existing governing institutions of law, education, religion, and the like. It is important to point out that this is how the Scots saw it. People in England, who, by the end of the twentieth century made up 85 per cent of the UK population, had no reason to distinguish between state and national identities, and appear not to separate the two in any clear-cut manner. Here is a comment by the writer Anthony Barnett, who tried to capture the variable geometry of identity in Britain:[14]

> What is the difference between being English and being British? If you ask a Scot or a Welsh person about their Britishness, the question makes sense to them. They might say that they feel Scots first and British second. Or that they enjoy a dual identity as Welsh-British, with both parts being equal. Or they might say, 'I'm definitely British first.' What they have in common is an understanding that there is a space between their nation and Britain, and they can assess the relationship between the two. The English, however, are more often baffled when asked how they relate their Englishness and Britishness to each

[13] M. W. Kirby, *The Decline of British Economic Power Since 1870* (London, 1981), pp. 79–80.
[14] A. Barnett, *This Time: Our Constitutional Revolution* (London, 1997), pp. 292–3.

other. They often fail to understand how the two can be contrasted at all. It seems like one of those puzzles that others can undo but you can't; Englishness and Britishness seem inseparable. They might prefer to be called one thing rather than the other—and today young people increasingly prefer English to British—but, like two sides of a coin, neither term has an independent existence from the other.

On reflection, I think this is a little unfair to the English, who appear to be using 'national' rather than 'state' identity labels more often these days, but it does capture nicely the alternative perspectives north and south of the border. For my purposes here it underscores the need not to assume that issues of citizenship and nationality operate according to the same framework in different parts of the kingdom.

Being British

So who *are* the British these days? We might be tempted—wrongly—to assume that Scots reject their British state identity just as they have become more Scottish. The short answer is that there is truth in the latter but not the former. We have only begun to measure these things in the last twenty years, since it became an interesting puzzle. Identity though, is not a zero-sum game. A few statistics might help. In 1979, 38 per cent of people in Scotland opted to say that 'British' was their preferred identity, and 56 per cent said it was Scottish. Twenty years later, the figures were 17 per cent and 77 per cent respectively.[15] Nevertheless, that is a stark and artificial choice to have to make, and most people—as many as 6 in 10—include some version of being British in accounts of who they are. By 2001, for example, 45 per cent say they are Scottish only, 41 per cent Scottish and British, and only 9 per cent British only. (In passing, we might note that in England only 33 per cent say they are British only, compared with 25 per cent who say they are English, and 40 per cent some mixture of the two.) In virtually all the surveys that have been done in the last two decades, people living in Scotland opt to forefront their national identity—being Scottish—but place (secondary) importance on being British also. What we find is some attachment to being British (only about 1 in 4 say they have none or very little), but it takes second place to being Scottish. In short, there does not seem to be an antipathy to being British among people in Scotland, but it does not ring with pride either: hence, perhaps, the usefulness of the 'withering away' metaphor. Being British may be dying, but more with a whimper than a bang.

[15] McCrone, *Understanding Scotland*, p. 160.

There are, of course, limits to surveys. They are good at gauging the spread of opinion, and less good at explaining what people mean. What people seem to do is to invest terms like 'British' (and 'Scottish' for that matter) with particular meanings and purposes as the need arises. In our survey analysis of the 1997 referendum,[16] for example, we found that while those claiming a British identity were marginally less likely to vote in favour of setting up a Scottish Parliament, it was a fairly weak predictor of so doing. In other words, identity preference and constitutional preference were not strongly correlated. Furthermore, we discovered that those people living in Scotland who emphasised their Britishness tended to have views on the right of the political spectrum, whereas in England the self-defining 'Brits' (as opposed to the 'English') were more liberal, and left-of-centre in their views, much as people who claimed to be 'Scottish' north of the border. In other words, we cannot jump to conclusions that people using 'British' north and south of the border actually mean similar things, something we have been exploring, in a series of studies, for almost a decade now.[17]

Put at its simplest, we have found that there is a repertoire of ways of being British for people living in Scotland. For those born and brought up in Scotland, 'British' can mean:

- a synonym for 'English'; some English-born migrants express puzzlement when their use of 'British' to imply commonality with the natives fails to work;
- simply a fact of bureaucratic life, expressed by having a British passport (in passing, we might note that in a putative choice, about two-thirds of people in Scotland would have a Scottish one, and only a quarter a British passport);
- evoking a (regrettable) imperialist legacy;
- evoking the (regrettable) end of empire;
- a statement of political unionism;
- a liberal, civic identity uniting diverse nations and ethnicities in the same state.

In truth, these meanings of being British cannot be reconciled with each other. What we cannot assume is that people are using items from this repertoire in the same way, and that is what we are currently exploring in our five-year research programme funded by the Leverhulme Trust.[18]

---

[16] A. Brown, D. McCrone, L. Paterson, and P. Surridge, *The Scottish Electorate: The 1997 Election and Beyond* (Basingstoke, 1999), p. 126.

[17] F. Bechhofer, D. McCrone, R. Kiely, and R. Stewart, 'Constructing national identity: arts and landed elites in Scotland', *Sociology* 33 (1999), pp. 515–34; R. Kiely, F. Bechhofer, R. Stewart, and D. McCrone, 'The markers and rules of Scottish national identity', *The Sociological Review* 49:1 (2001), pp. 33–55.

[18] http://www.institute–of–governance.org/forum/Leverhulme/TOC.html .

Whither the Union?

The most we can say is that there is nothing inevitable either about the survival of the union, nor about its demise. In any case, what 'union' means is somewhat elastic, and owes more to political aspiration than to constitutional practice. For example, one could imagine—hypothetically—that some sort of confederal arrangement might develop in these islands. Would the union be holding under those circumstances?—possibly, but not as we currently know it. What is striking about the constitutional questions which are subjects of debate in these islands is how diffuse and diverse they are. Distinct constitutional debates have taken place around (a) the Irish question, latterly the status of Northern Ireland *vis-à-vis* the UK and the Republic of Ireland; (b) devolution in Scotland and Wales; (c) sovereignty of the UK in the context of the European Union. Simply bundling up these distinctive debates in the hope of seeing some common thread is fruitless.

The low salience of constitutional debate is perhaps best grasped by the manner in which the UK government set up its Department of Constitutional Affairs in June 2003. Like a rabbit out of a hat, this initiative caught most commentators and analysts unawares when it was established largely to handle the fallout from the reform of the House of Lords, the role of the Lord Chancellor, and what to do about the territorial Secretaries of State for Scotland and Wales post-devolution. Proposals to set up a UK supreme court to replace the law lords has attracted criticism from senior Scottish law lords that it will 'anglicise' Scottish criminal law.[19] By March 2004, the British government had put on ice its proposals to abolish hereditary peers until it could come up with something more viable. The impression given was of fudge and muddle, and lack of a grand plan; instead, something dreamt up to get the government off a particular hook, only to impale itself on another. Certainly, there is no grand debate about the future of the United Kingdom, no systematic discussion of how the different elements of the famously unwritten constitution hold together, and how they might be made to, assuming that was desirable. One gets the sense that, for good or ill, matters of constitutional moment are of little interest to the political classes. After all, devolution in Scotland and Wales came about because of political pressure rather than a grand strategy, a nation-building programme for the twenty-first century. To say this is not to argue that it should be otherwise; merely that the United Kingdom is sustained more by accident than design, live and let live being the order of the day.

---

[19] http://www.dca.gov.uk/consult/supremecourt/scresp.htm .

Will the union hold? Let us review the arguments on either side. For those supporting the view that some version of the union will hold, the main ones seem to be as follows.

1. Liberal democracies, by and large, do not break up. Secession, as in the former East European states, happens when the central state falls apart, when it is unable to sustain its authority over the territory in question, and territories within the state go their separate ways. The obvious historical examples are the end of the Austro-Hungarian empire in the early part of the twentieth century, and the collapse of the Soviet Union towards the end of the century. Such collapse simply has not happened in modern, liberal democracies in the late twentieth century. It is true, of course, that the United Kingdom is smaller than it was one hundred years ago, for much of Ireland is independent. Surely, one might wonder, lightning might strike twice? This is to ignore the lessons of history, because Ireland's history was quite unlike that of Scotland, and even of Wales. Concepts such as 'internal colonialism' have limited value despite their superficial attractiveness.[20]

2. In a related fashion, the scale of grievances in Scotland at the present time is simply not sufficient to propel the country out of the British union. This is no oppressed colony seeking a struggle of liberation. Scotland has long been a semi-detached, self-defining nation in the United Kingdom, and political devolution simply makes explicit this status.

3. If anything, devolution removes the developing grievance that Scotland suffered from a democratic deficit, governed from London, and at the whim of the British ruling party. We should remind ourselves that the Irish question might have been solved if the Home Rule bills in the thirty years prior to the First World War had got through the House of Commons. Their failure so to do generated the end-game of full independence for much of the territory of the island of Ireland. As regards Scotland, if there are anomalies like the so-called West Lothian question remaining, then the issue is more one of managing those anomalies within the relatively unwritten constitution than in creating formal mechanisms which might have the unintended consequence of bringing about independence by default.

4. It is hard to make a claim that the British state is under threat as a result of too much centralisation rather than by too little, for

---

[20] McCrone, *Understanding Scotland*, p. 64–7.

allowing maximal autonomy within what is already a relaxed polity does not generate the desire to exit the state. The future of the United Kingdom would appear to lie in being a loose-linked, supra-national, multi-ethnic liberal state, set within a broader confederal Europe.

So far, so sanguine. There are, of course, arguments pointing in the other direction, towards the break-up of the British state.

1. First of all, the conditions which formed the state no longer hold. One might address the conditions under which the union survived, and why in particular the Scots joined, namely to have access to the developing riches and power of the burgeoning imperial system. These have long since ended. Empire—and global power—are no more. The declining significance of the marriage of convenience comes to rest upon the view that Scotland gets more financially out of the union than it puts in. This argument seems to rest on the view that the union will survive because it meets Scotland's pecuniary needs. Bribery, however, is a poor argument on which to build a state. Stay British, and the Barnett formula will deliver, is not much of a case for sustaining a union which has lasted almost 300 years.

2. There is also a cogent argument that what we are faced with is not a stark, zero-sum choice: in the union or cast into the outer dark-ness of the North Atlantic. What we have here are degrees of free-dom, a shift along the spectrum of self-government, which is a matter of degree not of kind as far as Scotland has always been con-cerned. To set up the case as all or nothing is to ignore the complex and subtle relationships between Scotland and England which have sustained the union, but nevertheless, the world has moved on. The past is a poor predictor of the future in a global, twenty-first-century world. In any event, the world in which the British union was created and prospered is no more. There is serious argument, in any case, that envisaging a world made up of independent, sover-eign nation-states has passed into history. The American sociolo-gist, Daniel Bell has observed that the nation-state these days is too small to solve the big problems of life, and too big to solve the small problems of life;[21] or, to shift the metaphor around, there is some-thing of a crisis of the hyphen in the modern nation-state.

3. Finally, there is what I call the *mentalité* factor. What is especially noticeable since 1999 in particular is how little cognisance is taken

---

[21] Quoted in A. McGrew, 'A global society?', in S. Hall et al. (eds), *Modernity and its Futures* (Cambridge, 1992), pp. 61–102, at p. 87.

of Scottish affairs south of the border. The media, written and electronic, carry less explicit Scottish news than ever before, albeit Loch
Ness monster-type stories, and those relying on stereotypes, still
survive. In short, we may live in a multi-national, quasi-federal
state, but living in England, one would hardly know. In truth,
maybe England is too big to notice what the peripheral minnows are
up to, nor does it care very much, apart from grousing that there are
too many Scots in the Westminster government.

This is the Britain we inhabit today, a Britain which the reforming constitutional world of modernity appears to have largely passed by. Just when we
have belatedly got round to constitutional reform, it seems to have gone out of
fashion. We can debate alternative scenarios, without being able to do a great
deal to bring them about. The pessimistic scenario is that British identity is so
thin and feeble: in the English case, simply a synonym—England and Britain
to be used interchangeably; and for the Celts, a state veneer which has served
its time at the height of empire, union and Protestantism (the reason why most
of the Irish could never be 'British', even if they wanted to). This matrix is no
more, and one prediction is that it will simply fade and give way to the 'genuine' nationalities of these islands. Empire no more: Britain no more. On the
other hand, more optimistically for those who believe in the United Kingdom,
this loose sense of Britishness might be tailor-made for postmodern times in
which pick 'n' mix identity is the order of the day. Be whoever you want to be.
Somehow, the UK has become a multicultural, postmodern society without
really trying, still less understanding how it has come about. Its constitutional
arrangements have leapt, as it were, from pre-modern to post-modern, largely
missing out the 'nation-building' phase which occurred in this period and
which constituted so much of modern nationalism.

How, then, are Anglo-Scottish relations to be managed in this brave, new
multinational world? There is a sense in which whether Scotland remains in
or out of the union matters less than we think. Pierre Trudeau, Prime Minster
of Canada in the 1960s, once remarked that Canada's relationship with the
United States was like that of a mouse in bed with an elephant. No matter
how friendly, one is affected by every twitch and grunt. Small nations, even
independent ones like Canada, are always going to be exasperated by the
failure of the bigger neighbour to notice, to act as if there is no one there but
themselves. Sharing the British island will always raise matters of *realpolitik*
regardless of constitutional status. There is the story that when God created
the world and made this archipelago of islands, the archangels were struck by
the riches and beauty of Scotland: temperate climate, oil, fish, mineral
wealth, what more could the Scots want in this paradise? Ah, said God, just
wait until they see the neighbours . . . In truth, that works both ways round.

14

Devolution and Communications Policy in Scotland

PHILIP SCHLESINGER

Scotland's Communicative Space

SCOTLAND HAS LONG HAD AN INDIGENOUS PRESS, which continues to exercise a strong grip on the country's readership, despite the inroads made by the Scottish editions of London-based titles. Most Scottish national titles (whether indigenous or editions of London papers) are published in Glasgow, Scotland's media capital. Significant papers are also published in Edinburgh, Dundee, and Aberdeen; and there is also a well-developed local press.

In the field of public service radio and television broadcasting, the whole country is served by BBC Scotland, with headquarters in Glasgow. Also regulated on public service lines are the ITV companies Scottish Television and Grampian Television, which cover virtually the whole country and are owned by SMG, the Scottish Media Group. A small slice of the television audience is served by Border Television. The dominant commercial radio player is Scottish Radio Holdings.

The BBC, Channel 3 (ITV1), Channel 4, and Channel 5 all have legal obligations to spend varying proportions of their programme-making budgets outside of London on first-run productions.[1] Part of this expenditure occurs in Scotland and is crucial to sustaining the creative economy there. Both the BBC and Channel 4 commission programmes for the network (as well as for Scotland) through their nations and regions offices in Glasgow. Some ITV programming produced in Scotland is also destined for the network. Scotland is presently one of the UK's leading audiovisual production centres, with Glasgow as the linchpin.

---

[1] Current figures are: BBC 33 per cent, C4 30 per cent, C5 10 per cent, and ITV 50 per cent.

Proceedings of the British Academy **128**, 217–230. © The British Academy 2005.

Devolution has thrown into relief relations that were once relatively implicit. The Scotland Act 1998 distinguished between 'devolved' and 'reserved' powers. Broadcasting—central to the new Communications Act 2003—was expressly 'reserved' to Westminster. So, too, was telecommunications. Powers over the press (most notably, in respect of cross-media ownership and concentration) are also reserved, coming under UK regulatory bodies. But Scotland does retain considerable autonomy over cultural arenas that relate directly to the 'converging' fields of broadcasting and telecommunications. Support for film and television production is handled by Scottish Screen. The arts generally are within the remit of the Scottish Arts Council. The business development end of the creative industries comes under the aegis of Scottish Enterprise.

Cultural and communicative activity in Scotland, then, is subject to distinct Scottish and UK jurisdictions. But devolution has created a new political system north of the border with the capacity to debate matters that still remain London's exclusive legislative and regulatory prerogative. From time to time, questions about communications, both Scottish and UK-wide, have been discussed in the Scottish Parliament. For instance, when the Communications Bill was passing through the Commons, there was also some debate at Holyrood. The main issue addressed was that of Scottish representation on the new regulatory body, the Office of Communications, Ofcom.[2] But this was muddled up with arguments about the sale of the *Herald* group of newspapers. In fact, the Scottish Parliament's pre-eminent concern about the media has been rather narrowly concerned with its own image in Scotland.

To date, the fact that communications is designated a reserved matter has inhibited thinking about broader policy questions both in the Executive and the Parliament. Although the SNP has periodically advocated greater control over broadcasting north of the border, on the whole political discussion has been both limited and sporadic. It remains to be seen whether this will change as the challenge represented by the Communications Act 2003, and the new regulatory body, Ofcom, increasingly impinges upon Scotland.

Tensions in Broadcasting

Because of its prominence in everyday life, broadcasting (especially television) tends to be a focus of jurisdictional tensions. These emerge occasionally

---

[2] Scottish Parliament Official Report, 'Broadcasting and the Print Media', Thursday 31 October 2002, www.scottish.parliament.uk/S1/official_report/session-02/sor1031-0.htm#Col14999-14810.

and often unpredictably—most often in the field of news and current affairs programming, which is at the heart of politics.

The most notorious recent row occurred in 1998, the year before devolution became a reality. The main lines of the story have been aired elsewhere.[3] The heart of the matter was whether or not BBC Scotland should be allowed to broadcast its own 6–7 p.m. hour of news and current affairs on BBC1. This would have entailed an opt-out from network news to follow a news agenda ordered according to Glasgow's priorities. For London, this was simply too much. For some—including John Birt, the BBC's then Director-General—the 'Scottish Six' was but one step away from the dissolution of the realm and the 'end of a single common experience of UK news' that would 'encourage separatist tendencies'.[4]

Senior ministers, most of them Scots, and the Prime Minister, were persuaded by this alarmist vision. Contrariwise, by the end of the various press campaigns, almost 70 per cent of Scots were said to be in favour of a Scottish Six.[5] For present purposes, what is so interesting about this case is its translation from a rather arcane and essentially private broadcasting row, debated for months between the Broadcasting Council for Scotland and the BBC Executive in London, into a major Scottish political story. The Scottish Six became a thoroughly national matter: one of having 'our' news denied to us by 'them'. And for the London-based opponents (the key ones being top Labour Party Scots), BBC Scotland's policy could easily be tarred with the brush of nationalism, and therefore dismissed.

For a while, the political heat dissipated. A little-noticed inquiry by the Scottish Affairs Committee at Westminster in spring 2002 showed no concern at all about the Scottish Six.[6] Further skirmishes came in autumn 2003 when it was reported that BBC Scotland had been producing pilot programmes for the BBC1 6–7 p.m. news and current affairs slot as part of BBC Scotland's review of its journalism output.[7]

These tussles were but the preamble to the publication on 17 December 2003 of BBC Scotland's *Journalism Review*.[8] Amongst a range of findings, what grabbed the headlines—predictably enough—was the report's virtual interment of the long-debated Scottish Six. While the research uncovered

---

[3] P. Schlesinger, D. Miller, and W. Dinan, *Open Scotland? Journalists, Spin Doctors and Lobbyists* (Edinburgh, 2001).

[4] J. Birt, *The Harder Path* (London, 2002), p. 484.

[5] Schlesinger, Miller, Dinan, *Open Scotland?*, p. 46.

[6] HC Scottish Affairs Committee on Post-Devolution News and Current Affairs Broadcasting in Scotland 3rd Report (HC Paper (2001–02) no. 549).

[7] M. Russell and K. Macintosh, 'Nations and regions: should there be a Scottish Six?', *Holyrood* 1 (December 2003), pp. 48–9.

[8] BBC Scotland, *Journalism Review 2003* (Glasgow, 2003).

some doubts about the relevance of news from London, the conclusion was that while 'the case for an integrated Scottish news hour does not appear strong enough to justify the change being made, the position should remain under review'.[9] So the door has not been entirely closed by the BBC.

Irrespective of what the corporation might decide, others seem determined to keep the matter on the public agenda. On 8 March 2004, the Scottish Consumer Council published a brief riposte to the BBC's research.[10] The report, based on a survey of attitudes towards the BBC's news provision, found that a majority of respondents was in favour of the creation of a Scottish Six. Paul McKinney, head of news and current affairs at Scottish Television, also took up the cudgels. He argued (with the endorsement of SMG) that Scottish broadcasters should broaden their horizons and put out an international, UK, and Scottish news programme on ITV in the slot currently occupied by ITN's late night news.[11]

Scotland's distinctive political map and electoral cycle occasionally throw up other complications. Even before devolution, the country's political culture would create the odd difficulty for London schedulers. Post-devolution, the same inherent tensions have persisted. When the ITV network broadcast *Ask the Prime Minister* in winter 2000, it faced protests about impartiality. The programme was due to be screened before a parliamentary by-election in Falkirk West. Speculation was then rife about whether there would be a UK General Election the following spring. Putting on an access show of this kind featuring Mr Blair meant that, in order to ensure due impartiality, ITV had to reschedule its programmes in Scotland. It also added a special edition of the election programme, *Hustings*, to meet the objections of the SNP. Such incidents tend to attract much press *Sturm und Drang*, some parliamentary expostulations, and, from a Scottish point of view, serve to rattle the cage of a presumed homogeneous Britishness.

Network broadcasters have had to rethink aspects of programming and scheduling in the wake of devolution. However, this has not posed any fundamental problems for them and the continuities are more striking than the changes. For instance, recent research has shown how London-based programme teams in the current affairs field have made adjustments to established formulae to meet Scottish needs, while at the same time keeping the entire UK audience in mind.[12]

---

[9] Ibid., pp. 17–23.

[10] Scottish Consumer Council, *Reaching Out: The Consumer Perspective on Communications in Scotland* (Glasgow, 2004).

[11] D. Fraser, 'STV news chief gives backing to independent "Scottish Six"', *Sunday Herald*, 14 March 2004, p. 7.

[12] B. McNair, M. Hibberd, and P. Schlesinger, *Mediated Access: Broadcasting and Democratic Participation in the Age of Mediated Politics* (Luton, 2003), pp. 48–54.

Press Competition

Press ownership also remains a sensitive question. To reduce its debt, in 2002 SMG decided to sell its newspaper holdings and put *The Herald*, *Sunday Herald*, and the *Evening Times* on the market. Given the pivotal opinion-forming role of the *Heralds*, not only for the west of Scotland, but also for the entire devolved political system, much hung on the purchaser. Both elements of Scotland's political class and sections of the blethering classes were somewhat exercised. The sale revealed much about how post-devolution politics over the press is conducted. In substance, it is just the same as pre-devolution politics. However, one thing is different: the stakes have risen.

Among the range of potential buyers for the *Herald* group was an investment vehicle for the Barclay brothers, who own Scotsman Publications. There was evidently widespread concern in the political class about the *Scotsman* stable making a successful bid. In the parliamentary debate already noted, Mike Russell MSP, the SNP's media and culture spokesman, quickly lodged a motion with the Scottish Parliament, calling for more diversity of ownership north of the border, thereby underlining the importance of decisions made in London for a devolved Scotland. By early November 2002, the SNP was calling for the power to regulate the media to be transferred to the Scottish Parliament from Westminster. Russell asked for the sale of SMG's papers to be subject to an inquiry by a parliamentary committee in Edinburgh.

Scottish Labour sought to avoid an open dispute with London and to lobby in time-worn fashion. Karen Gillon MSP, convener of the Scottish Parliament's education, culture and sport committee, wrote to the UK competition minister in the DTI, Melanie Johnson MP, raising questions about the impact of the sale on the diversity of content and the plurality of media ownership in Scotland. Ms Gillon echoed other MSPs' concerns about the risks of a 'predatory' bid by the Barclay brothers. Only the Scottish Conservatives appeared to favour a *Scotsman* take-over.[13] The issue and its wider implications spilled across the border in the shape of careful analyses influenced by cross-border media connections in both the *Financial Times* and *The Guardian*.[14]

Jack McConnell MSP, the Labour First Minister, is believed to have lobbied the UK Labour leadership. Robin Cook MP, Leader of the House of Commons, stated his preference for the *Herald* and *Scotsman* groups to remain separate. The Scottish Secretary, Helen Liddell MP, incurred the

---

[13] F. Horsburgh, 'Call for power to regulate Scottish media industry', *The Herald*, 1 November 2002, p. 9.
[14] Editorial, 'Scottish media', *Financial Times*, 6 November 2002; M. Brown, 'Tartan turmoil', *Media Guardian*, 11 November 2002, p. 6.

wrath of Andrew Neil, the *Scotsman* group's publisher, for her open concern about the sale.[15] Such expressions of opinion carried weight. The SMG board's judgement eventually went in favour of Gannett. Although commercial considerations predominated, the SMG board was also clearly sensitive to the political atmosphere and how it would look in its own backyard.[16]

The company opted to sell to Newsquest, the British arm of the US media giant, Gannett, for some £216m.[17] The sale was then investigated by the Competition Commission, which visited the Glasgow-based papers and held hearings in Scotland. The Commission, charged with considering public interest aspects of the sale, seemed aware that devolution had special implications for the Scottish media market. It opted for Newsquest and the Secretary of State for Trade and Industry accepted the recommendation.

The case showed the capacity of the Scottish Parliament to debate questions of media concentration but also its incapacity to act legislatively. Just as in the days of the Scottish Office, mobilising the old north–south lines of political influence to Westminster was the chosen path. Senior politicians' views, in all likelihood, were significant for the decision-making process, not least as the potential political consequences of making errors of judgement about media ownership in Scotland have grown considerably since 1999.

Influencing the Communications Act 2003

On 17 July, the Communications Act 2003 received Royal Assent. There are both political and economic calculations behind the refusal to devolve powers over the media. Politically, notably in relation to broadcasting, there has been a fear in key government circles and amongst some senior broadcasters that parcelling out powers will lead inevitably to separatism and the collapse of the union.

Economically, government policy is intended to make 'the UK the most dynamic and competitive communications market in the world'.[18] Increased competitiveness is conceived of as occurring within a 'convergent' digital electronic environment. UK government policy envisages a new communications economy in which broadcasting, telecommunications, and computing come

---

[15] D. Summers, 'Robin Cook intervenes over move to buy The Herald', *The Herald*, 22 November 2002, p. 12; J. Ashley, 'Interview: Haggis and press sneers fail to stop tough Scot', *The Guardian*, 27 January 2003, p. 10.

[16] C. Hope, 'Politicians welcome Gannett purchase of The Herald', *The Herald*, 1 November 2002, pp. 1–2.

[17] F. Kane, 'Herald of change in Scots press', *The Observer in Scotland*, Business, 23 June 2002, p. 8.

[18] www.communicationsbill.gov.uk/policynarrative/550806.html, p. 1.

together to create the basis for an 'information society'. For British policy-makers, the key reference point is the global economy and building 'UK plc's' strengths within that context. Permitting the emergence of bigger players—for instance, a single ITV—easing cross-media ownership rules, and encouraging foreign investment are all part of this picture. The Communications Act 2003 has been strongly driven by competition considerations.

The act was preceded by a lengthy period of consultation. First there was a White Paper, *A New Future for Communications*, published in December 2000. This was followed by the draft Communications Bill, on which consultation began in May 2002. The public consultation was paralleled by the pre-legislative scrutiny of a joint committee of the two Houses at Westminster, chaired by Lord Puttnam. The joint committee reported in August 2002. The government accepted a substantial number of amendments and a revised Communications Bill was issued at the end of 2002. The relatively open consultation process allowed a variety of lobbies to intervene.

Little public debate took place in Scotland during the act's lengthy gestation. The Voice of the Viewer and Listener (a UK body) held a public conference on the bill in Edinburgh in 2002. There was an occasional newspaper forum for articles on the Communications Bill.[19] There was the one, rather unfocused, Scottish Parliamentary debate in October 2002. More typical, apart from direct lobbying in London by a variety of interests, was the convening of small private meetings, such as a Glasgow lunch in February 2002 sponsored by the Scottish Consumer Council. The discussion showed that London policy-makers had given little thought to the implications for Scotland of their legislative proposals. The expression of strong views around the table did at least put Scottish concerns onto the agenda. The SCC worried about how market consolidation would affect 'regional identity, plurality and choice' in broadcasting and believed that Scotland was falling behind with respect to the Internet and digital television take-up.[20]

While at one level there are intense pressures on broadcasting to face outwards and address the global market, inherited constraints mean that audiences in the nations and regions have to be served in ways largely continuous with the past. The principled argument to retain 'regionality' was most effectively propounded by the outgoing regulator for commercial television, the ITC, in its *Charter for the Nations and Regions*, which noted that ITV had

---

[19] Communications Bill, www.communicationsbill.gov.uk/policynarrative/550806.html; R. Galbraith, 'What happened to the principles of independent TV?', *Sunday Herald*, Business, 9 June 2002, p. 7; K. Kemp, 'Broadcasting bill will promote regional identities', *Sunday Herald*, Business, 23 June 2002, p. 8; P. Schlesinger, 'Bill's new world order could be the death of regional diversity', *Sunday Herald*, Business, 2 June 2002, p. 8.
[20] Scottish Consumer Council, *Reaching Out*.

committed itself to an annual investment target of 50 per cent of expenditure on out-of-London originated programmes. A further commitment was made to extensive regional news coverage at peak time. At least 90 per cent of Scottish regional programmes were to be produced in Scotland. This commitment was an important influence on the climate of opinion during the legislative process. The ITC also argued strongly for the retention of offices in the nations and regions. Its research was used to bolster the arguments, identifying a considerable appetite for news provision that addressed local and regional concerns and indicating that regional programming was regarded as a vital service by the majority of viewers.[21]

Independent producer interests were effectively prosecuted by their trade organisation, PACT, which was instrumental in ensuring that favourable programme supply conditions were established as the bill was debated.[22] Independent television production for BBC Scotland, ITV, and Channel 4 (and other broadcasters) has contributed to building capacity in Scotland, particularly in Glasgow. The Communications Act 2003 has endorsed the demand for some decentralisation of the broadcast economy, a demand which long predated devolution. But (as previously) the present order does not favour Scottish interests as against those of any other nation or region. Ultimately, the performance of the broadcast economy in Scotland will be decided by its competitiveness within the wider UK framework.[23]

It was to address this issue that the Screen Industries Summit for Scotland was held in Glasgow on 3 November 2003. Participants were mainly broadcasters, independent production companies, and Scottish development agencies. Attended by over 150 people, this was the largest meeting to discuss the future of the audiovisual industries in Scotland for well over a decade. Of the UK's total of £4.8bn audiovisual content production in 2001, Scotland accounted for £240m, or 5 per cent.[24]

Subsequently, the Screen Industries Summit Group was formed, reflecting the range of interests present in Glasgow. Meetings held in early 2004 set about identifying key objectives for a potentially powerful Scottish lobbying exercise in the fields of television, film, the games industry, and research and development. It remains to be seen how effective the Scottish lobby will be in

[21] I. Hargreaves and J. Thomas, *New News, Old News* (London, 2002), pp. 62–8; M. Kidd and B. Taylor, *Television in the Nations and Regions* (London, 2002), pp. 44–5.
[22] ITC, *UK Programme Supply Review: A Report by the Independent Television Commission to the Secretary of State for Culture, Media and Sport* (London, 2002); PACT, *PACT Submission to the ITC Review of the Programme Supply Market* (London, 2002).
[23] The Research Centre, *Risky Business: Inside the Indies* (Glasgow, 2002); The Research Centre, *Inside the Commissioners* (Glasgow, 2003).
[24] D. Graham and Associates, *Audit of the Screen Industries in Scotland* (Glasgow, 2003), pp. 13–21.

fighting its case at the UK level at a time of considerable volatility in the media and communications sector.

Regulation and the Regulators

The distinct Scottish interest in communications has long been recognised, and in certain instances institutionalised, at the UK level. Until 2003, and the launch of Ofcom, the reigning model had been a politically inspired one, based on the seat in the UK cabinet accorded the Secretary of State for Scotland. As that office was demoted in significance during the summer of 2003, congruent changes were also taking place in the world of communications regulation.[25]

The BBC's Board of Governors has long had 'national' members for Scotland, Wales, and Northern Ireland. This system recognises the territorial distinctiveness of the smaller nations in the UK state. The practice was extended—by statute—to the Independent Television Commission (and its predecessor bodies, the ITA and the IBA), as well as to the Radio Authority. The Broadcasting Standards Commission also statutorily followed the national member model. In the field of telecommunications, there was a Scottish Advisory Committee on Telecommunications (SACOT), with a statutory duty to advise the then regulator, Oftel, on the needs of telecoms consumers in Scotland.

Before Ofcom, therefore, regulatory bodies dealing with broadcasting had Scottish representation at their highest levels. Scottish ire was aroused when it was decided that Ofcom's main board would drop the territorial principle for this strategic level of decision making. It was obvious from repeated ministerial statements, as well as the blank wall encountered during lobbying lunches such as that organised by the SCC, that the principle was not going to be conceded. The Office of Communications Act 2002, which set up the Ofcom board in advance of the Communications Act 2003, made no provision for territorial representation on the board of nine members.

The Puttnam committee, which reviewed the government's draft bill, expressly considered the 'representation of nations and regions'. It supported the UK government's approach to the composition of the main board. However, the committee asked that existing provisions in respect of the two key subordinate committees—the Content Board and the Consumer Panel—be strengthened. The committee was open to lobbying on this

---

[25] A. Trench, 'The more things change, the more things stay the same: intergovernmental relations four years on', in A. Trench (ed.), *Has Devolution Made a Difference? The State of the Nations 2004* (Exeter, 2004), pp. 165–92.

question and recommended that 'Ofcom be placed under a statutory duty to maintain offices in Scotland, Wales and Northern Ireland'; the regulator was also to report specifically on its activities in the nations.[26]

MPs, peers, and MSPs were vigorously lobbied by SACOT to strengthen the rather weak provisions on representation agreed by ministers.[27] The Scottish Executive lobbied on similar lines. The Puttnam committee was influenced in its thinking by these and other such efforts. In fact, the Scottish Executive had adopted a fallback position. The First Minister, Jack McConnell, took exception to the lack of representation on the Ofcom main board. But Tessa Jowell MP, the Secretary of State for Culture, Media and Sport at Westminster, rejected his argument.[28] The Executive's retreat from its original demands was fully exposed during the brief parliamentary debate initiated by Mike Russell MSP. Mr McConnell had also raised the issue with Helen Liddell, the Scottish Secretary. The Scotland Office, according to some insiders, toed the line being put out by the DCMS and DTI, which was hostile to any statutory provisions being made for Scottish representation.

At the end of 2002, the revised bill statutorily required offices to be set up in each of the UK's nations. The Content Board and Consumer Panel would each have a member for Scotland. SACOT argued that this was not enough capacity to attend to the country's needs and that 'the Bill should be amended to provide for a Committee for Scotland, reporting to the Ofcom Board, with input to and from both the Content Board and Consumer Panel'. The Committee for Scotland amendment was resisted by the Ofcom Board 'on the grounds that it was something they were going to do anyway. It was also resisted by the Government up to the final stages of the debate in Lords.'[29] Lobbying efforts, however, which included amendments to the bill drafted by SACOT, resulted in provision for a statutory national committee. Statutory status has entrenched the Scottish committee's functions. This status had to be fought for, and represents one of the signal outcomes of Scottish lobbying.

In the year-long run-up to the creation of a Scottish national advisory committee and the appointment of its Scottish director in March 2004, Ofcom's leadership kept open the lines to Scotland, providing both personal

---

[26] HL-HC Joint Committee on the Draft Communications Bill, vol. I Report (HL Paper (2001–02) no. 169–i; HC Paper (2001–02) no. 876–i), pp. 20–1.

[27] SACOT, *UK Communications Bill: Briefing for All MSPs* (Edinburgh, 2002).

[28] The Deputy Minister for Tourism, Culture and Sport, Dr Elaine Murray, candidly said in the parliamentary debate referred to above (n. 2): 'It is on record that the First Minister requested a seat on the central board. The DCMS feels strongly that it should not be a representative board . . .', col. 14807.

[29] Personal communication from Jeremy Mitchell, Chairman of SACOT, 4 September 2003.

briefings for key figures in broadcasting and telecommunications and meeting interested parties.

Where Next?

Most of the Holyrood political class has been reluctant to explore the boundaries between the devolved and the reserved. If that continues, 'ownership' of the communications agenda will surely remain with major interest groups that have the resources and motivation to get to grips with current policy debate. But at a period of far-reaching change there is a major public interest in communications being widely understood and discussed amongst all citizens as a counterweight to the elite and expert circles of influence which presently monopolise debate.

Across the UK as a whole, Ofcom now has a key role in policing the terms of trade for regional production that falls within a public service broadcaster's target. While BBC Scotland, the SMG companies, and, to a lesser extent, Channel 4, are significant players, the Scottish independent production companies—with few exceptions—are very small. Recent industry reports stress the need to improve the business skills of independents and to make them more market aware.[30] Glasgow's continued development as Scotland's media hub will be of decisive importance for inter-regional competition.

The newly merged ITV is imposing pressures on the regional-federal commercial model in force since 1955. That framework has been transformed increasingly by the growing concentration of ownership that has characterised the past two decades. Decentralised production for ITV depends on the future balance between competition and public service considerations in a rapidly changing commercial marketplace. Channels 4 and 5 also have to reposition themselves.

Against this volatile background, the Scottish ITV landscape is shifting. The future of SMG has been increasingly questioned, following the sale of its newspapers and then a key part of its radio assets to address its debt problems. If Scottish and Grampian are bought up and integrated into a consolidated ITV, this is likely to have major implications for the extent of TV production north of the border and for a Scottish voice on Channel 3. The stations could also be of interest to a non-UK buyer. The recurrent questions raised about the future ownership of ITV in Scotland means that how

---

[30] The Research Centre, *Risky Business*; The Research Centre, *Inside the Commissioners*.

effectively Ofcom defines and polices 'regionality' is likely to become an economic and political issue for the Scottish Executive and the Scottish Parliament.

As we head towards the government's goal of a digital switch-over by 2012, those who wish to argue for a different model of commissioning public service production, and for changing radically the nature of its distribution, point to the impact of new technology. Digitisation under regulated conditions expands the capacity for universal delivery. If a large number of channels were to become universally accessible, in principle the delivery of public service programming could be put out to tender on different principles from those that now pertain. The new conditional access technology could also transform the nature of payments for services. Such arguments raise fundamental questions about the future of the licence fee. Should it be maintained? Should it be top-sliced? Should it be distributed by a new public service broadcasting agency across a wider range of recipients, of which the BBC would be only one, even if the most significant?[31] Increasing numbers now buy their broadcast entertainment and mobile telephony as a matter of course, making unquestioning future public support for the licence fee as a special tax more and more doubtful. Longer-term changes in media consumption patterns are fertile ground for those who would argue that public service tax-based revenues should be parcelled out rather than earmarked for the BBC. How individual choice can be mobilised to sustain a public good has become the new heartland of debate about public service broadcasting.

The BBC's position as the principal vehicle of public service broadcasting has come increasingly under question. Ofcom's reviews during 2004 of spectrum pricing and of public service broadcasting, as well as the BBC's Charter Review (to conclude in 2006) will be severe tests for the corporation. At this time of writing, the BBC is still absorbing the impact of the Hutton Report, which found the BBC's journalistic rigour wanting.[32]

Hutton's strictures concerning the BBC's performance came precisely at a time of burgeoning debate about key aspects of the corporation's structure and functioning. The future role of the BBC Governors—already a matter of

---

[31] Such questions have been posed by the Elstein report for the Conservative Party, as well as by other protagonists in current debate. These ideas have been in circulation since the Peacock Committee reported in 1986. See D. Elstein (chairman) Broadcasting Policy Group, *Beyond the Charter: The BBC after 2006* (London, 2004); B. Cox, T. Gardam, and A. Singer, 'How to save shows like Operatunity', *Media Guardian*, 15 March 2004, pp. 2–3; for comments, see P. Schlesinger, 'Anti-Beeb brigade with a charter to work mischief', *Sunday Herald*, Business, 2 June 2002, p. 8; M. Wells, '£1bn culture cost in ending TV licence fee', *The Guardian*, 25 February 2004, p. 7.

[32] Lord Hutton, *Report of the Inquiry into the Circumstances Surrounding the Death of Dr David Kelly CMG*, www.the-hutton-inquiry.org.uk.

controversy amongst those who would either subordinate them to Ofcom or recast them in some other guise—was thrown further into question by Lord Hutton, who accused them of taking insufficient distance from BBC management during the Kelly affair. Any changes in the BBC's governance will have direct consequences for Scotland.

The Gaelic Media Service set up under the Communications Act 2003 has a line of responsibility to Ofcom in London. Public financial support for Gaelic falls under the remit of the Scottish Parliament, but broadcasting remains a reserved matter.[33] Alongside the Scottish Executive, the Scotland Office has a locus in the matter, as does the Department for Culture, Media and Sport. Policy development will therefore require a complex partnership between London and Edinburgh. The aspiration to run a coherent Gaelic television service on a digital channel will require funding, and coming debate about the feasibility of this might well, in turn, raise questions about the possibility of establishing a Scottish digital channel.

Telecommunications is far less accessible than broadcasting to widespread discussion and does not easily acquire headline status. But it is crucial for the functioning of everyday life and is central to the 'converged' legislation. The SCC's concern about Scotland falling behind in the 'communications revolution'—shared by SACOT—was also echoed by joint research from the ITC and the Broadcasting Standards Commission. Their survey of viewing habits, revealed 'that whilst the number of people with Internet access in the UK has almost doubled, 67 per cent of Scots can still not access the Internet'. Scottish digital take-up has also trailed all other parts of the UK, with 65 per cent not having access.[34]

In its final report, SACOT identified four key regulatory issues needing future attention by Ofcom. BT's market dominance in Scotland headed the queue. SACOT also pointed more generally to the need for accessible consumer information about telephony to make markets work more effectively; for more rapid progress to be made in the rolling out of broadband in Scotland; and for more consumer protection for young buyers of mobile phones.[35]

A Last Word

It is increasingly clear (though generally still not openly acknowledged) that the spectre of independence has haunted the calculations of devolutionist

---

[33] M. Cormack, 'Gaelic in the Media', *Scottish Affairs* 46 (2004), pp. 28–9.

[34] ITC, 'Scots behind in Internet access and digital take-up, says new ITC/BSC research', ITC news release, 16 February 2002, p. 1.

[35] SACOT, *The Final Report and the Future* (Edinburgh, 2003).

politicians.[36] This has produced an impasse and the scope and sophistication of contemporary debate must now urgently be addressed.

Scotland's institutional frameworks for handling culture and for dealing with media and communication are asymmetrical. That we cannot imagine a neatly bounded national space is one of the inherent complexities of the devolved Scottish condition. Although the image of a self-contained nation no longer reflects the realities of cultural and communicative flows in the era of 'globalisation', it does point to something important. The levers of state-hood still afford decisive policy advantages that those of mere autonomy within a state do not. The United Kingdom can still dispose of considerable room for manoeuvre in how it addresses culture and communications in the context of developing 'Europeanisation' and other forms of transnational governance.[37]

There is an opportunity to be seized in the next phase of devolution. The Communications Act 2003 has created a new, enlarged space for articulating Scottish perspectives on the media and communications industries. Ofcom's Scottish National Advisory Committee could become an important focus of informed debate north of the border as well as of influence in London. But for that to take place, it will first be essential for the Scottish Executive and Parliament, the civil service, and the Scottish public to be equipped to understand how the new communications agenda will impact on the country (and its culture).

Note. My thanks to Stuart Cosgrove, Donald Emslie, Sarah Jane Kerr, John McCormick, and Jeremy Mitchell for discussing the issues, to Mike Cormack and Simon Frith for helpful comments, and to Bill Miller for inviting my conference contribution. An earlier version of this chapter was published in *Scottish Affairs* 47 (2004).

[36] As clearly stated by J. McTernan in 'Too late review?', *Holyrood*, 8 September 2003, p. 26: 'Scotland has a Parliament because it is a nation, albeit one within a larger political unit. But because of the strength of nationalism over the last thirty years, there remains a residual fear that doing anything to build national identity is a gift to separatists.'

[37] P. Schlesinger, 'The Babel of Europe? An essay on networks and communicative spaces', ARENA Working Paper no. 22, November 2003 (Oslo), to be published in D. Castiglione and C. Longman (eds), *The Challenge of Multilingualism in Law and Politics* (Oxford, forthcoming).

15

Anglo-Scottish Relations:
A Borderland Perspective

JOHN TOMANEY

Introduction

BEFORE THE UNION OF THE CROWNS, the governance of the 'North Parts' was
a large challenge for the English Crown. The pacification of the region after
1603, together with the growth of industry from the eighteenth century
onward saw the integration of the region into a national economy and society. The region's sense of its distinctive identity did not disappear during this
period, but its expression tended to be restricted to cultural rather than
directly political fields, especially on the part of the region's aristocracy and
bourgeoisie.[1]

This chapter charts the rise of regionalism in North-East England during
the twentieth century. It argues that after 1914 North-East voices were central to the promotion of regional concerns in England and played a pivotal
role in the wider emergence of political regionalism. The prospect of Scottish
devolution accelerated elite debates about the governance of the North-East
at the end of the twentieth century, but a debate about the value of regional
government occurred throughout the century. In part, it fed off a sense of
social and economic injustices and in part, a sense of collective regional
identity that reflected cultural separateness.

Regionalism, however, gained political salience from the 1980s onward, as
a result of changes in the external and internal environment. Underpinning
North-East regionalism in the twentieth century was a large body of intellectual work, which sought to identify the distinctiveness of the region, both as
an 'imagined community' and as a victim of disadvantage. The development
of English regionalism as an economic and political project was heavily

[1] R. Colls and W. Lancaster, *Geordies: The Roots of Regionalism* (Edinburgh, 1992).

Proceedings of the British Academy **128**, 231–248. © The British Academy 2005.

influenced by contributors, notably geographers, with strong North-East connections, notably C. B. Fawcett, G. H. J. Daysh and J. W. House, although differences existed between such writers in their definitions, diagnoses, remedies, and practices.

The political expression of regionalism shifted significantly during the twentieth century. In the first half of the century regionalism was associated with bourgeois interests. In the second half of the twentieth century North-East Labourism eventually reached an accommodation with regionalism and became its main advocate. The story begins in 1919.

The North Country and 'Home Rule All Round'

C. B. Fawcett is regarded as one of the founders of modern British academic geography.[2] A student of Herbertson and Mackinder at Oxford, he contributed perhaps the founding text of English regionalism in his *Provinces of England*, first published in 1919.[3] This work emerged from the fertile, if complex and contradictory, intellectual milieu that surrounded Patrick Geddes and others in the period immediately before and just after First World War. This group placed great hope in the emerging possibilities of planning and saw the 'region' as the key focus of these possibilities. At the heart of Geddes's approach was the 'regional survey'—an attempt to view the region as an organism incorporating the natural and human worlds—which provided the foundation of modern town planning.[4] Geddes's ideas and those of his followers were outlined in a series of books and pamphlets with the general title of 'Making the Future'. Fawcett's study was a contribution to the Making the Future series and influenced by Geddes's reading of the French social scientist, Frédéric Le Play.

More immediately though, Fawcett's essay was a distinctive (northern) English contribution to the debate about 'Home Rule All Round'. Bogdanor has noted that the original Home Rule debates raised all the questions that dominated the discussion of devolution in the last quarter of the twentieth century.[5] With this in mind, the twenty-first-century reader of Fawcett's book

[2] T. W. Freeman, 'Charles Bungay Fawcett, 1883–1952', in T. W. Freeman (ed.), *Geographers: Biobibliographical Studies*, VI (International Geographical Union/International Union of History and Philosophy of Science, London, 1982), pp. 39–46.
[3] An earlier proposal to regionalise England was made by the Fabian Society. See W. S. Sanders, *Municipalisation by Provinces* (The New Heptarchy Series 1, Fabian Tract 125, London, 1905).
[4] D. F. T. Evans, 'Le Play House and the Regional Survey Movement in British Sociology, 1920–1955' (unpublished M.Phil. thesis, Birmingham Polytechnic/CNAA, 1986); H. Meller, *Patrick Geddes: Social Evolutionist and City Planner* (London, 1990).
[5] V. Bogdanor, *Devolution* (Oxford, 2001).

is struck by its far-sightedness and the degree to which it raises issues that had begun finally to be grappled with at the close of the twentieth century.

Fawcett begins by quickly rejecting the idea of an English parliament, which was proposed as a solution at the Speaker's conference on devolution in 1919, opining that it would dominate the federation in the manner that Prussia had dominated the German Empire before 1914. Moreover, such an English parliament would not speak to the desire for local autonomy and it would replicate the failures of the existing British parliament, which even in 1919 was 'overburdened by its manifest duties'.[6]

Fawcett also addresses what he regarded as the inadequacies of existing local government, especially the shires. By 1919, existing local authority boundaries were not fit for the purposes for which they had originally been designed, reflecting their origins in the pre-industrial age:

> The present planning authorities are the County Councils, but there is hardly any aspect of land use or development plans which does not immediately involve areas beyond the County boundary.[7]

Planning, in Fawcett's view, was best done at the regional level, as demonstrated by the design of the civil defence regions from 1918, which, broadly, represented the foundations for later regional boundaries. While some claimed that counties were the ancient and untouchable units of English governance, Fawcett shows that this argument is specious by reference to the hundreds of changes to existing local boundaries in the inter-census period 1901–11 alone, concluding, 'Evidently there is nothing sacrosanct in the boundaries of the administrative sub-divisions of England.'[8]

Fawcett outlines a set of principles for the creation of provinces, from which he produced a map of the 'Provinces of England'. In doing so he adapted Geddes's 'regional survey' method, which sought to link 'natural' geography with population distribution and questions of regional identity. But while acknowledging the importance of 'natural' divisions such as watersheds, Fawcett stipulates that regional boundaries should 'pay regard to local patriotism and to tradition'.[9] It is in relation to this latter dimension that the northern influence seems strongest.

Although couched in an austere language of scientific enquiry, there is little doubt that Fawcett's England is seen through a northern lens. Fawcett was born in Staindrop in Teesdale in 1883 of farming stock and went to

---

[6] C. B. Fawcett, *Provinces of England: A Study of Some Geographical Aspects of Devolution*, revised edn, eds W. G. East and S. W. Woolridge (London, 1961), p. 27.

[7] Fawcett, *Provinces of England*, p. 31.

[8] Ibid., p. 50.

[9] Ibid., p. 62.

school in Gainford.[10] After school he studied science at University College, Nottingham and, following a brief spell as a schoolteacher, joined the new School of Geography at Oxford University, where he was a student of Mackinder and Herbertson. Subsequently he lectured in geography at University College, Southampton and Leeds University before being appointed Professor of Geography at University College London, where he remained for twenty-one years until his retirement in 1949. He specialised in the study of population and political geography. In relation to the former he developed Geddes's pioneering concept of the 'conurbation', which had a bearing on his thinking about 'provinces', and was a founder member of the Le Play Society, which promoted regionalism and the virtues of planning.[11] He produced his monumental *Political Geography of the British Empire* in 1934. Fawcett died on 21 September 1952. Physically tall, spare, and tough, by all accounts Fawcett was a taciturn and diffident character, often regarded as aloof and unapproachable, although he also inspired loyalty among students and colleagues. His character was reflected in his work. According to one obituarist, 'he was so concerned to eliminate emotional elements that he kept his constructive imagination in over-strict subjection.'[12]

It seems appropriate that the founding text of modern English regionalism should be written by a man from County Durham. In an undemonstrative way, Fawcett maintained a deep feeling for his northern roots which, despite his reputation for studied detachment, was revealed in glimpses in his writings about his 'homeland'. Fawcett's approach to the subject is unobtrusively but avowedly influenced by a northern outlook. In describing his English provinces, Fawcett acknowledges that his treatment of 'North England' is dealt with first and at greater length than other provinces, 'partly, perhaps, because the writer is himself a Northcountryman'.[13] Fawcett's understanding of the provincial character of England appears heavily influenced by his firmly held view that the North-East was a region with its own identity which overlay more local identities:

> County identity is not prominent in Durham; and the inhabitants of that palatinate county are apt to think of themselves as Northcountrymen, and pride themselves on the fact, rather than as Men of Durham: their local patriotism is for the North Country, rather than the County.[14]

[10] According to one of his former students, 'Fawcett used to refer to his origins on a farm near Staindrop and claimed never to wear socks as a reminder of the fact. He derived quiet satisfaction from his progress from teaching in an elementary school to Faculty Dean' (Brian Fullerton, personal communication, 2003).
[11] Meller, *Patrick Geddes.*
[12] R. O. Buchanan, 'Obituary: Professor C. B. Fawcett, BLitt, DSc', *Geographical Journal* 118 (1953), pp. 514–16.
[13] Fawcett, *Provinces of England*, p. 60.
[14] Ibid., p. 69.

It was in the foreword to a short text about the geography of North-East England that Fawcett perhaps gave fullest expression to his feelings about the region and the way they had influenced his view about the political geography of England. In doing so he both freely adapted the language of his mentors Geddes and Mackinder and revealed a passion that was at odds with the emotional reticence others saw in his work:

> A knowledge of Geography is like Charity, in that it should begin at home and extend from there to the whole world. It is only by knowing the geography of our Homeland and our Home Folk that we can lay the foundation for a sound knowledge of other lands and peoples.[15]

He sets the contemporary region in a long historical timeframe:

> Most of the districts which now form North-East England were then the central parts of the strong Angle kingdom of Northumbria, formed of the coastal areas between the Humber and the Forth.[16]

Fawcett describes how during the Middle Ages 'our Homeland was a border country under the rule of many feudal lords, ... a land of barbaric border warfare which was both savage and bitter at the time, though it appears romantic now that it is seen through the softening mists of time'.[17] The region, though, was transformed by the industrial revolution: 'Then the prosperity of our Homeland was built up by the men who were able to make the best use of its natural resources.'[18]

In *Provinces of England* this view of the region as a land apart was explicated more fully:

> Medieval England, at least as an administrative unit, did not effectively incorporate Yorkshire and the North Country. These regions acknowledged the overlordship of the kings who ruled over the English lowlands but, like Wales and the Welsh Marches, they were too remote from the capital at London to be easily or directly controlled from there. Towards the end of the Middle Ages they were ruled by the Council of the North; and not until after the time of the Tudors and the Commonwealth do these remoter regions appear to have been really integral parts of England.[19]

---

[15] C. B. Fawcett, 'Foreword', in E. M. Coulthard, *From Tweed to Tees: A Short Geography of North Eastern England* (Edinburgh, 1934), pp. 5–8, at p. 5. The text in question was aimed at schoolchildren and is a classic 'regional survey'. It was written by Miss E. M. Coulthard, 'geography mistress at the Bishop Auckland Girls' County School'. Miss Coulthard's interest in her 'adopted land' was 'first stirred' by Fawcett (p. 10).

[16] Fawcett, 'Foreword', p. 5.

[17] Ibid., p. 17.

[18] Ibid., p. 7.

[19] Fawcett, *Provinces of England*, pp. 60–1.

Fawcett's view of the historical position of the region has generally been bolstered during the twentieth century by the 'new British historiography' which, among other things, emphasises the ambiguous position of North-East England as a largely self-governing province during the Middle Ages. For Fawcett, the North-East 'is still in many respects an intermediate region between the English and Scottish lowlands, rather than part of either',[20] with its distinctiveness accentuated by the uneven geographical impact of the industrial revolution. Although his geographical interests were wide—what we could today call 'global'—Fawcett returned periodically to write about his 'homeland', contributing classical regional surveys of the North-East, complete with river section, the leitmotif of the Le Play Society.[21] In continually emphasising the geographical and historic distinctiveness of the region, Fawcett set a template for future studies, such as that of A. E. Smailes, a native of Tynedale and Professor of Geography at Queen Mary College, University of London, which also sought to emphasise the region's special character within an English context.[22]

The opportunities for political regionalism were fleeting at the end of the First World War. On the one hand, the debate about devolution evaporated, following the partition of Ireland and the creation of the Irish Free State, while the inter-war period was characterised by a grave economic crisis in the North-East which required urgent action. However, although the political conditions for devolution had disappeared, the geographically uneven character of the inter-war crisis meant that the North-East became the focus of a new debate about regional policy.

The North-East as a 'Problem Region'

Following the First World War, the North-East experienced a deepening focus on it as an object of study, especially as far as its social and economic problems were concerned. Geographers, planners, and, to a lesser extent, economists contributed to the notion of the North-East as a distinctive region, but now with particular economic problems associated with the collapse of its dominating traditional industries of coal-mining, steel-making, and shipbuilding. Indeed the region became the archetypal 'problem region'

---

[20] Ibid., p. 75.
[21] C. B. Fawcett, 'A regional study of North-East England', *Geographical Teacher* 10 (1920), pp. 224–360; C. B. Fawcett, 'North-East England', in A. G. Ogilvie (ed.), *Great Britain: Essays in Regional Geography* (Cambridge, 1928), pp. 332–48.
[22] A. E. Smailes, *North England* (London, 1960).

and the focus of multiple 'regional policies' over the following decades. Linked to these developments, the inter-war period saw an emerging regionalism, driven to a large degree by bourgeois forces, especially those with large 'sunk costs' tied up in the traditional industries.

While the region was emerging during this period as a Labour heartland, the Labour Party's role in regionalism remained modest. Hugh Dalton, MP for Bishop Auckland, showed an interest in regional policy as a solution to the unemployment problem and took up the idea in his role of Chancellor of the Exchequer in the 1945 Labour government. In the era of the General Strike, the Miners' Lockout, and the Jarrow Crusade, class conflict was a more immediate concern.[23] Moreover, the powerful miners' unions began to see the solution to the problems of the Great Northern Coalfield in terms of 'nationalisation'—as did miners in Scotland and Wales—while labour leaders such as Peter Lee sought to capture existing local government for the Labour Party.[24]

The idea of the North-East as a region with special claims was reinforced, though, by a new series of 'regional surveys' in the inter-war and immediate post-Second World War periods, which sought to quantify and explain the character of the regions' economic crisis.[25] Such studies formed part of the background to the designation of the North-East as a 'Special Area' under the terms of the Special Areas Acts of 1934 and 1937.

A key figure in the study of the region and the promotion of its interests, before and after the Second World War, was Henry Daysh, a geographer at Armstrong College in Newcastle (which in 1937 became King's College, University of Durham and then, in 1967, the University of Newcastle upon Tyne). Daysh ended his career as Deputy Vice-Chancellor of Newcastle University, but made his name as the author of Armstrong College's influential studies of the region's economic conditions in the late 1920s and early 1930s. His career included a spell during the Second World War as Director of the Research Division in the Ministry of Town and Planning, during which he served as the Ministry's representative on the Inter-departmental

[23] E. Wilkinson, *The Town That Was Murdered: The Life Story of Jarrow* (London, 1939).
[24] B. Austrin and H. Beynon, *Masters and Servants. Class and Patronage in the Making of a Labour Organisation: The Durham Miners and the English Political Tradition* (London, 1994).
[25] Armstrong College, *The Industrial Position of the North East Coast of England* (Report for the North East Development Board, Newcastle upon Tyne, 1931); Armstrong College, *A Survey of Industrial Facilities of the North East Coast* (Report for the North East Development Board, Newcastle upon Tyne, 1936); G. Pepler and P. W. MacFarlane, *The North East Development Plan*, Report to the Minister of Town and Country Planning (London, 1949); H. Mess, *Industrial Tyneside: A Social Survey made for the Bureau of Social Research for Tyneside* (London, 1928).

Committee on regional policy which contributed to the White Paper on Employment Policy.[26]

In addition to undertaking influential research on the North-East, Daysh also promoted action to address the regional problem. With the Teesside industrialist Sir Sadler Forster, he was the moving force behind the establishment of the North East Development Board (NEDB), building on earlier local efforts to promote economic revival.[27] The NEDB proved to be the first in a series of organisations that sought to promote the region as a location for investment and as requiring special assistance from government. Although NEDB folded with the outbreak of the Second World War, Daysh was influential in setting up a successor body, the North East Development Association (NEDA), in 1943 (see Figure 15.1). While such bodies focused primarily on economic development, they also sought to promote regional identity. For instance, the North East Industrial Development Association (NEIDA), which replaced NEDA in 1953, sponsored a regional history textbook for schoolchildren.[28]

Daysh, originally from Hampshire, was heavily involved in regional politics. According to a colleague he was 'essentially a businessman' and 'an active Conservative—what we would nowadays call a "one-nation" Tory'. His experience in the North-East and in wartime planning meant he eschewed *laissez-faire* policies and, instead, was 'much in favour of government support to the depressed areas and [much in favour] of an element of regional devolution and planning',[29] and saw the North-East as being characterised by a 'regionalism of discontent'.[30] However, according to a former colleague, in Daysh's view:

> Regional development was best achieved through the co-operation of influential individuals from industry and government, applying information supplied by geographers, economists and statisticians as they saw fit.

The idea that regional problems could be best tackled by regional bodies dominated by regional elites was established as the *modus operandi* of North-East regionalism in the inter-war period and continued after the Second

---

[26] K. C. Edwards, 'Foreword: academic', in J. W. House (ed.), *Northern Geographical Essays in honour of G. H. J. Daysh* (Newcastle upon Tyne, 1966); S. Forster, 'Foreword: personal' in ibid.; R. Hudson, *Wrecking a Region: State Policies, Party Politics and Regional Change in North East England* (Studies in Society and Space, London, 1989).

[27] Edwards, 'Foreword: academic'.

[28] See H. G. Bowling, L. C. Coombes, and R. Walker, *The Land of Three Rivers: The Tyne and Wear and the Tees* (North East Industrial Development Association, London, 1958).

[29] Brian Fullerton, personal communication, 2003.

[30] J. W. House, 'Regionalism and the sense of community', *Geographical Journal* 136:1 (1970), pp. 6–12.

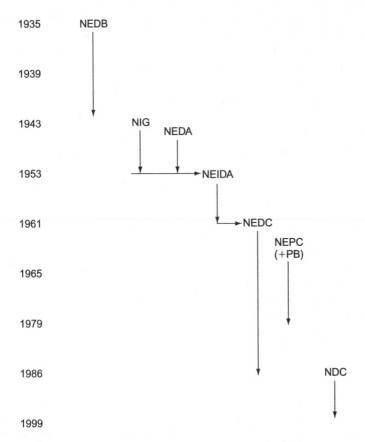

Figure 15.1.   Schematic history of regional bodies in North-East England.
NEDB: North East Development Board
NIG: Northern Industrial Group
NEDA: North East Development Association
NEIDA: North East Industrial Development Association
NEDC: North East Development Council
NEPC: Northern Economic Planning Council; (+PB: Planning Board)
NDC: Northern Development Company

World War, but was very much associated with the capitalist interest.[31] The character of the regional economy as a form of 'carboniferous capitalism' meant that coal-owners and others had large amounts of the wealth tied up in fixed assets in the region. Consequently the early regional organisations

---

[31] Benwell Community Development Project, *The Making of a Ruling Class: Two Centuries of Capital Development on Tyneside* (Newcastle upon Tyne, 1979); J. M. Cousins et al., 'Aspects of contradiction in regional policy: the case of North East England', *Regional Studies* 8 (1974), pp. 133–44.

were dominated by figures from coal-owning families such as Lord Ridley. Ironically it was nationalisation of coal and railways in 1947 which liquidised these assets and led both to a switch from productive to rentier investments and to capital flight from the region and signified the beginning of the end of the leading role of such families in regional politics.[32]

During the 1930s official analyses began to draw a connection between the failure to address the economic crisis in the region and the need to reform structures of governance. The government commissioned a series of studies into conditions in the 'depressed areas' in 1934. The study of Durham and Tyneside was conducted by Captain D. Euan Wallace, MP. Wallace concluded, somewhat radically given the context, that the cause of the region's problem lay outside the control of its inhabitants and that the region needed urgent government help. Among Wallace's recommendations was the formation of an 'industrial development company' and the appointment of a Royal Commission to investigate the reorganisation of local government.[33] The resulting Royal Commission reported in 1937. It concluded that the existing system of local government hindered the efficient administration of local services. Among the recommendations of the Royal Commission was that a 'regional council' should be established to administer 'national services' that required control over a large area.[34]

At the same time some influential voices in the North-East made the case for political devolution. A key figure was the diplomat, Conservative politician, and bearer of a great Northumbrian name, Lord Eustace Percy. Percy explicitly raised the notion of devolution to the region in language not dissimilar to that of Fawcett, but linked it also to the failure to deal with the inter-war crisis. In the introduction to a series of essays by his fellow Conservative MP Sir Cuthbert Headlam he argued:

> English government is at bottom provincial government. To-day, when we are beginning to realize that our existing units of local administration can no longer meet all our local needs, it is good to be reminded once again that there are larger units, marked out by geography and by history, which deserve some share of the local patriotism which we have hitherto devoted to county and municipality . . . The time may come when this Northern Province will find in a regional council the solution of some of those social problems which have baffled our statesmanship during recent years.[35]

[32] Benwell, *The Making of a Ruling Class*.
[33] *Reports of investigations into the industrial conditions in certain depressed areas of* I: *Cumberland and Haltwhistle*, II: *Durham and Tyneside*, III: *South Wales and Monmouthshire*, IV: *Scotland*, Sessional Papers 1933–4, XIII, Cmd. 4728 (London, 1934).
[34] *Local Government in the Tyneside Area*, Report of Royal Commission, Sessional Papers 1936/7, xiii, Cmd. 5402.
[35] E. Percy, 'Introduction', in C. Headlam (ed.), *The Three Northern Counties of England* (Gateshead, 1939), pp. xi–xiii.

Percy was Minister for Health in 1923–4 and then President of the Board of Education until 1929. However, he wanted Baldwin to give him a different office. According to a contemporary:

> He had wanted to become Minister for his economically depressed native North-East [but] Neville Chamberlain, the Chancellor of the Exchequer, was determined to retain any Government action in the regions in his own hands.[36]

Economic intervention remained firmly in the hands of central government. The limited forms of intervention in the region by central authorities to promote rationalisation of industry—notably by the Bank of England and the Treasury—were concerned with precluding more radical demands. The Governor of the Bank of England, Montagu Norman, appreciated the scale of the problem in regions like the North-East, but sanctioned intervention only so long as it was 'limited, temporary and exceptional'. It involved modest efforts to promote mergers in the traditional industries, but only on a voluntary basis, and generally neglected issues of technological change and productivity. These efforts were far from enough to offset the Bank's commitment to financial orthodoxy, which eroded further the competitiveness of the region's export base.[37]

The government did eventually act during this period to address the regional unemployment problem, albeit in a modest way. The intervention came in the form of the Special Areas Acts of 1934 and 1937. Four Special Areas were designated, of which one was in the North-East. These Acts provided loans and aid to firms willing to invest in the designated areas and for the construction of publicly funded 'Trading Estates'. The first of these in the country was the Team Valley Trading Estate at Gateshead. It aimed to attract the new type of consumer industries, which were growing quickly in the Midlands and South. Although operating on a tiny scale, when compared to the scale of the problem, this approach set the pattern for regional policy in subsequent decades. In particular, it defined the regional problem as one of over-reliance on 'old' industries, such as coal-mining, and defined the solution as 'diversification' of the industrial bases (that is, the creation of 'new' plants in 'new' sectors).

---

[36] H. Loebl, *Outside In: Memoirs of Business and Public Work in the North East of England 1951–1984* (Newcastle upon Tyne, 2001), p. 232.
[37] C. Heim, 'Inter-war responses to regional decline', in B. Elbaum and W. Lazonick (eds), *The Decline of the British Economy* (Oxford, 1986), pp. 240–65.

Regionalism in the Era of Nationalisation

The North-East's unemployment problem was solved by war and its build-up, as the demand for coal, steel, and ships expanded, rather than by regional policy. Regionalism, moreover, had a good war. Regional planning was integral to the war effort and appeared replete with possibility when peace returned. Its attractions were acknowledged across the political spectrum. In a contribution to Sir Ernest Barker's famous effort to find the 'spirit of England' immediately after the Second World War, the Conservative historian, G. M. Young opined:

> We may not have a demand for Home Rule in Northumbria or the East Midlands. [But] we may very likely hear a claim for Regional Rights; for a legal delimitation of the powers of Parliament and the regional assembly; for an infusion of Federalism into the constitution.[38]

On the Left, for the Fabians, 'Regionaliter', acknowledging the contribution of Fawcett, proposed that, building on the experience of wartime Regional Commissioners, directly elected 'regional councils' should be created with the purpose of improving regional planning and securing 'intelligent coordinated action' among the various government departments operating at the regional level.[39]

The economic and political conditions immediately after the war did not lend themselves to the regionalist argument in the North-East, any more than they did to nationalism in Wales and Scotland. The Labour Party consolidated its hold over local government in the region, but the basic industries, notably coal-mining, were *nationalised*, eventually leaving the North-East a 'state managed region'.[40] Although the White Paper on Employment Policy drew attention to the need for a 'balanced distribution of industry and employment' and an apparatus of regional policy was established, the basic industries during this period were working to full capacity, reflecting the exigencies of post-war reconstruction and the demands of the Korean War. After 1951, the Conservative government reduced regional policy, although strong voices within the North-East (now designated a 'Development Area')—and even some in Whitehall—acknowledged that the staple industries were still characterised by major structural weaknesses. For instance, in 1951 Board of Trade officials prepared a note for the incoming

[38] G. M. Young, 'Government', in Ernest Barker (ed.), *The Character of England* (Oxford, 1947), p. 111.

[39] 'Regionaliter', *Regional Government* (Fabian Research Series 63, London, 1942); see also G. D. H. Cole, *Local and Regional Government* (London, 1947), who acknowledges his debt to Fawcett.

[40] Hudson, *Wrecking a Region*, p. 355.

(Conservative) minister Peter Thorneycroft giving a pessimistic view of the economic outlook in the 'Development Areas'. Thorneycroft ignored this warning. The Treasury, in particular, saw no economic case for regional policy and was sanguine about prospects for staple industries.

Voices in the North-East, however, were raised to complain about the ineffectiveness of the government's approach. The chairman of North East Trading Estates, Sadler Forster, complained to the House of Commons Select Committee on Estimates in 1962 that the inconsistency and short-termism of the government's approach hindered development of a long-term strategy in the North-East.[41] Such prognostications were borne out when recession at the end of the 1950s led to a sharp rise in unemployment in the region with problems concentrated in shipbuilding.

The Conservative government's response was to appoint Lord Hailsham as 'Minister for the North East'. Hailsham, famously sporting a worker's flat cap, visited the region to assess its problems. The outcome was the Hailsham Plan of 1963, which was published as a government White Paper, although it was largely produced by officials from within the region. Although the stimulus to its preparation had been a rise in unemployment, the focus for the Plan was the promotion of economic growth rather than the direct alleviation of unemployment. Accordingly, new development was to be focused on 'growth points', including 'new towns', rather than existing mining communities. The Plan advocated an integrated programme of infrastructure development, advance factories, and grants to firms.[42] According to one later commentator, though, Hailsham's 'contribution is to be measured not in terms of millions of pounds invested in motorways but rather as a crucial step forward in regional thinking on the broadest possible front'.[43]

Hailsham's approach was endorsed by the incoming Labour government of 1964, which, as part of its more interventionist approach to the 'underperformance' of UK industry, massively expanded expenditure on regional policy to levels which were more or less maintained by governments of both parties until the late 1970s. An important innovation of the Labour government was the introduction of a Regional Economic Planning Council (REPC), which brought together government, business, and trade unions, to advise ministers about regional investment priorities. REPCs were established in all regions of England, but had no executive powers. Moreover, central government activity in the region remained split between many different

[41] P. Scott, 'The worst of both worlds: British regional policy', *Business History* 38:4 (1996), pp. 41–64.

[42] Board of Trade, *The North-East: A Programme for Regional Development*, Cmnd. 2206 'The Hailsham Report' (London, 1963).

[43] Dan Smith, *An Autobiography* (Newcastle upon Tyne, 1970), p. 79.

departments, whose activities were determined by national priorities. The notion that the governance of the English regions was both too centralised and too fragmented to be effective, especially in poorly performing regions like the North-East, was to become an important theme of the debate about regional development.

Despite its handicaps, the Northern Economic Planning Council, however, developed a relatively high profile under the charismatic (and controversial) leadership of the local Labour politician T. Dan Smith. Smith had ambitions for a more active role for the REPC, for instance, in developing a science policy for the region. These ambitions, though, went far beyond what the government had in mind, and, given the dominance of central government in the framing of regional policy, little came of them.[44] The arrival of T. Dan Smith on the regional stage can be seen as marking a transition from the old 'bourgeois regionalism' to a new 'Labourist regionalism'. Smith was its flag-bearer. His entrance was a reflection of the hegemony of Labour in the local state on the one hand and, on the other, the political decline of the coal-owners and landed families of previous eras.

Smith claimed that it was following discussion with the Labour Party in the North that the Wilson government created Regional Economic Planning Councils. But, in Smith's view, the growth of economic regionalism should be used to fuel a more explicit political regionalism. Smith advocated a unified Tyneside (and Teesside) as the appropriate local government arrangements to accompany a devolved government, drawing on a debate that stretched back to the inter-war period,[45] and sought to secure the role of 'regional capital' for Newcastle.

Smith's voice was not the only one in the Labour Party calling for devolution. For instance the Tyneside Fabian Society made a case for a 'regional government for North East England', which emphasised how there had been a rapid growth in 'regional administration' following the Second World War, but that this tier of regional administration was poorly co-ordinated and lacked accountability.[46] The argument prefigured those that would be used in the White Paper, *Your Region Your Choice*, in 2002. Political regionalism, though, remained a minority taste inside the Labour Party during this period, notwithstanding the support of some MPs such as the former minister, Arthur Blenkinsop.[47]

[44] Ibid.
[45] See Mess, *Industrial Tyneside*.
[46] Tyneside Fabian Society, *Regional Government for North East England* (Newcastle upon Tyne, 1966), pp. 4, 12.
[47] R. Guthrie and I. McLean, 'Another part of the periphery: reactions to devolution in an English Development Area', *Parliamentary Affairs* 31 (1978), pp. 190–200.

The mantle of intellectual regionalism in the 1960s fell on Henry Daysh's successor as Professor of Geography at Newcastle, John House, who later became Mackinder Professor of Geography at Oxford. House pursued a more avowedly academic approach than Daysh, but nevertheless contributed to policy debates and was a member of the Northern Economic Planning Council. Like others before him, he strongly endorsed the regional concept, acknowledging that he had been 'reared on the contribution of C. B. Fawcett'.[48] House saw the region as becoming more relevant as modern society developed. Contemporary social and economic changes, according to House, were generating 'community-forming forces at higher scale' than the locality and 'prospectively creating a corporate sense out of what were initially no more than a set of functional relationships'. For House, the 'province' was one of a number of inter-related 'concepts of community'. The creation of bodies such as the Regional Economic Planning Council both reflected and contributed to the growth of regionalism. But regionalism was also a product of growing personal mobility and a less parochial sense of life. House maintained that 'provincial level loyalties' in England were fostered in the 1960s by the emergence of regional television, industrial promotion policies and regional marketing strategies, and the emergence of bodies such as regional arts associations which, in particular, had contributed to a 'strong sense of provincial community in the North East'.[49] These developments, together with the growing importance of regional planning raised the question of regional governance. House, indeed, endorsed the view of Lewis Mumford that 'the reanimation and rebuilding of regions as deliberate works of collective action is the grand task of politics in the coming generation'.[50] Regionalism was by now firmly linked to the agenda of modernisation.[51]

The fate of North-East regionalism remained linked to the powerful figure of Dan Smith, however. The ignominious end to Smith's career—he ended up convicted and jailed on corruption charges in 1971—was a damaging blow to regionalism, especially inside the Labour movement. The emerging Left was suspicious of regionalism, offering the analysis that 'regional problems are no more than constellations of social-structural problems'.[52] At the same time, however, during the 1970s rising Scottish nationalism meant that the devolution debate continued to exercise the attention of the region's political elite.

---

[48] House, 'Regionalism and the sense of community', p. 11.
[49] Ibid., p. 7.
[50] Ibid., p. 11.
[51] E. Allen, 'Breakthrough to regionalism', in House (ed.), *Northern Geographical Essays in honour of G. H. J. Daysh*, pp. 14–124.
[52] Cousins et al., 'Aspects of contradiction', p. 143.

The rise of Scottish nationalism was generally viewed, with some exceptions, as a threat to the region. Local authority leaders in the North-East and the Northern Group of MPs were the chief opponents of the Scotland Bill in 1977. The Northern Group of Labour MPs was disproportionately represented among those who rebelled in the House of Commons on the guillotine proposals motion on 22 February 1977, which effectively killed the devolution Bill.[53]

Structures and Opportunities

The North-East region played a pivotal role in debates about English regional government after 1979. At the end of the 1970s the idea of a powerful government in Edinburgh—which, after all, is the North-East's nearest capital city—had been regarded as a threat by most economic and political interests in the North-East. For a variety of reasons this attitude gradually changed during the 1980s. The region struggled to cope with rapid deindustrialisation and its social fallout. It found itself politically and culturally at odds with Margaret Thatcher's supporters in Middle England and its Labourist voting traditions were reinforced. Local authorities, trade unions, and business, stimulated partly by European pressures, sought to co-operate and develop the region's distinctive institutions in order to attract new industry. In short, a series of factors reinforced the 'regionalism of discontent' identified by Daysh half a century earlier.

Attitudes among sections of the regional elite were transformed during the 1980s, such that by the early 1990s, the regional Labour Party had endorsed the idea of an elected assembly as its policy. A number of factors underpinned this development. In part, leading figures in the regional labour movement recognised that, despite the defeat of 1979, Scottish devolution was unlikely to disappear from the political agenda. At the same time, the miners' strike of 1984–5 and a series of high-profile battles to save shipyards and steelworks looked like old class-struggles, but their failure cast doubt on the traditional approaches of Labourism in the face social and economic change. Such defeats highlighted the extent to which they were an expression of regional, as well as class, concerns. Thatcherism provided a cold political climate for the North-East (and vice versa). By 1997, Labour held twenty-eight out of thirty parliamentary seats in the North-East.

Following their fall from grace with Dan Smith, regionalist arguments were redeemed inside the Labour Party. In the 1980s, it was the younger, left-

---

[53] Guthrie and McLean, 'Another part of the periphery'.

wing critics of the Labour old guard in parliament and at the local level who attached themselves to regionalism and linked it to a radical analysis of the North-East's social and political weaknesses. A significant contribution came from Alan Milburn, later Secretary of State for Health, who drafted the regional party's policy.[54] These efforts were connected to—and helped to influence—a wider debate in the Labour Party, in which future Ministers such as John Prescott were involved. By 1992, the Labour Party's manifesto included a commitment to create elected assemblies in the English regions. Increasingly this was linked to a programme aimed at addressing the persistent economic inequalities that marked England.

The debate at this point, however, moved out of what were the increasingly narrow confines of the Labour Party. In 1992, the 'Campaign for a Northern Assembly' was formed, with an explicitly cross-party character and which cast the argument for a regional assembly in cultural as well as economic terms.[55] Later still, in 1999, inspired by if not exactly mimicking the Scottish Constitutional Convention, a North East Constitutional Convention (NECC) was established and sought to sketch out a workable model of an elected assembly.[56] These developments proved both challenging and innovative in such a Labour bastion.

In 1997 Labour was elected with a commitment to legislate for elected assemblies in those regions that wanted them, but in office it moved slowly. Regional Development Agencies were established across England, but in the North-East these could be seen as the latest development in a process of institution building going back to the 1930s, rather than a radical step forward. Key figures within New Labour remained sceptical of the regional agenda, although its weight inside government gradually increased, so that by 2003 the prospect of referendums was offered to three northern regions for late 2004. The outcomes of this process were by no means certain: devolution was no longer an inspiring prospect, but an imperfect reality and a pervasive cynicism about politics was an obstacle to a 'Yes' vote.

Scottish devolution heightened the argument about a North East Assembly at the close of the twentieth century, but this chapter has shown that a long and distinctive debate about the merits of regional government can be traced throughout the century. This debate emphasised the particular identity of the region and the need for institutional innovation to address longstanding social and economic problems. The proposal to hold a

---

[54] A. Milburn and P. Corrigan, 'The case for regional government', Discussion Paper, Northern Region Labour Party (1992).

[55] R. Forbes (ed.), *Governing Ourselves* (Newcastle upon Tyne, 1992).

[56] J. Tomaney, 'Democratically elected regional government in England: the work of the North East Constitutional Convention', *Regional Studies* 34:4 (2000), pp. 383–8.

referendum on a North East Assembly in 2004 provided an opportunity for the people of the region to pass judgement on a century's debate.

In November 2004 the people of North-East England voted decisively against the establishment of elected Assembly. The reasons for this outcome are beyond the scope of the current paper, but it is worth noting some historical similarities with result in Wales in 1979. As well as the margins of defeat being similar, so too were some of the political conditions—a government of declining popularity, less than enthusiastic about devolution, was the proponent of change. (Of course there were also important differences between the North-East and Wales, including an absence of a 'language question' and equivalent administrative devolution.) Morover, it seems likely that a more pervasive cynicism about politics played a prominent role in the defeat of the proposition. Writing in the aftermath of the Welsh referendum defeat, the great Welsh historian Gwyn A. Williams, reflecting the despair felt by supporters of devolution there, wrote that the 'Welsh electorate in 1979 wrote *finis* to nearly two hundred years of Welsh history. They declared bankrupt the political creeds which the modern Welsh had embraced. They may in the process have warranted the death of Wales itself.'[57] There are those who will draw similar conclusions from the result in North-East England. However, things changed in Wales. Moreover, even in the aftermath of the 1979 defeat, some in Wales adopted a less baleful outlook. Kenneth O. Morgan suggested that 'the idea of Welsh devolution did not disappear from history in March 1979.'[58] Morgan, ultimately, was proved correct. The social, economic, and political problems which generated the quest for regionalism in the North-East during the twentieth certainly did not disappear in November 2004. It remains to be seen whether the people of the North-East will ever embrace devolution as a solution to these problems.

[57] G. A. Williams, *When Was Wales?* (Harmondsworth, 1985), p. 295.
[58] K. O. Morgan, 'Foreword', in D. Foulkes, J. B. Jones, and R. A. Wilford (eds), *The Welsh Veto: The Wales Act 1978 and the Referendum* (Cardiff, 1983), pp. i–x, at p. x.

16

New Unions for Old

NEIL MacCORMICK

THE CONSTITUTIONAL POLICY OF THE SCOTTISH NATIONAL PARTY, of which I was until 2004 a Vice-President and an elected representative in the European Parliament, proposes 'Independence in Europe' for Scotland, but with a continuation of the shared British monarchy. Headship of State in Scotland should continue to be vested in Queen Elizabeth and her successors as these are determined in future by the law of Scotland. The present European Union Membership of Scotland (as part of the United Kingdom) should continue, as should that of other successor states to the United Kingdom (save if one or more took advantage of an implicit or, possibly, explicit, right to right to discontinue that membership).

The political case for this view presents it as a way to avoid certain of the implicit difficulties built into the variable geometry of the current UK constitution under multi-speed devolution. What is offered is, among other things, one solution to the problems of political identity which bulk so large in these islands, and throughout the European Union, at the present time. Certainly, not all my political colleagues agree about the continuing Union of Crowns. Some disagree on grounds of republican principle. Others disagree on the ground that a dual Headship of State would be unworkable or at any rate damaging to at least one party during a period of negotiation for a consensual dissolution of the current incorporating union as it has evolved since first adopted in 1706/7. The compromise that we all accept says that a referendum should be conducted following the establishment of Scottish independence on the question whether to substitute an elective for a hereditary head of state.

Unlike many of my political friends I contend in a quite unembarrassed way that there ought to remain some form of union between Scotland and England in the time to come as in the past four hundred years. We share an

Proceedings of the British Academy **128**, 249–255. © The British Academy 2005.

island, a huge amount of trade and of personal and familial interpenetration. This merits some political recognition and even celebration. But, in my view, this should not be at the cost of demoting Scotland to the status simply of a 'region', one among many, in the European Union as this is evolving. The idea of a 'union' of some kind, very different from the present, is one I inherit from, among others, the patriot Andrew Fletcher of Saltoun. A union through shared membership of the great confederation of the European Union, with a shared head of state but not of government seems to me a good version of 'new unions for old'.

I argued this at length in the concluding chapter of my book *Questioning Sovereignty* in 1999,[1] and I have not seen reason to change my opinion much in the past five years. Indeed, with the enlargement of the EU and the entry of ten new states, six smaller than Scotland and one (the Slovak Republic) the same in size, the case seems yet more compelling. A further part of that argument deserves a reprise also. It is possible to envisage, and to welcome, an evolution of the current 'British/Irish Council', or 'Council of the Isles' into a collaboration of independent but cognate countries akin to the Nordic League (which Scotland should seek also to join) or to Benelux.

Malcolm Rifkind once criticised the 'new unions for old' idea on the ground that it repeats a formula previously tried, tested, and failed. The Union of the Crowns was in itself a failed union, says Rifkind. It was saved at the last gasp only by being turned into a full incorporating union under the Union Treaty of 1706 ratified by the Scottish and English Acts of Union enacted by the two parliaments in 1707. A close friend and political colleague put the same point to me as recently as 1 November 2003 at a Scottish National Party meeting in Glasgow. The Union of the Crowns did not work well in the seventeenth century, and would work no better in the twenty-first, it is argued.

A part of the motivation for this volume on Anglo-Scottish relations is that 2003 marked the quatercentenary of the Union of the Crowns. In such a context, and in the light of present controversies, it seems fitting to reflect further on the Union of 1603, the personal union, the Union of the Crowns under James VI and I. Is it true that a regal union of that kind failed, and indeed true that it was foredoomed to failure? Would such a failure inevitably be repeated in contemporary circumstances?

The succession in 1603 by James VI, King of Scots, to the Crown of England and Ireland was a personal, but also a dynastic and diplomatic, triumph. The Marriage of the Thistle and the Rose, between James IV of Scots and Margaret Tudor, sister to the future Henry VIII, had borne fruit a century after its celebration. The long-held ambition of kings of England to

---

[1] See N. MacCormick, *Questioning Sovereignty: Law, State and Nation in the European Commonwealth* (Oxford, 1999), ch. 12, which elaborates some of the present arguments.

engross Scotland within their territories was achieved with a curious inversion. For a Scottish king, reared and educated in Scotland under the tutelage of the eminent universal-humanist but also intensely Scottish scholar George Buchanan, had, after all, engrossed England into his domains. (Of course, not even James really saw matters that way. The moment the news of Elizabeth's death and her naming himself as heir reached him, he was off to London to lodge himself in the greater kingdom with almost indecent haste.)

As so many able students do, James rejected totally the teachings of his tutor—in so far at least as concerned political theory. Buchanan's contractual theory of monarchy, with its corollary of the people's right to depose a misruling monarch, met its exact antithesis in James's version of the Divine Right of Kings. As a believer in divine right, James necessarily perceived his accession to the English throne as a God-given opportunity. As a lover of peace, he thought that the union of three kingdoms through his own person could bring an end to strife. He posed the aim of procuring a union of all his kingdoms in peace and under moderate religious toleration, albeit under episcopacy, not presbyterian rule.

James's ambition for an immediate political union of all his kingdoms into a single one never got far off the ground. In the early seventeenth century, a full union proved as unacceptable to the English as to the Scottish Parliament, to say nothing of Irish problems. Schemes such as those drafted by the jurist-courtier Thomas Craig of Riccartoun fell stillborn from the authorial pen, although the beginnings of comparative Anglo-Scottish law then took shape, Craig's *Ius Feudale*, itself a distinguished first fruit of the process.

The argument of this chapter was originally submitted to the joint attention of the Royal Society and the British Academy on a date very close to 5 November 2003. The coincidence gave a poignant reminder of the circumstances that brought about the early demise of James's hope for a broad and tolerant approach in religious matters. The Gunpowder Plot of 1605 triggered virulent anti-Catholicism, and set a tone that never completely disappeared from the culture of the island of Great Britain until the later years of the twentieth century, if even then. Among the baleful consequences was the plantation of Ulster with Protestants who forcibly excluded the indigenous Gaelic-speaking and Catholic Ulstermen from all but the poorest land. As a strategy for ridding the Anglo-Scottish border of unruly elements, plantation may have had some success. As an element in a strategy for the governance of Ireland, it was a disaster.

James nevertheless succeeded in maintaining peace in the islands during his long reign—long in England itself, longer yet in Scotland. He it was who could at long range govern Scotland with his pen as his ancestors had failed to do with the sword. Charles I, heir through the death of his brother Henry, tried to carry on his father's policies yet more ambitiously, but without any real personal knowledge of the land of his own birth. He disastrously mis-judged opinion in Scotland. The Bishops' War was an inevitable conse-quence, and it in turn led inexorably to the overlapping but distinct Civil Wars of the three kingdoms. Of these, the long drawn-out aftermath was found in Cromwell's protectorate and its savage coercion of Ireland during a time that also extended to Scottish merchants the advantages of coming within the scheme of the English Navigation Acts.

Charles's approach, if it showed anything, should be supposed to have shown that haste for full union through uniformity in worship and in admin-istration was by no means a path toward civic tranquillity. Other aspects of the drive to uniformity shade over towards a long and slow-burning form of genocide. From the point of view of Gaelic Ireland, the seventeenth century finally cut the head off a great culture, particularly in its most flourishing domain in the North. Thus, too, it contributed to the long-term decay of Scotland's Gaelic heritage, with its close historical connections to that of Ulster. The fate of Montrose's ally, Alasdair MacDonald, of Dunyveg and the Glens of Antrim, son of Colkitto and successor to the tradition of the Lords of the Isles, should remind us that the tragedy of Gaelic was played out on both sides of the North Channel. If at last there are still glimmering hopes for a slow outbreak of peace in Ulster in the early twenty-first century, it is nevertheless salutary to reflect on how sour things have been for so long.

After 1603, Scotland, while sharing a king with England, remained a dis-tinct kingdom, but a kingdom without a king. At that time, we have to acknowledge that a kingdom without a king was a practical contradiction in terms. For then the king was the active head of government as well as formal head of state. Kings depended on ministers, but on ministers as the servants of the royal will and policy, advisers on its formation. They were not, as they have become, the true wielders of power, wielding it only formally in the monarch's name. Of course, this is over-stated. Scotland was not quite a king-dom without a king; it was a kingdom with an absentee king. The absentee king was somewhat precarious on the throne of his larger and more prosper-ous realm. Political prudence required a policy primarily aimed at sustaining favourable opinion there, while not pressing minority realms beyond the limits of serious resistance. James VI and I could achieve this, and so could Charles II after the restoration. Charles I and James VII and II failed comprehensively.

Certainly, things began to change in the later seventeenth century, follow-ing on the Revolutions of 1688 and 1689. These laid what hindsight shows to have been the early foundations of fully constitutional monarchy. That it should have turned out so was not a fore-ordained certainty, for who can say how it would all have worked out but for the succession in 1714 of Hanoverians with a manifest lack of personal charisma, and little ability or inclination to do business in the English language? Up till then, and certainly throughout the seventeenth century, kings had been in any event active political, ecclesiastical, and military leaders, whether successful or unsuccessful in these roles.

A king's or a queen's ministers were the advisers they chose for themselves. These ministers were obliged at least sometimes to consult parliaments, and they had to be able to keep some kind of grip on parliaments. They had also to keep a weather eye on the risks of impeachment. The clear outcome of the English Civil War, achieved at the Restoration, was the demonstration that parliament had to authorise the supply of financial resources to the king. In England this was a potent weapon. In Scotland, against monarchs with an English base but shared Scottish legitimacy, it was less so. The Scottish finances could go quite far awry for quite a long time without immediate catastrophe for the head of state.

The point of this all became clear during the final struggles of the Scottish Parliament in the first six years of the eighteenth century. The arguments by Fletcher of Saltoun for election of Scottish ministers by the Scottish Parliament and for the monarch's duty to assent to measures carried by a majority in parliament no doubt seemed at the time to be extravagantly republican. But in the twentieth century they gradually came to seem commonplace, and it is striking how much of Fletcher's original ideas have come to pass in the devolution legislation in Scotland.

More generally, in Westminster as well as Edinburgh and elsewhere, real power has come to be invested in parliaments, and thus in the governments that command parliamentary majorities through the dominance of political parties. By this means, a kind of last-resort sovereignty has effectively shifted to the people themselves as the sovereign electorate within parliamentary systems of government. None of this was remotely true for seventeenth-century Scotland. Parliaments were founded on a narrow base mainly of aristocracy and gentry. They were open to all sorts of manipulation. Indeed, in Scotland, James and his successors were able to manage parliamentary business as they chose, through the Lords of the Articles, whose power was curbed only in the last two decades of the old Scottish Parliament following the 1689 Revolution.

A very rough equivalent of the Lords of the Articles can be found in the business bureau of the contemporary Scottish Parliament, save for the democratic legitimation of the latter. James not implausibly claimed that he could sit in London and govern Scotland with a pen more effectively than his predecessors had ever been able to do with the sword. This is the essential reason why the Union of the Crowns was a disaster for Scotland. Scotland entered the seventeenth century at a time of a new intellectual quickening, triggered by the *nova erectio*, or refoundation, of the ancient universities in Glasgow,

St Andrews, and Aberdeen and by the foundation of Edinburgh University. But the removal of political power and court patronage from its heart was a discouraging circumstance, and the wars of religion and wars concerning royal succession that plagued the next hundred years added their dire effects.

Moreover, since the king was the real head of government, he was inevitably going to pursue the same policies and alliances in relation to all three kingdoms. There was little possibility for independent action in any one. It was inevitable that the interest of the largest would predominate in all decision making. The classic example of this was provided by the Darien Disaster in the 1690s. The Company of Scotland set out on the ambitious project to establish a trading colony on the Darien isthmus, strategically placed for both Pacific and Atlantic trade. Nearly everyone in Scotland with available capital invested it in the project.

English colonists in North America objected, Spain was against it, and King William, influenced by his English ministers, decided to let the Scottish colonists suffer their own fate without naval or military assistance. Commercial Scotland was ruined overnight. Whatever the venture's prospects would have been in favourable circumstances, the opposition of Scotland's only effective government made sure of the very worst of possible outcomes. In the aftermath, Scots learned the lesson. Unless the Scottish Parliament could elect Scotland's ministers, there would never be a possibility of independent and answerable government in Scotland. That might need a re-separation of the Crowns, and, if so, let it be so.

The English government recoiled in horror from that prospect, negotiations for union were put in hand, armies marched towards the Scottish border, Scottish Commissioners were persuaded that a treaty for an incorporating union was the only alternative to conquest, and the imposition of yet worse terms. The parliament reluctantly approved the agreed Articles of Union, and on 1 May 1707 the old Scottish kingdom breathed its last. So did the English, but nobody noticed, because it did not really. New Great Britain was old England writ a little larger. Regal union under seventeenth-century assumptions had an inexorable drive towards either of two resolutions: renewed separation under separate monarchs, with possible resumption of old hostilities; or transformation into full political and parliamentary union. Despite fierce popular opposition, especially in Scotland, incorporating union was the chosen outcome in our case.

The relevant seventeenth-century assumptions, however, do not hold good in relation to constitutional monarchy as this has evolved, especially in the context of the Commonwealth. The development of constitutional monarchy has made it possible for genuinely independent countries to share a formal head of state if that is what they wish. Formally, Queen Elizabeth is Head of State in Australia, New Zealand, and Canada, as well as in the

United Kingdom. Democratic parliamentary government having prevailed, sharing a head of state is not a bar to the genuine mutual independence of countries. They elect their own parliaments and democratically chosen governments, and these pursue their own policies broadly as mandated electorally. The same headship of state is compatible with very different political approaches in different countries over the same stretch of time. There is surely a lesson here for contemporary Scotland, though it is an open question whether anyone wishes to learn and profit from it. The expansion of the present Scottish Parliament's powers to completeness, coupled with a negotiated and consensual severance of responsibility of the Westminster Parliament and UK government, would lead to the same state of affairs obtaining as between other mutually independent monarchies in the Commonwealth. Membership of a successor state in the European Union under its prevailing constitutional provisions concerning accession of states to membership would be a matter of further negotiation and adjustment, but not on the face of it particularly difficult or controversial.

In fact, the real difficulty, when you press the argument to its conclusion, does not concern a shared head of state, if this involves a constitutional monarch exercising only formal powers under a constitution. The problem of the Union of the Crowns was a problem arising from having a single head of government for two polities with two parliaments.

Were we to look for a contemporary analogy to this, where might we find it? The answer I would tentatively offer is this: in the United Kingdom under devolution. Especially under a Prime Minister with the remarkable personal traits and political effectiveness of Mr Blair, it is clear that there is only one UK head of government. Scotland's, or indeed Wales's First Minister is by no means comparable to the leader of a parish council. But the pre-eminence of Blair over the whole scope of UK policy is scarcely in doubt. The military engagement in Iraq seems to me a striking illustration of this.

The present system works so long as party ties make more or less unquestioned the loyalty of the head of a devolved Scottish government to the head of the United Kingdom government. Think how different things would be were Mrs Thatcher to return to power, or even Mr Howard to score a shock victory at the next UK General Election. And then think again of the prospect of a Scottish National Party leader's taking office in Scotland in 2007, were that to happen after the May 2007 election in the tercentenary year of the incorporating union.

The present contribution is offered primarily as a scholarly, not a political one. Let me therefore not even seem to engage in polemics or even partisan rhetoric. It is enough if it has sketched grounds for taking seriously the question what 'new unions for old' might mean.

Index